J. S. WESBY & SONS, INC.
WORCESTER, MASS.

Name of Library: Bradford Junior College Library
Bradford, Massachusetts

"PLEASE CHECK"

Buckram Color No. 2573 ....

No. of Volumes ....

	Bind as is	☐
Covers	Out	☐
	In	☐
Front Covers Only		☐
Ads	Out	☐
	In	☐

Editorials and Feature Articles

	Out	☐
	In	☐
Index	Front	☐
	Back	☐
	Do not trim	☐
	Recase in old cover	☐
	Bindery has pattern	☐
	Rub sent	☐
	Sample sent	☐
1st Binding	Make pattern	☐
Lettering on spine:	Horizontal	☐
	Vertical	☐
	Gold Lettering	☐
	Black Lettering	☐
	White Lettering	☐
	Color Foil Lettering	☐
Insert stubs for:	Missing Issues	☐
	Missing Pages	☐
	Index	☐

Shaw. G B.

Androcles and the lion

Special Instructions:

ANDROCLES AND THE LION
OVERRULED   PYGMALION ✓
BY BERNARD SHAW.

BRENTANO'S ◆ NEW YORK
PUBLISHERS

PRINTED IN THE UNITED STATES OF AMERICA

CONTENTS

Contents

Contents

Contents

ANDROCLES AND THE LION
XXIII

1912

PREFACE ON THE PROSPECTS OF CHRISTIANITY

Why not give Christianity a Trial?

THE question seems a hopeless one after 2000 years of resolute adherence to the old cry of "Not this man, but Barabbas." Yet it is beginning to look as if Barabbas was a failure, in spite of his strong right hand, his victories, his empires, his millions of money, and his moralities and churches and political constitutions. "This man" has not been a failure yet; for nobody has ever been sane enough to try his way. But he has had one quaint triumph. Barabbas has stolen his name and taken his cross as a standard. There is a sort of compliment in that. There is even a sort of loyalty in it, like that of the brigand who breaks every law and yet claims to be a patriotic subject of the king who makes them. We have always had a curious feeling that though we crucified Christ on a stick, he somehow managed to get hold of the right end of it, and that if we were better men we might try his plan. There have been one or two grotesque attempts at it by inadequate people, such as the Kingdom of God in Munster, which was ended by a crucifixion so much more atrocious than the one on Calvary that the bishop who took the part of Annas went home and died of horror. But responsible people have never made such attempts. The moneyed, respectable, capable world has been steadily anti-Christian and Barabbasque since the crucifixion; and the specific doctrine of Jesus has not in all that time been put into political

or general social practice. I am no more a Christian
than Pilate was, or you, gentle reader; and yet, like
Pilate, I greatly prefer Jesus to Annas and Caiaphas;
and I am ready to admit that after contemplating the
world and human nature for nearly sixty years, I see
no way out of the world's misery but the way which
would have been found by Christ's will if he had un-
dertaken the work of a modern practical statesman.

Pray do not at this early point lose patience with me
and shut the book. I assure you I am as sceptical and
scientific and modern a thinker as you will find anywhere. I grant you I know a great deal more about
economics and politics than Jesus did, and can do things
he could not do. I am by all Barabbasque standards
a person of much better character and standing, and
greater practical sense. I have no sympathy with vagabonds and talkers who try to reform society by taking
men away from their regular productive work and making vagabonds and talkers of them too; and if I had
been Pilate I should have recognized as plainly as he
the necessity for suppressing attacks on the existing
social order, however corrupt that order might be, by
people with no knowledge of government and no power
to construct political machinery to carry out their views,
acting on the very dangerous delusion that the end of
the world was at hand. I make no defence of such
Christians as Savonarola and John of Leyden: they were
scuttling the ship before they had learned how to build
a raft; and it became necessary to throw them overboard
to save the crew. I say this to set myself right with
respectable society; but I must still insist that if Jesus
could have worked out the practical problems of a Communist constitution, an admitted obligation to deal with
crime without revenge or punishment, and a full assumption by humanity of divine responsibilities, he would
have conferred an incalculable benefit on mankind, be-

cause these distinctive demands of his are now turning
out to be good sense and sound economics.

I say distinctive, because his common humanity and
his subjection to time and space (that is, to the Syrian
life of his period) involved his belief in many things,
true and false, that in no way distinguish him from other
Syrians of that time. But such common beliefs do not
constitute specific Christianity any more than wearing
a beard, working in a carpenter's shop, or believing that
the earth is flat and that the stars could drop on it from
heaven like hailstones. Christianity interests practical
statesmen now because of the doctrines that distinguished
Christ from the Jews and the Barabbasques generally,
including ourselves.

Why Jesus more than Another ?

I do not imply, however, that these doctrines were
peculiar to Christ. A doctrine peculiar to one man would
be only a craze, unless its comprehension depended on a
development of human faculty so rare that only one ex-
ceptionally gifted man possessed it. But even in this
case it would be useless, because incapable of spreading.
Christianity is a step in moral evolution which is independent of any individual preacher. If Jesus had never
existed (and that he ever existed in any other sense
than that in which Shakespear's Hamlet existed has been
vigorously questioned) Tolstoy would have thought and
taught and quarrelled with the Greek Church all the
same. Their creed has been fragmentarily practised to
a considerable extent in spite of the fact that the laws
of all countries treat it, in effect, as criminal. Many of
its advocates have been militant atheists. But for some
reason the imagination of white mankind has picked
out Jesus of Nazareth as *the* Christ, and attributed all
the Christian doctrines to him; and as it is the doctrine

and not the man that matters, and, as, besides, one symbol is as good as another provided everyone attaches the
same meaning to it, I raise, for the moment, no question
as to how far the gospels are original, and how far they
consist of Greek and Chinese interpolations. The record
that Jesus said certain things is not invalidated by a
demonstration that Confucius said them before him.
Those who claim a literal divine paternity for him cannot
be silenced by the discovery that the same claim was made
for Alexander and Augustus. And I am not just now
concerned with the credibility of the gospels as records
of fact; for I am not acting as a detective, but turning
our modern lights on to certain ideas and doctrines in
them which disentangle themselves from the rest because
they are flatly contrary to common practice, common
sense, and common belief, and yet have, in the teeth of
dogged incredulity and recalcitrance, produced an irresistible impression that Christ, though rejected by his
posterity as an unpractical dreamer, and executed by his
contemporaries as a dangerous anarchist and blasphemous madman, was greater than his judges.

Was Jesus a Coward ?

I know quite well that this impression of superiority
is not produced on everyone, even of those who profess
extreme susceptibility to it. Setting aside the huge mass
of inculcated Christ-worship which has no real significance because it has no intelligence, there is, among people who are really free to think for themselves on the
subject, a great deal of hearty dislike of Jesus and of
contempt for his failure to save himself and overcome his
enemies by personal bravery and cunning as Mahomet
did. I have heard this feeling expressed far more impatiently by persons brought up in England as Christians than by Mahometans, who are, like their prophet,

very civil to Jesus, and allow him a place in their esteem
and veneration at least as high as we accord to John the
Baptist. But this British bulldog contempt is founded
on a complete misconception of his reasons for submitting voluntarily to an ordeal of torment and death.
The modern Secularist is often so determined to regard
Jesus as a man like himself and nothing more, that he
slips unconsciously into the error of assuming that Jesus
shared that view. But it is quite clear from the New
Testament writers (the chief authorities for believing
that Jesus ever existed) that Jesus at the time of his
death believed himself to be the Christ, a divine personage. It is therefore absurd to criticize his conduct before Pilate as if he were Colonel Roosevelt or Admiral
von Tirpitz or even Mahomet. Whether you accept his
belief in his divinity as fully as Simon Peter did, or reject it as a delusion which led him to submit to torture
and sacrifice his life without resistance in the conviction
that he would presently rise again in glory, you are
equally bound to admit that, far from behaving like a
coward or a sheep, he shewed considerable physical fortitude in going through a cruel ordeal against which he
could have defended himself as effectually as he cleared
the moneychangers out of the temple. "Gentle Jesus,
meek and mild' is a snivelling modern invention, with
no warrant in the gospels. St. Matthew would as soon
have thought of applying such adjectives to Judas Mac-
cabeus as to Jesus; and even St. Luke, who makes Jesus
polite and gracious, does not make him meek. The picture of him as an English curate of the farcical comedy
type, too meek to fight a policeman, and everybody's
butt, may be useful in the nursery to soften children;
but that such a figure could ever have become a centre
of the world's attention is too absurd for discussion;
grown men and women may speak kindly of a harmless
creature who utters amiable sentiments and is a helpless

nincompoop when he is called on to defend them; but
they will not follow him, nor do what he tells them,
because they do not wish to share his defeat and disgrace.

Was Jesus a Martyr?

It is important therefore that we should clear our
minds of the notion that Jesus died, as some of are in
the habit of declaring, for his social and political opinions.   There have been many martyrs to those opinions;
but he was not one of them, nor, as his words shew, did
he see any more sense in martyrdom than Galileo did.
He was executed by the Jews for the blasphemy of
claiming to be a God; and Pilate, to whom this was a
mere piece of superstitious nonsense, let them execute
him as the cheapest way of keeping them quiet, on the
formal plea that he had committed treason against Rome
by saying that he was the King of the Jews. He was
not falsely accused, nor denied full opportunities of defending himself. The proceedings were quite straight-
forward and regular; and Pilate, to whom the appeal
lay, favored him and despised his judges, and was evidently willing enough to be conciliated. But instead of
denying the charge, Jesus repeated the offence. He
knew what he was doing: he had alienated numbers of his
own disciples and been stoned in the streets for doing
it before. He was not lying: he believed literally what
he said. The horror of the High Priest was perfectly
natural: he was a Primate confronted with a heterodox
street preacher uttering what seemed to him an appall-
ing and impudent blasphemy. The fact that the blasphemy was to Jesus a simple statement of fact, and that
it has since been accepted as such by all western nations,
does not invalidate the proceedings, nor give us the right
to regard Annas and Caiaphas as worse men than the
Archbishop of Canterbury and the Head Master of

Eton. If Jesus had been indicted in a modern court, he would have been examined by two doctors; found to be obsessed by a delusion; declared incapable of pleading; and sent to an asylum: that is the whole difference. But please note that when a man is charged before a modern tribunal (to take a case that happened the other day) of having asserted and maintained that he was an officer returned from the front to receive the Victoria Cross at the hands of the King, although he was in fact a mechanic, nobody thinks of treating him as afflicted with a delusion. He is punished for false pretences, because his assertion is credible and therefore misleading. Just so, the claim to divinity made by Jesus was to the High Priest, who looked forward to the coming of a Messiah, one that might conceivably have been true, and might therefore have misled the people in a very dangerous way. That was why he treated Jesus as an imposter and a blasphemer where we should have treated him as a madman.

The Gospels without Prejudice.

All this will become clear if we read the gospels without prejudice. When I was young it was impossible to read them without fantastic confusion of thought. The confusion was so utterly confounded that it was called the proper spirit to read the Bible in. Jesus was a baby; and he was older than creation. He was a man who could be persecuted, stoned, scourged, and killed; and he was a god, immortal and all-powerful, able to raise the dead and call millions of angels to his aid. It was a sin to doubt either view of him: that is, it was a sin to reason about him; and the end was that you did not reason about him, and read about him only when you were compelled. When you heard the gospel stories read in church, or learnt them from painters and poets, you came out with an impression of their contents that would have astonished a Chinaman who had read the story without prepossession. Even sceptics who were specially on their guard, put the Bible in the dock, and read the gospels with the object of detecting discrepancies in the four narratives to shew that the writers were as subject to error as the writers of yesterday's newspaper.

All this has changed greatly within two generations. Today the Bible is so little read that the language of the Authorized Version is rapidly becoming obsolete; so that even in the United States, where the old tradition of the verbal infallibility of "the book of books" lingers more strongly than anywhere else except perhaps in Ulster, retranslations into modern English have been introduced perforce to save its bare intelligibility. It is quite easy today to find cultivated persons who have never read the New Testament, and on whom therefore it is possible to try the experiment of asking them to read the gospels and state what they have gathered as to the history and views and character of Christ.

The Gospels now unintelligible to Novices.

But it will not do to read the gospels with a mind furnished only for the reception of, say, a biography of Goethe. You will not make sense of them, nor even be able without impatient weariness to persevere in the task of going steadily through them, unless you know something of the history of the human imagination as applied to religion. Not long ago I asked a writer of distinguished intellectual competence whether he had made a study of the gospels since his childhood. His reply was that he had lately tried, but "found it all such nonsense that I could not stick it." As I do not want to send anyone to the gospels with this result, I had better here give a brief exposition of how much of the history of religion is needed to make the gospels and the conduct and ultimate fate of Jesus intelligible and interesting.

Worldliness of the Majority.

The first common mistake to get rid of is that mankind consists of a great mass of religious people and a few eccentric atheists. It consists of a huge mass of worldly people, and a small percentage of persons deeply interested in religion and concerned about their own souls and other peoples'; and this section consists mostly of those who are passionately affirming the established religion and those who are passionately attacking it, the genuine philosophers being very few. Thus you never have a nation of millions of Wesleys and one Tom Paine. You have a million Mr. Worldly Wisemans, one Wesley, with his small congregation, and one Tom Paine, with *his* smaller congregation. The passionately religious are a people apart; and if they were not hopelessly outnumbered by the worldly, they would turn the world upside down, as St. Paul was reproached, quite justly, for wanting to do. Few people can number among their personal acquaintances a single atheist or a single Plymouth Brother. Unless a religious turn in ourselves has led us to seek the little Societies to which these rare birds belong, we pass our lives among people who, whatever creeds they may repeat, and in whatever temples they may avouch their respectability and wear their Sunday clothes, have robust consciences, and hunger and thirst, not for righteousness, but for rich feeding and comfort and social position and attractive mates and ease and pleasure and respect and consideration: in short, for love and money. To these people one morality is as good as another provided they are used to it and can put up with its restrictions without unhappiness; and in the maintenance of this morality they will fight and punish and coerce without scruple. They may not be the salt of the earth, these Philistines; but they are the substance of civilization; and they save society from ruin by criminals and conquerors as well as by Savonarolas and Knipperdollings. And as they know, very sensibly, that a little religion is good for children and serves morality, keeping the poor in good humor or in awe by promising rewards in heaven or threatening torments in hell, they encourage the religious people up to a certain point; for instance, if Savonarola only tells the ladies of Florence that they ought to tear off their jewels and finery and sacrifice them to God, they offer him a cardinal's hat, and praise him as a saint; but if he induces them to actually do it, they burn him as a public nuisance.

Religion of the Minority.   Salvationism.

The religion of the tolerated religious minority has always been essentially the same religion: that is why its changes of name and form have made so little difference. That is why, also, a nation so civilized as the English can convert negroes to their faith with great ease, but cannot convert Mahometans or Jews. The negro finds in civilized Salvationism an unspeakably more comforting version of his crude creed; but neither Saracen nor Jew sees any advantage in it over his own version. The Crusader was surprised to find the Saracen quite as religious and moral as himself, and rather more than less civilized. The Latin Christian has nothing to offer the Greek Christian that Greek Christianity has not already provided. They are all, at root, Salvationists.

Let us trace this religion of Salvation from its beginnings. So many things that man does not himself contrive or desire are always happening: death, plagues, tempests, blights, floods, sunrise and sunset, growths and

harvests and decay, and Kant's two wonders of the
starry heavens above us and the moral law within us,
that we conclude that somebody must be doing it all, or
that somebody is doing the good and somebody else
doing the evil, or that armies of invisible persons, benef-
icent and malevolent, are doing it; hence you postulate
gods and devils, angels and demons. You propitiate
these powers with presents, called sacrifices, and flatteries, called praises. Then the Kantian moral law within
you makes you conceive your god as a judge; and
straightway you try to corrupt him, also with presents
and flatteries. This seems shocking to us; but our objection to it is quite a recent development: no longer ago
than Shakespear's time it was thought quite natural that
litigants should give presents to human judges; and the
buying off of divine wrath by actual money payments to
priests, or, in the reformed churches which discounten-
ance this, by subscriptions to charities and church building and the like, is still in full swing. Its practical disadvantage is that though it makes matters very easy for
the rich, it cuts off the poor from all hope of divine
favor. And this quickens the moral criticism of the poor
to such an extent, that they soon find the moral law within them revolting against the idea of buying off the deity
with gold and gifts, though they are still quite ready to
buy him off with the paper money of praise and professions of repentance. Accordingly, you will find that
though a religion may last unchanged for many centuries in primitive communities where the conditions of
life leave no room for poverty and riches, and the process
of propitiating the supernatural powers is as well within
the means of the least of the members as within those of
the headman, yet when commercial civilization arrives,
and capitalism divides the people into a few rich and a
great many so poor that they can barely live, a movement for religious reform will arise among the poor, and

will be essentially a movement for cheap or entirely
gratuitous salvation.

To understand what the poor mean by propitiation, we
must examine for a moment what they mean by justice.

The Difference between Atonement and Punishment.

The primitive idea of justice is partly legalized revenge and partly expiation by sacrifice. It works out
from both sides in the notion that two blacks make a
white, and that when a wrong has been done, it should
be paid for by an equivalent suffering. It seems to the
Philistine majority a matter of course that this compen-
sating suffering should be inflicted on the wrongdoer for
the sake of its deterrent effect on other would-be wrong-
doers; but a moment's reflection will shew that this utili-
tarian application corrupts the whole transaction. For
example, the shedding of innocent blood cannot be balanced by the shedding of guilty blood. Sacrificing a
criminal to propitiate God for the murder of one of his
righteous servants is like sacrificing a mangy sheep or
an ox with the rinderpest: it calls down divine wrath instead of appeasing it. In doing it we offer God as a sacrifice the gratification of our own revenge and the protection of our own lives without cost to ourselves; and
cost to ourselves is the essence of sacrifice and expiation.
However much the Philistines have succeeded in confusing these things in practice, they are to the Salvationist
sense distinct and even contrary. The Baronet's cousin
in Dickens's novel, who, perplexed by the failure of the
police to discover the murderer of the baronet's solicitor,
said "Far better hang wrong fellow than no fellow," was
not only expressing a very common sentiment, but trembling on the brink of the rarer Salvationist opinion that

it is much better to hang the wrong fellow: that, in fact, the wrong fellow is the right fellow to hang.

The point is a cardinal one, because until we grasp it not only does historical Christianity remain unintelligible to us, but those who do not care a rap about historical Christianity may be led into the mistake of supposing that if we discard revenge, and treat murderers exactly as God treated Cain: that is, exempt them from punishment by putting a brand on them as unworthy to be sacrificed, and let them face the world as best they can with that brand on them, we should get rid both of punishment and sacrifice. It would not at all follow: on the contrary, the feeling that there must be an expiation of the murder might quite possibly lead to our putting some innocent person—the more innocent the better—to a cruel death to balance the account with divine justice.

Salvation at first a Class Privilege; and the Remedy.

Thus, even when the poor decide that the method of purchasing salvation by offering rams and goats or bringing gold to the altar must be wrong because they cannot afford it, we still do not feel "saved" without a sacrifice and a victim. In vain do we try to substitute mystical rites that cost nothing, such as circumcision, or, as a substitute for that, baptism. Our sense of justice still demands an expiation, a sacrifice, a sufferer for our sins. And this leaves the poor man still in his old difficulty; for if it was impossible for him to procure rams and goats and shekels, how much more impossible is it for him to find a neighbor who will voluntarily suffer for his sins: one who will say cheerfully "You have committed a murder Well, never mind: I am willing to be hanged for it in your stead?"

Our imagination must come to our rescue. Why **not**, instead of driving ourselves to despair by insisting on a separate atonement by a separate redeemer for every sin, have one great atonement and one great redeemer to compound for the sins of the world once for all? Nothing easier, nothing cheaper. The yoke is easy, the burden light. All you have to do when the redeemer is once found (or invented by the imagination) is to believe in the efficacy of the transaction, and you are saved. The rams and goats cease to bleed; the altars which ask for expensive gifts and continually renewed sacrifices are torn down; and the Church of the single redeemer and the single atonement rises on the ruins of the old temples, and becomes a single Church of the Christ.

Retrospective Atonement; and the Expectation of the Redeemer.

But this does not happen at once. Between the old costly religion of the rich and the new gratuitous religion of the poor there comes an interregnum in which the redeemer, though conceived by the human imagination, is not yet found. He is awaited and expected under the names of the Christ, the Messiah, Baldur the Beautiful, or what not; but he has not yet come. Yet the sinners are not therefore in despair. It is true that they cannot say, as we say, "The Christ has come, and has redeemed us;" but they can say "The Christ will come, and will redeem us," which, as the atonement is conceived as retrospective, is equally consoling. There are periods when nations are seething with this expectation and crying aloud with prophecy of the Redeemer through their poets. To feel that atmosphere we have only to take up the Bible and read Isaiah at one end of such a period and Luke and John at the other.

Completion of the Scheme by Luther and Calvin.

We now see our religion as a quaint but quite intelligible evolution from crude attempts to propitiate the destructive forces of Nature among savages to a subtle theology with a costly ritual of sacrifice possible only to the rich as a luxury, and finally to the religion of Luther and Calvin. And it must be said for the earlier forms that they involved very real sacrifices. The sacrifice was not always vicarious, and is not yet universally so. In India men pay with their own skins, torturing themselves hideously to attain holiness. In the west, saints amazed the world with their austerities and self-scourgings and confessions and vigils. But Luther delivered us from all that. His reformation was a triumph of imagination and a triumph of cheapness. It brought you complete salvation and asked you for nothing but faith. Luther did not know what he was doing in the scientific sociological way in which we know it; but his instinct served him better than knowledge could have done; for it was instinct rather than theological casuistry that made him hold so resolutely to Justification by Faith as the trump card by which he should beat the Pope, or, as he would have put it, the sign in which he should conquer. ⎸ He may be said to have abolished the charge for admission to heaven.⎸ Paul had advocated this; but Luther and Calvin did it.

John Barleycorn

There is yet another page in the history of religion which must be conned and digested before the career of Jesus can be fully understood. People who can read long books will find it in Frazer's Golden Bough. Simpler folk will find it in the peasant's song of John Bar-

leycorn, now made accessible to our drawingroom
amateurs in the admirable collections of Somersetshire
Folk Songs by Mr. Cecil Sharp. From Frazer's *mag-
num opus* you will learn how the same primitive logic
which makes the Englishman believe today that by eating
a beefsteak he can acquire the strength and courage of
the bull, and to hold that belief in the face of the most
ignominious defeats by vegetarian wrestlers and racers
and bicyclists, led the first men who conceived God as
capable of incarnation to believe that they could acquire
a spark of his divinity by eating his flesh and drinking
his blood. And from the song of John Barleycorn you
may learn how the miracle of the seed, the growth, and
the harvest, still the most wonderful of all the miracles
and as inexplicable as ever, taught the primitive hus-
bandman, and, as we must now affirm, taught him quite
rightly, that God is in the seed, and that God is immortal. And thus it became the test of Godhead that
nothing that you could do to it could kill it, and that
when you buried it, it would rise again in renewed life
and beauty and give mankind eternal life on condition
that it was eaten and drunk, and again slain and buried,
to rise again for ever and ever. You may, and indeed
must, use John Barleycorn "right barbarouslee," cutting
him "off at knee" with your scythes, scourging him with
your flails, burying him in the earth; and he will not resist you nor reproach you, but will rise again in golden
beauty amidst a great burst of sunshine and bird music,
and save you and renew your life. And from the inter-
weaving of these two traditions with the craving for the
Redeemer, you at last get the conviction that when the
Redeemer comes he will be immortal; he will give us his
body to eat and his blood to drink; and he will prove his
divinity by suffering a barbarous death without resistance or reproach, and rise from the dead and return to
the earth in glory as the giver of life eternal.

Looking for the End of the World.

Yet another persistent belief has beset the imagination of the religious ever since religion spread among the poor, or, rather, ever since commercial civilization produced a hopelessly poor class cut off from enjoyment in this world. That belief is that the end of this world is at hand, and that it will presently pass away and be replaced by a kingdom of happiness, justice, and bliss in which the rich and the oppressors and the unjust shall have no share. We are all familiar with this expectation: many of us cherish some pious relative who sees in every great calamity a sign of the approaching end. Warning pamphlets are in constant circulation: advertisements are put in the papers and paid for by those who are convinced, and who are horrified at the indifference of the irreligious to the approaching doom. And revivalist preachers, now as in the days of John the Baptist, seldom fail to warn their flocks to watch and pray, as the great day will steal upon them like a thief in the night, and cannot be long deferred in a world so wicked. This belief also associates itself with Barleycorn's second coming; so that the two events become identified at last.

There is the other and more artificial side of this belief, on which it is an inculcated dread. The ruler who appeals to the prospect of heaven to console the poor and keep them from insurrection also curbs the vicious by threatening them with hell. In the Koran we find Mahomet driven more and more to this expedient of government; and experience confirms his evident belief that it is impossible to govern without it in certain phases of civilization. We shall see later on that it gives a powerful attraction to the belief in a Redeemer, since it adds to remorse of conscience, which hardened men bear very lightly, a definite dread of hideous and eternal torture.

The Honor of Divine Parentage.

One more tradition must be noted. The consummation
of praise for a king is to declare that he is the son of no
earthly father, but of a god. His mother goes into the
temple of Apollo, and Apollo comes to her in the shape
of a serpent, or the like. The Roman emperors, following the example of Augustus, claimed the title of God.
Illogically, such divine kings insist a good deal on their
royal human ancestors. Alexander, claiming to be the
son of Apollo, is equally determined to be the son of
Philip. As the gospels stand, St. Matthew and St. Luke
give genealogies (the two are different) establishing
the descent of Jesus through Joseph from the royal
house of David, and yet declare that not Joseph but the
Holy Ghost was the father of Jesus. It is therefore now
held that the story of the Holy Ghost is a later interpolation borrowed from the Greek and Roman imperial
tradition. But experience shews that simultaneous faith
in the descent from David and the conception by the
Holy Ghost is possible. Such double beliefs are enter-
tained by the human mind without uneasiness or consciousness of the contradiction involved. Many instances
might be given: a familiar one to my generation being
that of the Tichborne claimant, whose attempt to pass
himself off as a baronet was supported by an association
of laborers on the ground that the Tichborne family, in
resisting it, were trying to do a laborer out of his rights.
It is quite possible that Matthew and Luke may have
been unconscious of the contradiction: indeed the interpolation theory does not remove the difficulty, as the in-
terpolators themselves must have been unconscious of it.
A better ground for suspecting interpolation is that St.
Paul knew nothing of the divine birth, and taught that
Jesus came into the world at his birth as the son of
Joseph, but rose from the dead after three days as the

son of God. Here again, few notice the discrepancy: the three views are accepted simultaneously without intellectual discomfort. We can provisionally entertain half a dozen contradictory versions of an event if we feel either that it does not greatly matter, or that there is a category attainable in which the contradictions are reconciled.

But that is not the present point. All that need be noted here is that the legend of divine birth was sure to be attached sooner or later to very eminent persons in Roman imperial times, and that modern theologians, far from discrediting it, have very logically affirmed the miraculous conception not only of Jesus but of his mother.

With no more scholarly equipment than a knowledge of these habits of the human imagination, anyone may now read the four gospels without bewilderment, and without the contemptuous incredulity which spoils the temper of many modern atheists, or the senseless credulity which sometimes makes pious people force us to shove them aside in emergencies as impracticable lunatics when they ask us to meet violence and injustice with dumb submission in the belief that the strange demeanor of Jesus before Pilate was meant as an example of normal human conduct. Let us admit that without the proper clues the gospels are, to a modern educated person, nonsensical and incredible, whilst the apostles are unreadable. But with the clues, they are fairly plain sailing. Jesus becomes an intelligible and consistent person. His reasons for going "like a lamb to the slaughter" instead of saving himself as Mahomet did, become quite clear. The narrative becomes as credible as any other historical narrative of its period.

MATTHEW.

The Annunciation: the Massacre: the Flight.

Let us begin with the gospel of Matthew, bearing in mind that it does not profess to be the evidence of an eyewitness. It is a chronicle, founded, like other chronicles, on such evidence and records as the chronicler could get hold of. The only one of the evangelists who professes to give first-hand evidence as an eyewitness naturally takes care to say so; and the fact that Matthew makes no such pretension, and writes throughout as a chronicler, makes it clear that he is telling the story of Jesus as Holinshed told the story of Macbeth, except that, for a reason to be given later on, he must have collected his material and completed his book within the lifetime of persons contemporary with Jesus. Allowance must also be made for the fact that the gospel is written in the Greek language, whilst the first-hand traditions and the actual utterances of Jesus must have been in Aramaic, the dialect of Palestine. These distinctions were important, as you will find if you read Holinshed or Froissart and then read Benvenuto Cellini. You do not blame Holinshed or Froissart for believing and repeating the things they had read or been told, though you cannot always believe these things yourself. But when Cellini tells you that he saw this or did that, and you find it impossible to believe him, you lose patience with him, and are disposed to doubt everything in his autobiography. Do not forget, then, that Matthew is Holinshed and not Benvenuto. The very first pages of his narrative will put your attitude to the test.

Matthew tells us that the mother of Jesus was betrothed to a man of royal pedigree named Joseph, who was rich enough to live in a house in Bethlehem to which kings could bring gifts of gold without provoking any comment. An angel announces to Joseph that Jesus is the son of the Holy Ghost, and that he must not accuse her of infidelity because of her bearing a son of which he is not the father; but this episode disappears from the subsequent narrative: there is no record of its having been told to Jesus, nor any indication of his having any knowledge of it. The narrative, in fact, proceeds in all respects as if the annunciation formed no part of it.

Herod the Tetrarch, believing that a child has been born who will destroy him, orders all the male children to be slaughtered; and Jesus escapes by the flight of his parents into Egypt, whence they return to Nazareth when the danger is over. Here it is necessary to anticipate a little by saying that none of the other evangelists accept this story, as none of them except John, who throws over Matthew altogether, shares his craze for treating history and biography as mere records of the fulfillment of ancient Jewish prophecies. This craze no doubt led him to seek for some legend bearing out Hosea's "Out of Egypt have I called my son," and Jeremiah's Rachel weeping for her children: in fact, he says so. Nothing that interests us nowadays turns on the credibility of the massacre of the innocents and the flight into Egypt. We may forget them, and proceed to the important part of the narrative, which skips at once to the manhood of Jesus.

John the Baptist.

At this moment, a Salvationist prophet named John is stirring the people very strongly. John has declared that the rite of circumcision is insufficient as a dedication of the individual to God, and has substituted the rite of baptism. To us, who are accustomed to baptism as a matter of course, and to whom circumcision is a rather ridiculous foreign practice of no consequence, the sensational effect of such a heresy as this on the Jews is not apparent: it seems to us as natural that John should have baptized people as that the rector of our village should do so. But, as St. Paul found to his cost later on, the discarding of circumcision for baptism was to the Jews as startling a heresy as the discarding of transubstantiation in the Mass was to the Catholics of the XVI century.

Jesus joins the Baptists.

Jesus entered as a man of thirty (Luke says) into the religious life of his time by going to John the Baptist and demanding baptism from him, much as certain well-to-do young gentlemen forty years ago "joined the Socialists." As far as established Jewry was concerned, he burnt his boats by this action, and cut himself off from the routine of wealth, respectability, and orthodoxy. He then began preaching John's gospel, which, apart from the heresy of baptism, the value of which lay in its bringing the Gentiles (that is, the uncircumcized) within the pale of salvation, was a call to the people to repent of their sins, as the kingdom of heaven was at hand. Luke adds that he also preached the communism of charity; told the surveyors of taxes not to over-assess the taxpayers; and advised soldiers to be content with their wages and not to be violent or lay false accusations. There is no record of John going beyond this.

The Savage John and the Civilized Jesus.

Jesus went beyond it very rapidly, according to Matthew. Though, like John, he became an itinerant preacher, he departed widely from John's manner of life.

John went into the wilderness, not into the synagogues; and his baptismal font was the river Jordan. He was an ascetic, clothed in skins and living on locusts and wild honey, practising a savage austerity. He courted martyrdom, and met it at the hands of Herod. Jesus saw no merit either in asceticism or martyrdom. In contrast to John he was essentially a highly-civilized, cultivated person. According to Luke, he pointed out the contrast himself, chaffing the Jews for complaining that John must be possessed by the devil because he was a teetotaller and vegetarian, whilst, because Jesus was neither one nor the other, they reviled him as a gluttonous man and a winebibber, the friend of the officials and their mistresses. He told straitlaced disciples that they would have trouble enough from other people without making any for themselves, and that they should avoid martyrdom and enjoy themselves whilst they had the chance. "When they persecute you in this city," he says, "flee into the next." He preaches in the synagogues and in the open air indifferently, just as they come. He repeatedly says, "I desire mercy and not sacrifice," meaning evidently to clear himself of the inveterate superstition that suffering is gratifying to God. "Be not, as the Pharisees, of a sad countenance," he says. He is convivial, feasting with Roman officials and sinners. He is careless of his person, and is remonstrated with for not washing his hands before sitting down to table. The followers of John the Baptist, who fast, and who expect to find the Christians greater ascetics than themselves, are disappointed at finding that Jesus and his twelve friends do not fast; and Jesus tells them that they should rejoice in him instead of being melancholy. He is jocular and tells them they will all have as much fasting as they want soon enough, whether they like it or not. He is not afraid of disease, and dines with a leper. A woman, apparently to protect him against infection, pours a costly unguent on his head, and is rebuked because what it cost might have been given to the poor. He poohpoohs that lowspirited view, and says, as he said when he was reproached for not fasting, that the poor are always there to be helped, but that he is not there to be anointed always, implying that you should never lose a chance of being happy when there is so much misery in the world. He breaks the Sabbath; is impatient of conventionality when it is uncomfortable or obstructive; and outrages the feelings of the Jews by breaches of it. He is apt to accuse people who feel that way of hypocrisy. Like the late Samuel Butler, he regards disease as a department of sin, and on curing a lame man, says "Thy sins are forgiven" instead of "Arise and walk," subsequently maintaining, when the Scribes reproach him for assuming power to forgive sin as well as to cure disease, that the two come to the same thing. He has no modest affectations, and claims to be greater than Solomon or Jonah. When reproached, as Bunyan was, for resorting to the art of fiction when teaching in parables, he justifies himself on the ground that art is the only way in which the people can be taught. He is, in short, what we should call an artist and a Bohemian in his manner of life.

Jesus not a Proselytist.

A point of considerable practical importance today is that he expressly repudiates the idea that forms of religion, once rooted, can be weeded out and replanted with the flowers of a foreign faith. "If you try to root up the tares you will root up the wheat as well." Our proselytizing missionary enterprises are thus flatly contrary to his advice; and their results appear to bear him out in his view that if you convert a man brought up in another creed, you inevitably demoralize him. He acts

on this view himself, and does not convert his disciples
from Judaism to Christianity. To this day a Christian
would be in religion a Jew initiated by baptism instead
of circumcision, and accepting Jesus as the Messiah,
and his teachings as of higher authority than those of
Moses, but for the action of the Jewish priests, who, to
save Jewry from being submerged in the rising flood of
Christianity after the capture of Jerusalem and the destruction of the Temple, set up what was practically a
new religious order, with new Scriptures and elaborate
new observances, and to their list of the accursed added
one Jeschu, a bastard magician, whose comic rogueries
brought him to a bad end like Punch or Til Eulen-
spiegel: an invention which cost them dear when the
Christians got the upper hand of them politically. The
Jew as Jesus, himself a Jew, knew him, never dreamt of
such things, and could follow Jesus without ceasing to
be a Jew.

The Teachings of Jesus.

So much for his personal life and temperament. His
public career as a popular preacher carries him equally
far beyond John the Baptist. He lays no stress on
baptism or vows, and preaches conduct incessantly. He
advocates communism, the widening of the private family
with its cramping ties into the great family of mankind
under the fatherhood of God, the abandonment of revenge and punishment, the counteracting of evil by good
instead of by a hostile evil, and an organic conception
of society in which you are not an independent individual
but a member of society, your neighbor being another
member, and each of you members one of another, as two
fingers on a hand, the obvious conclusion being that unless you love your neighbor as yourself and he recipro-
cates you will both be the worse for it. He conveys all

this with extraordinary charm, and entertains his hearers with fables (parables) to illustrate them. He has no synagogue or regular congregation, but travels from place to place with twelve men whom he has called from their work as he passed, and who have abandoned it to follow him.

The Miracles.

He has certain abnormal powers by which he can perform miracles. He is ashamed of these powers, but, being extremely compassionate, cannot refuse to exercise them when afflicted people beg him to cure them, when multitudes of people are hungry, and when his disciples are terrified by storms on the lakes. He asks for no reward, but begs the people not to mention these powers of his. There are two obvious reasons for his dislike of being known as a worker of miracles. One is the natural objection of all men who possess such powers, but have far more important business in the world than to exhibit them, to be regarded primarily as charlatans, besides being pestered to give exhibitions to satisfy curiosity. The other is that his view of the effect of miracles upon his mission is exactly that taken later on by Rousseau. He perceives that they will discredit him and divert attention from his doctrine by raising an entirely irrelevant issue between his disciples and his opponents.

Possibly my readers may not have studied Rousseau's Letters Written From The Mountain, which may be regarded as the classic work on miracles as credentials of divine mission. Rousseau shews, as Jesus foresaw, that the miracles are the main obstacle to the acceptance of Christianity, because their incredibility (if they were not incredible they would not be miracles) makes people sceptical as to the whole narrative, credible enough in the main, in which they occur, and suspicious of the doc-

trine with which they are thus associated. "Get rid of
the miracles," said Rousseau, "and the whole world will
fall at the feet of Jesus Christ." He points out that
miracles offered as evidence of divinity, and failing to
convince, make divinity ridiculous. He says, in effect,
there is nothing in making a lame man walk: thousands
of lame men have been cured and have walked without
any miracle. Bring me a man with only one leg and
make another grow instantaneously on him before my
eyes; and I will be really impressed; but mere cures of
ailments that have often been cured before are quite useless as evidence of anything else than desire to help and
power to cure.

Jesus, according to Matthew, agreed so entirely with
Rousseau, and felt the danger so strongly, that when
people who were not ill or in trouble came to him and
asked him to exercise his powers as a sign of his mission,
he was irritated beyond measure, and refused with an
indignation which they, not seeing Rousseau's point,
must have thought very unreasonable. To be called "an
evil and adulterous generation" merely for asking a
miracle worker to give an exhibition of his powers, is
rather a startling experience. Mahomet, by the way,
also lost his temper when people asked him to perform
miracles. But Mahomet expressly disclaimed any unusual powers; whereas it is clear from Matthew's story
that Jesus (unfortunately for himself, as he thought)
had some powers of healing. It is also obvious that the
exercise of such powers would give rise to wild tales of
magical feats which would expose their hero to condem-
nation as an impostor among people whose good opinion
was of great consequence to the movement started by his
mission.

But the deepest annoyance arising from the miracles
would be the irrelevance of the issue raised by them.
Jesus's teaching has nothing to do with miracles. If his

mission had been simply to demonstrate a new method of restoring lost eyesight, the miracle of curing the blind would have been entirely relevant. But to say "You should love your enemies; and to convince you of this I will now proceed to cure this gentleman of cataract" would have been, to a man of Jesus's intelligence, the proposition of an idiot. If it could be proved today that not one of the miracles of Jesus actually occurred, that proof would not invalidate a single one of his didactic utterances; and conversely, if it could be proved that not only did the miracles actually occur, but that he had wrought a thousand other miracles a thousand times more wonderful, not a jot of weight would be added to his doctrine. And yet the intellectual energy of sceptics and divines has been wasted for generations in arguing about the miracles on the assumption that Christianity is at stake in the controversy as to whether the stories of Matthew are false or true. According to Matthew himself, Jesus must have known this only too well; for wherever he went he was assailed with a clamor for miracles, though his doctrine created bewilderment.

So much for the miracles! Matthew tells us further, that Jesus declared that his doctrines would be attacked by Church and State, and that the common multitude were the salt of the earth and the light of the world. His disciples, in their relations with the political and ecclesiastical organizations, would be as sheep among wolves.

Matthew imputes Bigotry to Jesus.

Matthew, like most biographers, strives to identify the opinions and prejudices of his hero with his own. Although he describes Jesus as tolerant even to carelessness, he draws the line at the Gentile, and represents Jesus as a bigoted Jew who regards his mission as addressed exclusively to "the lost sheep of the house of Israel." When a woman of Canaan begged Jesus to cure her daughter, he first refused to speak to her, and then told her brutally that "It is not meet to take the children's bread and cast it to the dogs." But when the woman said, "Truth, Lord; yet the dogs eat of the crumbs which fall from their master's table," she melted the Jew out of him and made Christ a Christian. To the woman whom he had just called a dog he said, "O woman, great is thy faith: be it unto thee even as thou wilt." This is somehow one of the most touching stories in the gospel; perhaps because the woman rebukes the prophet by a touch of his own finest quality. It is certainly out of character; but as the sins of good men are always out of character, it is not safe to reject the story as invented in the interest of Matthew's determination that Jesus shall have nothing to do with the Gentiles. At all events, there the story is; and it is by no means the only instance in which Matthew reports Jesus, in spite of the charm of his preaching, as extremely uncivil in private intercourse.

The Great Change.

So far the history is that of a man sane and interesting apart from his special gifts as orator, healer, and prophet. But a startling change occurs. One day, after the disciples have discouraged him for a long time by their misunderstanings of his mission, and their speculations as to whether he is one of the old prophets come again, and if so, which, his disciple Peter suddenly solves the problem by exclaiming, "Thou are the Christ, the son of the living God." At this Jesus is extraordinarily pleased and excited. He declares that Peter has had a revelation straight from God. He makes a pun on

Peter's name, and declares him the founder of his
Church. And he accepts his destiny as a god by announcing that he will be killed when he goes to Jerusalem; for if he is really the Christ, it is a necessary
part of his legendary destiny that he shall be slain.
Peter, not understanding this, rebukes him for what
seems mere craven melancholy; and Jesus turns fiercely
on him and cries, "Get thee behind me, Satan."

Jesus now becomes obsessed with a conviction of his
divinity, and talks about it continually to his disciples,
though he forbids them to mention it to others. They
begin to dispute among themselves as to the position they
shall occupy in heaven when his kingdom is established.
He rebukes them strenuously for this, and repeats his
teaching that greatness means service and not domina-
tion; but he himself, always instinctively somewhat
haughty, now becomes arrogant, dictatorial, and even
abusive, never replying to his critics without an insulting
epithet, and even cursing a fig-tree which disappoints
him when he goes to it for fruit. He assumes all the traditions of the folk-lore gods, and announces that, like
John Barleycorn, he will be barbarously slain and
buried, but will rise from the earth and return to life.
He attaches to himself the immemorial tribal ceremony
of eating the god, by blessing bread and wine and handing them to his disciples with the words "This is my
body: this is my blood." He forgets his own teaching
and threatens eternal fire and eternal punishment. He
announces, in addition to his Barleycorn resurrection,
that he will come to the world a second time in glory
and establish his kingdom on earth. He fears that this
may lead to the appearance of impostors claiming to be
himself, and declares explicitly and repeatedly that no
matter what wonders these impostors may perform, his
own coming will be unmistakable, as the stars will fall
from heaven, and trumpets be blown by angels. Further

he declares that this will take place during the lifetime of persons then present.

Jerusalem and the Mystical Sacrifice.

In this new frame of mind he at last enters Jerusalem amid great popular curiosity; drives the moneychangers and sacrifice sellers out of the temple in a riot; refuses to interest himself in the beauties and wonders of the temple building on the ground that presently not a stone of it shall be left on another; reviles the high priests and elders in intolerable terms; and is arrested by night in a garden to avoid a popular disturbance. He makes no resistance, being persuaded that it is part of his destiny as a god to be murdered and to rise again. One of his followers shews fight, and cuts off the ear of one of his captors. Jesus rebukes him, but does not attempt to heal the wound, though he declares that if he wished to resist he could easily summon twelve million angels to his aid. He is taken before the high priest and by him handed over to the Roman governor, who is puzzled by his silent refusal to defend himself in any way, or to contradict his accusers or their witnesses, Pilate having naturally no idea that the prisoner conceives himself as going through an inevitable process of torment, death, and burial as a prelude to resurrection. Before the high priest he has also been silent except that when the priest asks him is he the Christ, the Son of God, he replies that they shall all see the Son of Man sitting at the right hand of power, and coming on the clouds of heaven. He maintains this attitude with frightful fortitude whilst they scourge him, mock him, torment him, and finally crucify him between two thieves. His prolonged agony of thirst and pain on the cross at last breaks his spirit, and he dies with a cry of "My God: why hast Thou forsaken me?"

Not this Man but Barabbas.

Meanwhile he has been definitely rejected by the people as well as by the priests. Pilate, pitying him, and unable to make out exactly what he has done (the blasphemy that has horrified the high priest does not move the Roman) tries to get him off by reminding the people that they have, by custom, the right to have a prisoner released at that time, and suggests that he should release Jesus. But they insist on his releasing a prisoner named Barabbas instead, and on having Jesus crucified. Matthew gives no clue to the popularity of Barabbas, describing him simply as "a notable prisoner." The later gospels make it clear, very significantly, that his offence was sedition and insurrection; that he was an advocate of physical force; and that he had killed his man. The choice of Barabbas thus appears as a popular choice of the militant advocate of physical force as against the unresisting advocate of mercy.

The Resurrection.

Matthew then tells how after three days an angel opened the family vault of one Joseph, a rich man of Arimathea, who had buried Jesus in it, whereupon Jesus rose and returned from Jerusalem to Galilee and resumed his preaching with his disciples, assuring them that he would now be with them to the end of the world.

At that point the narrative abruptly stops. The story has no ending.

Date of Matthew's Narrative.

One effect of the promise of Jesus to come again in glory during the lifetime of some of his hearers is to date the gospel without the aid of any scholarship. It must have been written during the lifetime of Jesus's contemporaries: that is, whilst it was still possible for the promise of his Second Coming to be fulfilled. The death of the last person who had been alive when Jesus said "There be some of them that stand here that shall in no wise taste death till they see the Son of Man coming in his kingdom" destroyed the last possibility of the promised Second Coming, and bore out the incredulity of Pilate and the Jews. And as Matthew writes as one believing in that Second Coming, and in fact left his story unfinished to be ended by it, he must have produced his gospel within a lifetime of the crucifixion. Also, he must have believed that reading books would be one of the pleasures of the kingdom of heaven on earth.

Class Type of Matthew's Jesus.

One more circumstance must be noted as gathered from Matthew. Though he begins his story in such a way as to suggest that Jesus belonged to the privileged classes, he mentions later on that when Jesus attempted to preach in his own country, and had no success there, the people said, "Is not this the carpenter's son?" But Jesus's manner throughout is that of an aristocrat, or at the very least the son of a rich bourgeois, and by no means a lowly-minded one at that. We must be careful therefore to conceive Joseph, not as a modern proletarian carpenter working for weekly wages, but as a master craftsman of royal descent. John the Baptist may have been a Keir Hardie; but the Jesus of Matthew is of the Ruskin-Morris class.

This haughty characterization is so marked that if we had no other documents concerning Jesus than the gospel of Matthew, we should not feel as we do about him.

We should have been much less loth to say, "There is a man here who was sane until Peter hailed him as the Christ, and who then became a monomaniac." We should have pointed out that his delusion is a very common delusion among the insane, and that such insanity is quite consistent with the retention of the argumentative cunning and penetration which Jesus displayed in Jerusalem after his delusion had taken complete hold of him. We should feel horrified at the scourging and mocking and crucifixion just as we should if Ruskin had been treated in that way when he also went mad, instead of being cared for as an invalid. And we should have had no clear perception of any special significance in his way of calling the Son of God the Son of Man. We should have noticed that he was a Communist; that he regarded much of what we call law and order as machinery for robbing the poor under legal forms; that he thought domestic ties a snare for the soul; that he agreed with the proverb "The nearer the Church, the farther from God;" that he saw very plainly that the masters of the community should be its servants and not its oppressors and parasites; and that though he did not tell us not to fight our enemies, he did tell us to love them, and warned us that they who draw the sword shall perish by the sword. All this shews a great power of seeing through vulgar illusions, and a capacity for a higher morality than has yet been established in any civilized community; but it does not place Jesus above Confucius or Plato, not to mention more modern philosophers and moralists.

MARK.

The Women Disciples and the Ascension.

Let us see whether we can get anything more out of Mark, whose gospel, by the way, is supposed to be older

than Matthew's. Mark is brief; and it does not take
long to discover that he adds nothing to Matthew except
the ending of the story by Christ's ascension into heaven,
and the news that many women had come with Jesus to
Jerusalem, including Mary Magdalene, out of whom he
had cast seven devils. On the other hand Mark says
nothing about the birth of Jesus, and does not touch his
career until his adult baptism by John. He apparently
regards Jesus as a native of Nazareth, as John does,
and not of Bethlehem, as Matthew and Luke do, Bethlehem being the city of David, from whom Jesus is said
by Matthew and Luke to be descended. He describes
John's doctrine as "Baptism of repentance unto remission of sins": that is, a form of Salvationism. He tells
us that Jesus went into the synagogues and taught, not
as the Scribes but as one having authority: that is, we
infer, he preaches his own doctrine as an original moralist instead of repeating what the books say. He describes the miracle of Jesus reaching the boat by walking across the sea, but says nothing about Peter trying
to do the same. Mark sees what he relates more vividly
than Matthew, and gives touches of detail that bring
the event more clearly before the reader. He says, for
instance, that when Jesus walked on the waves to the
boat, he was passing it by when the disciples called out to
him. He seems to feel that Jesus's treatment of the
woman of Canaan requires some apology, and therefore
says that she was a Greek of Syrophenician race, which
probably excused any incivility to her in Mark's eyes.
He represents the father of the boy whom Jesus cured
of epilepsy after the transfiguration as a sceptic who
says "Lord, I believe: help thou mine unbelief." He
tells the story of the widow's mite, omitted by Matthew.
He explains that Barabbas was "lying bound with them
that made insurrection, men who in the insurrection had
committed murder." Joseph of Arimathea, who buried

Jesus in his own tomb, and who is described by Matthew
as a disciple, is described by Mark as "one who also
himself was looking for the kingdom of God," which
suggests that he was an independent seeker. Mark earns
our gratitude by making no mention of the old prophecies, and thereby not only saves time, but avoids the
absurd implication that Christ was merely going through
a predetermined ritual, like the works of a clock, instead
of living. Finally Mark reports Christ as saying, after
his resurrection, that those who believe in him will be
saved and those who do not, damned; but it is impossible
to discover whether he means anything by a state of
damnation beyond a state of error. The paleographers
regard this passage as tacked on by a later scribe.

On the whole Mark leaves the modern reader where
Matthew left him.

LUKE.

Luke the Literary Artist.

When we come to Luke, we come to a later story-
teller, and one with a stronger natural gift for his art.
Before you have read twenty lines of Luke's gospel you
are aware that you have passed from the chronicler writing for the sake of recording important facts, to the
artist, telling the story for the sake of telling it. At the
very outset he achieves the most charming idyll in the
Bible: the story of Mary crowded out of the inn into the
stable and laying her newly-born son in the manger, and
of the shepherds abiding in the field keeping watch over
their flocks by night, and how the angel of the Lord
came upon them, and the glory of the Lord shone around
them, and suddenly there was with the angel a multitude
of the heavenly host. These shepherds go to the stable
and take the place of the kings in Matthew's chronicle.

So completely has this story conquered and fascinated our imagination that most of us suppose all the gospels to contain it; but it is Luke's story and his alone: none of the others have the smallest hint of it.

The Charm of Luke's Narrative.

Luke gives the charm of sentimental romance to every incident. The Annunciation, as described by Matthew, is made to Joseph, and is simply a warning to him not to divorce his wife for misconduct. In Luke's gospel it is made to Mary herself, at much greater length, with a sense of the ecstasy of the bride of the Holy Ghost. Jesus is refined and softened almost out of recognition: the stern peremptory disciple of John the Baptist, who never addresses a Pharisee or a Scribe without an insulting epithet, becomes a considerate, gentle, sociable, almost urbane person; and the Chauvinist Jew becomes a pro-Gentile who is thrown out of the synagogue in his own town for reminding the congregation that the prophets had sometimes preferred Gentiles to Jews. In fact they try to throw him down from a sort of Tarpeian rock which they use for executions; but he makes his way through them and escapes: the only suggestion of a feat of arms on his part in the gospels. There is not a word of the Syrophenician woman. At the end he is calmly superior to his sufferings; delivers an address on his way to execution with unruffled composure; does not despair on the cross; and dies with perfect dignity, commending his spirit to God, after praying for the forgiveness of his persecutors on the ground that "They know not what they do." According to Matthew, it is part of the bitterness of his death that even the thieves who are crucified with him revile him. According to Luke, only one of them does this; and he is rebuked by the other, who begs Jesus to remember him when he

4

comes into his kingdom. To which Jesus replies, "This day shalt thou be with me in Paradise," implying that he will spend the three days of his death there. In short, every device is used to get rid of the ruthless horror of the Matthew chronicle, and to relieve the strain of the Passion by touching episodes, and by representing Christ as superior to human suffering. It is Luke's Jesus who has won our hearts.

The Touch of Parisian Romance.

Luke's romantic shrinking from unpleasantness, and his sentimentality, are illustrated by his version of the woman with the ointment. Matthew and Mark describe it as taking place in the house of Simon the Leper, where it is objected to as a waste of money. In Luke's version the leper becomes a rich Pharisee; the woman becomes a Dame aux Camellias; and nothing is said about money and the poor. The woman washes the feet of Jesus with her tears and dries them with her hair; and he is reproached for suffering a sinful woman to touch him. It is almost an adaptation of the unromantic Matthew to the Parisian stage. There is a distinct attempt to increase the feminine interest all through. The slight lead given by Mark is taken up and developed. More is said about Jesus's mother and her feelings. Christ's following of women, just mentioned by Mark to account for their presence at his tomb, is introduced earlier; and some of the women are named; so that we are introduced to Joanna the wife of Chuza, Herod's steward, and Susanna. There is the quaint little domestic episode between Mary and Martha. There is the parable of the Prodigal Son, appealing to the indulgence romance has always shewn to Charles Surface and Des Grieux. Women follow Jesus to the cross; and he makes them a speech beginning "Daughters of Jerusalem." Slight as these changes may seem, they make a great change in the atmosphere. The Christ of Matthew could never have become what is vulgarly called a woman's hero (though the truth is that the popular demand for sentiment, as far as it is not simply human, is more manly than womanly); but the Christ of Luke has made possible those pictures which now hang in many ladies' chambers, in which Jesus is represented exactly as he is represented in the Lourdes cinematograph, by a handsome actor. The only touch of realism which Luke does not instinctively suppress for the sake of producing this kind of amenity is the reproach addressed to Jesus for sitting down to table without washing his hands; and that is retained because an interesting discourse hangs on it.

Waiting for the Messiah.

Another new feature in Luke's story is that it begins in a world in which everyone is expecting the advent of the Christ. In Matthew and Mark, Jesus comes into a normal Philistine world like our own of today. Not until the Baptist foretells that one greater than himself shall come after him does the old Jewish hope of a Messiah begin to stir again; and as Jesus begins as a disciple of John, and is baptized by him, nobody connects him with that hope until Peter has the sudden inspiration which produces so startling an effect on Jesus. But in Luke's gospel men's minds, and especially women's minds, are full of eager expectation of a Christ not only before the birth of Jesus, but before the birth of John the Baptist, the event with which Luke begins his story. Whilst Jesus and John are still in their mothers' wombs, John leaps at the approach of Jesus when the two mothers visit one another. At the circumcision of Jesus pious men and women hail the infant as the Christ.

The Baptist himself is not convinced; for at quite a late period in his former disciple's career he sends two young men to ask Jesus is he really the Christ. This is noteworthy because Jesus immediately gives them a deliberate exhibition of miracles, and bids them tell John what they have seen, and ask him what he thinks *now*. This is in complete contradiction to what I have called the Rousseau view of miracles as inferred from Matthew. Luke shews all a romancer's thoughtlessness about miracles; he regards them as "signs": that is, as proofs of the divinity of the person performing them, and not merely of thaumaturgic powers. He revels in miracles just as he revels in parables: they make such capital stories. He cannot allow the calling of Peter, James, and John from their boats to pass without a comic miraculous overdraft of fishes, with the net sinking the boats and provoking Peter to exclaim, "Depart from me; for I am a sinful man, O Lord," which should probably be translated, "I want no more of your miracles: natural fishing is good enough for my boats."

There are some other novelties in Luke's version. Pilate sends Jesus to Herod, who happens to be in Jerusalem just then, because Herod had expressed some curiosity about him; but nothing comes of it: the prisoner will not speak to him. When Jesus is ill received in a Samaritan village James and John propose to call down fire from heaven and destroy it; and Jesus replies that he is come not to destroy lives but to save them. The bias of Jesus against lawyers is emphasized, and also his resolution not to admit that he is more bound to his relatives than to strangers. He snubs a woman who blesses his mother. As this is contrary to the traditions of sentimental romance, Luke would presumably have avoided it had he not become persuaded that the brotherhood of Man and the Fatherhood of God are superior even to sentimental considerations. The story

of the lawyer asking what are the two chief command-
ments is changed by making Jesus put the question to
the lawyer instead of answering it.

As to doctrine, Luke is only clear when his feelings
are touched. His logic is weak; for some of the sayings
of Jesus are pieced together wrongly, as anyone who has
read them in the right order and context in Matthew
will discover at once. He does not make anything new
out of Christ's mission, and, like the other evangelists,
thinks that the whole point of it is that Jesus was the
long expected Christ, and that he will presently come
back to earth and establish his kingdom, having duly
died and risen again after three days. Yet Luke not
only records the teaching as to communism and the discarding of hate, which have, of course, nothing to do
with the Second Coming, but quotes one very remarkable saying which is not compatible with it, which is,
that people must not go about asking where the kingdom of heaven is, and saying "Lo, here!" and "Lo,
there!" because the kingdom of heaven is within them.
But Luke has no sense that this belongs to a quite different order of thought to his Christianity, and retains un-
disturbed his view of the kingdom as a locality as definite as Jerusalem or Madagascar.

JOHN.

A New Story and a New Character.

The gospel of John is a surprise after the others.
Matthew, Mark and Luke describe the same events in
the same order (the variations in Luke are negligible),
and their gospels are therefore called the synoptic gospels. They tell substantially the same story of a wandering preacher who at the end of his life came to Jerusalem. John describes a preacher who spent practically

exactly as he does. Hence I conclude that the dates of
the original narratives cannot be ascertained, and that
we must make the best of the evangelists' own accounts
of themselves. There is, as we have seen, a very marked
difference between them, leaving no doubt that we are
dealing with four authors of well-marked diversity; but
they all end in an attitude of expectancy of the Second
Coming which they agree in declaring Jesus to have positively and unequivocally promised within the lifetime of
his contemporaries. Any believer compiling a gospel
after the last of these contemporaries had passed away,
would either reject and omit the tradition of that promise
on the ground that since it was not fulfilled, and could
never now be fulfilled, it could not have been made, or
else have had to confess to the Jews, who were the keen-
est critics of the Christians, that Jesus was either an
impostor or the victim of a delusion. Now all the evangelists except Matthew expressly declare themselves to
be believers; and Matthew's narrative is obviously not
that of a sceptic. I therefore assume as a matter of
common sense that, interpolations apart, the gospels are
derived from narratives written in the first century A.D.
I include John, because though it may be claimed that
he hedged his position by claiming that Christ, who
specially loved him, endowed him with a miraculous life
until the Second Coming, the conclusion being that John
is alive at this moment, I cannot believe that a literary
forger could hope to save the situation by so outrageous
a pretension. Also, John's narrative is in many passages
nearer to the realities of public life than the simple
chronicle of Matthew or the sentimental romance of Luke.
This may be because John was obviously more a man of
the world than the others, and knew, as mere chroniclers
and romancers never know, what actually happens away
from books and desks. But it may also be because he saw
and heard what happened instead of collecting traditions

about it. The paleographers and daters of first quotations may say what they please: John's claim to give evidence as an eyewitness whilst the others are only compiling history is supported by a certain verisimilitude which appeals to me as one who has preached a new doctrine and argued about it, as well as written stories. This verisimilitude may be dramatic art backed by knowledge of public life; but even at that we must not forget that the best dramatic art is the operation of a divinatory instinct for truth. Be that as it may, John was certainly not the man to believe in the Second Coming and yet give a date for it after that date had passed. There is really no escape from the conclusion that the originals of all the gospels date from the period within which there was still a possibility of the Second Coming occurring at the promised time.

The Peculiar Theology of Jesus.

In spite of the suspicions roused by John's idiosyncrasies, his narrative is of enormous importance to those who go to the gospels for a credible modern religion. For it is John who adds to the other records such sayings as that "I and my father are one"; that "God is a spirit"; that the aim of Jesus is not only that the people should have life, but that they should have it "more abundantly" (a distinction much needed by people who think a man is either alive or dead, and never consider the important question how much alive he is); and that men should bear in mind what they were told in the 82nd Psalm: that they are gods, and are responsible for the doing of the mercy and justice of God. The Jews stoned him for saying these things, and, when he remonstrated with them for stupidly stoning one who had done nothing to them but good works, replied "For a good work we stone thee not; but for blasphemy, because that thou, be-

ing a man, makest thyself God." He insists (referring
to the 82nd psalm) that if it is part of their own religion
that they are gods on the assurance of God himself, it
cannot be blasphemy for him, whom the Father sanctified
and sent into the world, to say "I am the son of God."
But they will not have this at any price; and he has to
escape from their fury. Here the point is obscured by
the distinction made by Jesus between himself and other
men. He says, in effect, "If you are gods, then, *à for-
tiori,* I am a god." John makes him say this, just as he
makes him say "I am the light of the world." But Matthew makes him say to the people "Ye are the light of
the world." John has no grip of the significance of
these scraps which he has picked up: he is far more interested in a notion of his own that men can escape death
and do even more extraordinary things than Christ himself: in fact, he actually represents Jesus as promising
this explicitly, and is finally led into the audacious hint
that he, John, is himself immortal in the flesh. Still, he
does not miss the significant sayings altogether. However
inconsistent they may be with the doctrine he is con-
sciously driving at, they appeal to some sub-intellectual
instinct in him that makes him stick them in, like a child
sticking tinsel stars on the robe of a toy angel.

John does not mention the ascension; and the end of
his narrative leaves Christ restored to life, and appear-
ing from time to time among his disciples. It is on one
of these occasions that John describes the miraculous
draught of fishes which Luke places at the other end of
Christ's career, at the call of the sons of Zebedee.

John agreed as to the Trial and Crucifixion.

Although John, following his practice of shewing
Jesus's skill as a debater, makes him play a less passive
part at his trial, he still gives substantially the same ac-

count of it as all the rest. And the question that would occur to any modern reader never occurs to him, any more than it occurred to Matthew, Mark, or Luke. That question is, Why on earth did not Jesus defend himself, and make the people rescue him from the High Priest? He was so popular that they were unable to prevent him driving the money-changers out of the temple, or to arrest him for it. When they did arrest him afterwards, they had to do it at night in a garden. He could have argued with them as he had often done in the temple, and justified himself both to the Jewish law and to Caesar. And he had physical force at his command to back up his arguments: all that was needed was a speech to rally his followers; and he was not gagged. The reply of the evangelists would have been that all these inquiries are idle, because if Jesus had wished to escape, he could have saved himself all that trouble by doing what John describes him as doing: that is, casting his captors to the earth by an exertion of his miraculous power. If you asked John why he let them get up again and torment and execute him, John would have replied that it was part of the destiny of God to be slain and buried and to rise again, and that to have avoided this destiny would have been to repudiate his Godhead. And that is the only apparent explanation. Whether you believe with the evangelists that Christ could have rescued himself by a miracle, or, as a modern Secularist, point out that he could have defended himself effectually, the fact remains that according to all the narratives he did not do so. He had to die like a god, not to save himself "like one of the princes." [1] The consensus on this

[1] Jesus himself had refered to that psalm (LXXXII) in which men who have judged unjustly and accepted the persons of the wicked (including by anticipation practically all the white inhabitants of the British Isles and the North American continent, to mention no other places) are condemned in the words, "I have said, ye are gods; and all of ye are children of the Most High; but ye shall die like men, and fall like one of the princes."

point is important, because it proves the absolute sincerity of Jesus's declaration that he was a god. No impostor would have accepted such dreadful consequences without an effort to save himself. No impostor would have been nerved to endure them by the conviction that he would rise from the grave and live again after three days. If we accept the story at all, we must believe this, and believe also that his promise to return in glory and establish his kingdom on earth within the lifetime of men then living, was one which he believed that he could, and indeed must fulfil. Two evangelists declare that in his last agony he despaired, and reproached God for forsaking him. The other two represent him as dying in unshaken conviction and charity with the simple remark that the ordeal was finished. But all four testify that his faith was not deceived, and that he actually rose again after three days. And I think it unreasonable to doubt that all four wrote their narratives in full faith that the other promise would be fulfilled too, and that they themselves might live to witness the Second Coming.

Credibility of the Gospels.

It will be noted by the older among my readers, who are sure to be obsessed more or less by elderly wrangles as to whether the gospels are credible as matter-of-fact narratives, that I have hardly raised this question, and have accepted the credible and incredible with equal complacency. I have done this because credibility is a subjective condition, as the evolution of religious belief clearly shews. Belief is not dependent on evidence and reason. There is as much evidence that the miracles occurred as that the battle of Waterloo occurred, or that a large body of Russian troops passed through England in 1914 to take part in the war on the western front. The rea-

sons for believing in the murder of Pompey are the same
as the reasons for believing in the raising of Lazarus.
Both have been believed and doubted by men of equal
intelligence. Miracles, in the sense of phenomena we
cannot explain, surround us on every hand; life itself is
the miracle of miracles. Miracles in the sense of events
that violate the normal course of our experience are
vouched for every day: the flourishing Church of Christ
Scientist is founded on a multitude of such miracles. Nobody believes all the miracles: everybody believes some
of them. I cannot tell why men who will not believe that
Jesus ever existed yet believe firmly that Shakespear was
Bacon. I cannot tell why people who believe that angels
appeared and fought on our side at the battle of Mons,
and who believe that miracles occur quite frequently at
Lourdes, nevertheless boggle at the miracle of the lique-
faction of the blood of St. Januarius, and reject it as a
trick of priestcraft. I cannot tell why people who will
not believe Matthew's story of three kings bringing costly
gifts to the cradle of Jesus, believe Luke's story of the
shepherds and the stable. I cannot tell why people,
brought up to believe the Bible in the old literal way as
an infallible record and revelation, and rejecting that
view later on, begin by rejecting the Old Testament,
and give up the belief in a brimstone hell before they give
up (if they ever do) the belief in a heaven of harps,
crowns, and thrones. I cannot tell why people who will
not believe in baptism on any terms believe in vaccination
with the cruel fanaticism of inquisitors. I am convinced
that if a dozen sceptics were to draw up in parallel
columns a list of the events narrated in the gospels which
they consider credible and incredible respectively, their
lists would be different in several particulars. Belief is
literally a matter of taste.

Fashions of Belief.

Now matters of taste are mostly also matters of fashion. We are conscious of a difference between medieval fashions in belief and modern fashions. For instance, though we are more credulous than men were in the Middle Ages, and entertain such crowds of fortune-tellers, magicians, miracle workers, agents of communication with the dead, discoverers of the elixir of life, transmuters of metals, and healers of all sorts, as the Middle Ages never dreamed of as possible, yet we will not take our miracles in the form that convinced the Middle Ages. Arithmetical numbers appealed to the Middle Ages just as they do to us, because they are difficult to deal with, and because the greatest masters of numbers, the Newtons and Leibnitzes, rank among the greatest men. But there are fashions in numbers too. The Middle Ages took a fancy to some familiar number like seven; and because it was an odd number, and the world was made in seven days, and there are seven stars in Charles's Wain, and for a dozen other reasons, they were ready to believe anything that had a seven or a seven times seven in it. Seven deadly sins, seven swords of sorrow in the heart of the Virgin, seven champions of Christendom, seemed obvious and reasonable things to believe in simply because they were seven. To us, on the contrary, the number seven is the stamp of superstition. We will believe in nothing less than millions. A medieval doctor gained his patient's confidence by telling him that his vitals were being devoured by seven worms. Such a diagnosis would ruin a modern physician. The modern physician tells his patient that he is ill because every drop of his blood is swarming with a million microbes; and the patient believes him abjectly and instantly. Had a bishop told William the Conqueror that the sun was seventy-seven miles distant from the earth, William would have believed him not only out of respect for the Church, but because he would have felt that seventy-seven miles was the proper distance. The Kaiser, knowing just as little about it as the Conqueror, would send that bishop to an asylum. Yet he (I presume) unhesitatingly accepts the estimate of ninety-two and nine-tenths millions of miles, or whatever the latest big figure may be.

Credibility and Truth.

And here I must remind you that our credulity is not to be measured by the truth of the things we believe. When men believed that the earth was flat, they were not credulous: they were using their common sense, and, if asked to prove that the earth was flat, would have said simply, "Look at it." Those who refuse to believe that it is round are exercising a wholesome scepticism. The modern man who believes that the earth is round is grossly credulous. Flat Earth men drive him to fury by confuting him with the greatest ease when he tries to argue about it. Confront him with a theory that the earth is cylindrical, or annular, or hour-glass shaped, and he is lost. The thing he believes may be true, but that is not why he believes it: he believes it because in some mysterious way it appeals to his imagination. If you ask him why he believes that the sun is ninety-odd million miles off, either he will have to confess that he doesnt know, or he will say that Newton proved it. But he has not read the treatise in which Newton proved it, and does not even know that it was written in Latin. If you press an Ulster Protestant as to why he regards Newton as an infallible authority, and St. Thomas Aquinas or the Pope as superstitious liars whom, after his death, he will have the pleasure of watching from his place in heaven whilst they roast in eternal flame, or if you ask me why I take into serious consideration Colonel Sir

Almroth Wright's estimates of the number of streptococci
contained in a given volume of serum whilst I can only
laugh at the earlier estimates of the number of angels
that can be accommodated on the point of a needle, no
reasonable reply is possible except that somehow sevens
and angels are out of fashion, and billions and streptococci are all the rage.   I simply cannot tell you why Bacon, Montaigne, and Cervantes had a quite different
fashion of credulity and incredulity from the Venerable
Bede and Piers Plowman and the divine doctors of the
Aquinas-Aristotle school, who were certainly no stupider,
and had the same facts before them.   Still less can I
explain why, if we assume that these leaders of thought
had all reasoned out their beliefs, their authority seemed
conclusive to one generation and blasphemous to another,
neither generation having followed the reasoning or gone
into the facts of the matter for itself at all.

It is therefore idle to begin disputing with the reader
as to what he should believe in the gospels and what he
should disbelieve.   He will believe what he can, and disbelieve what he must.   If he draws any lines at all, they
will be quite arbitrary ones.   St. John tells us that when
Jesus explicitly claimed divine honors by the sacrament
of his body and blood, so many of his disciples left him
that their number was reduced to twelve.   Many modern
readers will not hold out so long: they will give in at the
first miracle.   Others will discriminate.   They will accept
the healing miracles, and reject the feeding of the multitude.   To some the walking on the water will be a legendary exaggeration of a swim, ending in an ordinary rescue of Peter; and the raising of Lazarus will be only a
similar glorification of a commonplace feat of artificial
respiration, whilst others will scoff at it as a planned
imposture in which Lazarus acted as a confederate.   Between the rejection of the stories as wholly fabulous and
the acceptance of them as the evangelists themselves

mean them to be accepted, there will be many shades of belief and disbelief, of sympathy and derision. It is not a question of being a Christian or not. A Mahometan Arab will accept literally and without question parts of the narrative which an English Archbishop has to reject or explain away; and many Theosophists and lovers of the wisdom of India, who never enter a Christian Church except as sightseers, will revel in parts of John's gospel which mean nothing to a pious matter-of-fact Bradford manufacturer. Every reader takes from the Bible what he can get. In submitting a précis of the gospel narratives I have not implied any estimate either of their credibility or of their truth. I have simply informed him or reminded him, as the case may be, of what those narratives tell us about their hero.

Christian Iconolatry and the Peril of the Iconoclast.

I must now abandon this attitude, and make a serious draft on the reader's attention by facing the question whether, if and when the medieval and Methodist will-to-believe the Salvationist and miraculous side of the gospel narratives fails us, as it plainly has failed the leaders of modern thought, there will be anything left of the mission of Jesus: whether, in short, we may not throw the gospels into the waste-paper basket, or put them away on the fiction shelf of our libraries. I venture to reply that we shall be, on the contrary, in the position of the man in Bunyan's riddle who found that "the more he threw away, the more he had." We get rid, to begin with, of the idolatrous or iconographic worship of Christ. By this I mean literally that worship which is given to pictures and statues of him, and to finished and unalterable stories about him. The test of the prevalence of this is that

5

if you speak or write of Jesus as a real live person, or even as a still active God, such worshippers are more horrified than Don Juan was when the statue stepped from its pedestal and came to supper with him. You may deny the divinity of Jesus; you may doubt whether he ever existed; you may reject Christianity for Judaism, Mahometanism, Shintoism, or Fire Worship; and the iconolaters, placidly contemptuous, will only classify you as a freethinker or a heathen. But if you venture to wonder how Christ would have looked if he had shaved and had his hair cut, or what size in shoes he took, or whether he swore when he stood on a nail in the carpenter's shop, or could not button his robe when he was in a hurry, or whether he laughed over the repartees by which he baffled the priests when they tried to trap him into sedition and blasphemy, or even if you tell any part of his story in the vivid terms of modern colloquial slang, you will produce an extraordinary dismay and horror among the iconolaters. You will have made the picture come out of its frame, the statue descend from its pedestal, the story become real, with all the incalculable consequences that may flow from this terrifying miracle. It is at such moments that you realize that the iconolaters have never for a moment conceived Christ as a real person who meant what he said, as a fact, as a force like electricity, only needing the invention of suitable political machinery to be applied to the affairs of mankind with revolutionary effect.

Thus it is not disbelief that is dangerous in our society: it is belief. The moment it strikes you (as it may any day) that Christ is not the lifeless harmless image he has hitherto been to you, but a rallying centre for revolutionary influences which all established States and Churches fight, you must look to yourselves; for you have brought the image to life; and the mob may not be able to bear that horror.

The Alternative to Barabbas.

But mobs must be faced if civilization is to be saved. It did not need the present war to shew that neither the iconographic Christ nor the Christ of St. Paul has succeeded in effecting the salvation of human society. Whilst I write, the Turks are said to be massacring the Armenian Christians on an unprecedented scale; but Europe is not in a position to remonstrate; for her Christians are slaying one another by every device which civilization has put within their reach as busily as they are slaying the Turks. Barabbas is triumphant everywhere; and the final use he makes of his triumph is to lead us all to suicide with heroic gestures and resounding lies. Now those who, like myself, see the Barabbasque social organization as a failure, and are convinced that the Life Force (or whatever you choose to call it) cannot be finally beaten by any failure, and will even supersede humanity by evolving a higher species if we cannot master the problems raised by the multiplication of our own numbers, have always known that Jesus had a real message, and have felt the fascination of his character and doctrine. Not that we should nowadays dream of claiming any supernatural authority for him, much less the technical authority which attaches to an educated modern philosopher and jurist. But when, having entirely got rid of Salvationist Christianity, and even contracted a prejudice against Jesus on the score of his involuntary connection with it, we engage on a purely scientific study of economics, criminology, and biology, and find that our practical conclusions are virtually those of Jesus, we are distinctly pleased and encouraged to find that we were doing him an injustice, and that the nimbus that surrounds his head in the pictures may be interpreted some day as a light of science rather than a declaration of sentiment or a label of idolatry.

The doctrines in which Jesus is thus confirmed are, roughly, the following:

1. The kingdom of heaven is within you. You are the son of God; and God is the son of man. God is a spirit, to be worshipped in spirit and in truth, and not an elderly gentleman to be bribed and begged from. We are members one of another; so that you cannot injure or help your neighbor without injuring or helping yourself. God is your father: you are here to do God's work; and you and your father are one.

2. Get rid of property by throwing it into the common stock. Dissociate your work entirely from money payments. If you let a child starve you are letting God starve. Get rid of all anxiety about tomorrow's dinner and clothes, because you cannot serve two masters: God and Mammon.

3. Get rid of judges and punishment and revenge. Love your neighbor as yourself, he being a part of yourself. And love your enemies: they are your neighbors.

4. Get rid of your family entanglements. Every mother you meet is as much your mother as the woman who bore you. Every man you meet is as much your brother as the man she bore after you. Don't waste your time at family funerals grieving for your relatives: attend to life, not to death: there are as good fish in the sea as ever came out of it, and better. In the kingdom of heaven, which, as aforesaid, is within you, there is no marriage nor giving in marriage, because you cannot devote your life to two divinities: God and the person you are married to.

Now these are very interesting propositions; and they become more interesting every day, as experience and science drive us more and more to consider them favorably. In considering them, we shall waste our time unless we give them a reasonable construction. We must assume that the man who saw his way through such a mass of popular passion and illusion as stands between us and a sense of the value of such teaching was quite aware of all the objections that occur to an average stockbroker in the first five minutes. It is true that the world is governed to a considerable extent by the considerations that occur to stockbrokers in the first five minutes; but as the result is that the world is so badly governed that those who know the truth can hardly bear to live in it, an objection from an average stockbroker constitutes in itself a *prima facie* case for any social reform.

The Reduction to Modern Practice of Christianity.

All the same, we must reduce the ethical counsels and proposals of Jesus to modern practice if they are to be of any use to us. If we ask our stockbroker to act simply as Jesus advised his disciples to act, he will reply, very justly, "You are advising me to become a tramp." If we urge a rich man to sell all that he has and give it to the poor, he will inform us that such an operation is impossible. If he sells his shares and his lands, their purchaser will continue all those activities which oppress the poor. If all the rich men take the advice simultaneously the shares will fall to zero and the lands be unsaleable. If one man sells out and throws the money into the slums, the only result will be to add himself and his dependents to the list of the poor, and to do no good to the poor beyond giving a chance few of them a drunken spree. We must therefore bear in mind that whereas, in the time of Jesus, and in the ages which grew darker and darker after his death until the darkness, after a brief false dawn in the Reformation and the Renascence, culminated in the commercial night of the nineteenth century, it was believed that you could not make men good by Act of

Parliament, we now know that you cannot make them good in any other way, and that a man who is better than his fellows is a nuisance. The rich man must sell up not only himself but his whole class; and that can be done only through the Chancellor of the Exchequer. The disciple cannot have his bread without money until there is bread for everybody without money; and that requires an elaborate municipal organization of the food supply, rate supported. Being members one of another means One Man One Vote, and One Woman One Vote, and universal suffrage and equal incomes and all sorts of modern political measures. Even in Syria in the time of Jesus his teachings could not possibly have been realized by a series of independent explosions of personal righteousness on the part of the separate units of the population. Jerusalem could not have done what even a village community cannot do, and what Robinson Crusoe himself could not have done if his conscience, and the stern compulsion of Nature, had not imposed a common rule on the half dozen Robinson Crusoes who struggled within him for not wholly compatible satisfactions. And what cannot be done in Jerusalem or Juan Fernandez cannot be done in London, New York, Paris, and Berlin.

In short, Christianity, good or bad, right or wrong, must perforce be left out of the question in human affairs until it is made practically applicable to them by complicated political devices; and to pretend that a field preacher under the governorship of Pontius Pilate, or even Pontius Pilate himself in council with all the wisdom of Rome, could have worked out applications of Christianity or any other system of morals for the twentieth century, is to shelve the subject much more effectually than Nero and all its other persecutors ever succeeded in doing. Personal righteousness, and the view that you cannot make people moral by Act of Parliament, is, in fact, the favorite defensive resort of the people who, con-sciously or subconsciously, are quite determined not to have their property meddled with by Jesus or any other reformer.

Modern Communism.

Now let us see what modern experience and modern sociology has to say to the teaching of Jesus as summarized on page lxviii. First, get rid of your property by throwing it into the common stock. One can hear the Pharisees of Jerusalem and Chorazin and Bethsaida saying, "My good fellow, if you were to divide up the wealth of Judea equally today, before the end of the year you would have rich and poor, poverty and affluence, just as you have today; for there will always be the idle and the industrious, the thrifty and the wasteful, the drunken and the sober; and, as you yourself have very justly observed, the poor we shall have always with us." And we can hear the reply, "Woe unto you, liars and hypocrites; for ye have this very day divided up the wealth of the country yourselves, as must be done every day (for man liveth not otherwise than from hand to mouth, nor can fish and eggs endure for ever); and ye have divided it unjustly; also ye have said that my reproach to you for having the poor always with you was a law unto you that this evil should persist and stink in the nostrils of God to all eternity; wherefore I think that Lazarus will yet see you beside Dives in hell." Modern Capitalism has made short work of the primitive pleas for inequality. The Pharisees themselves have organized communism in capital. Joint stock is the order of the day. An attempt to return to individual properties as the basis of our production would smash civilization more completely than ten revolutions. You cannot get the fields tilled today until the farmer becomes a co-operator. Take the shareholder to his railway, and ask him to point out to you

the particular length of rail, the particular seat in the
railway carriage, the particular lever in the engine that
is his very own and nobody elses; and he will shun you
as a madman, very wisely.   And if, like Ananias and
Sapphira, you try to hold back your little shop or what
not from the common stock, represented by the Trust, or
Combine, or Kartel, the Trust will presently freeze you
out and rope you in and finally strike you dead indus-
trially as thoroughly as St. Peter himself.   There is no
longer any practical question open as to Communism in
production: the struggle today is over the distribution of
the product: that is, over the daily dividing-up which is
the first necessity of organized society.

Redistribution.

Now it needs no Christ to convince anybody today that
our system of distribution is wildly and monstrously
wrong.   We have million-dollar babies side by side with
paupers worn out by a long life of unremitted drudgery.
One person in every five dies in a workhouse, a public
hospital, or a madhouse.   In cities like London the proportion is very nearly one in two.   Naturally so outrageous a distribution has to be effected by violence pure and
simple.   If you demur, you are sold up.   If you resist the
selling up you are bludgeoned and imprisoned, the
process being euphemistically called the maintenance of
law and order.   Iniquity can go no further.   By this time
nobody who knows the figures of the distribution defends
them.   The most bigoted British Conservative hesitates
to say that his king should be much poorer than Mr.
Rockefeller, or to proclaim the moral superiority of
prostitution to needlework on the ground that it pays
better.   The need for a drastic redistribution of income
in all civilized countries is now as obvious and as generally admitted as the need for sanitation.

Shall He Who Makes, Own.

It is when we come to the question of the proportions in which we are to redistribute that controversy begins. We are bewildered by an absurdly unpractical notion that in some way a man's income should be given to him, not to enable him to live, but as a sort of Sunday School Prize for good behavior. And this folly is complicated by a less ridiculous but quite as unpractical belief that it is possible to assign to each person the exact portion of the national income that he or she has produced. To a child it seems that the blacksmith has made a horse-shoe, and that therefore the horse-shoe is his. But the blacksmith knows that the horse-shoe does not belong solely to him, but to his landlord, to the rate collector and tax-gatherer, to the men from whom he bought the iron and anvil and the coals, leaving only a scrap of its value for himself; and this scrap he has to exchange with the butcher and baker and the clothier for the things that he really appropriates as living tissue or its wrappings, paying for all of them more than their cost; for these fellow traders of his have also their landlords and moneylenders to satisfy. If, then, such simple and direct village examples of apparent individual production turn out on a moment's examination to be the products of an elaborate social organization, what is to be said of such products as dreadnoughts, factory-made pins and needles, and steel pens? If God takes the dreadnought in one hand and a steel pen in the other, and asks Job who made them, and to whom they should belong by maker's right, Job must scratch his puzzled head with a potsherd and be dumb, unless indeed it strikes him that God is the ultimate maker, and that all we have a right to do with the product is to feed his lambs.

Labor Time.

So maker's right as an alternative to taking the advice
of Jesus would not work. In practice nothing was possible in that direction but to pay a worker by labor time:
so much an hour or day or week or year. But how much?
When that question came up, the only answer was "as
little as he can be starved into accepting," with the
ridiculous results already mentioned, and the additional
anomaly that the largest share went to the people who
did not work at all, and the least to those who worked
hardest. In England nine-tenths of the wealth goes into
the pockets of one-tenth of the population.

The Dream of Distribution According to Merit.

Against this comes the protest of the Sunday School
theorists "Why not distribute according to merit?" Here
one imagines Jesus, whose smile has been broadening
down the ages as attempt after attempt to escape from
his teaching has led to deeper and deeper disaster, laughing outright. Was ever so idiotic a project mooted as the
estimation of virtue in money? The London School of
Economics is, we must suppose, to set examination papers
with such questions as, "Taking the money value of the
virtues of Jesus as 100, and of Judas Iscariot as zero,
give the correct figures for, respectively, Pontius Pilate,
the proprietor of the Gadarene swine, the widow who put
her mite in the poor-box, Mr. Horatio Bottomley, Shakespear, Mr. Jack Johnson, Sir Isaac Newton, Palestrina,
Offenbach, Sir Thomas Lipton, Mr. Paul Cinquevalli,
your family doctor, Florence Nightingale, Mrs. Siddons,
your charwoman, the Archbishop of Canterbury, and the
common hangman." Or "The late Mr. Barney Barnato

received as his lawful income three thousand times as much money as an English agricultural laborer of good general character. Name the principal virtues in which Mr. Barnato exceeded the laborer three thousandfold; and give in figures the loss sustained by civilization when Mr. Barnato was driven to despair and suicide by the reduction of his multiple to one thousand." The Sunday School idea, with its principle "to each the income he deserves" is really too silly for discussion. Hamlet disposed of it three hundred years ago. "Use every man after his deserts, and who shall scape whipping?" Jesus remains unshaken as the practical man; and we stand exposed as the fools, the blunderers, the unpractical visionaries. The moment you try to reduce the Sunday School idea to figures you find that it brings you back to the hopeless plan of paying for a man's time; and your examination paper will read "The time of Jesus was worth nothing (he complained that the foxes had holes and the birds of the air nests whilst he had not a place to lay his head). Dr. Crippen's time was worth, say, three hundred and fifty pounds a year. Criticize this arrangement; and, if you dispute its justice, state in pounds, dollars, francs and marks, what their relative time wages ought to have been." Your answer may be that the question is in extremely bad taste and that you decline to answer it. But you cannot object to being asked how many minutes of a bookmaker's time is worth two hours of an astronomer's?

Vital Distribution.

In the end you are forced to ask the question you should have asked at the beginning. What do you give a man an income for? Obviously to keep him alive. Since it is evident that the first condition on which he can be kept alive without enslaving somebody else is that he shall produce an equivalent for what it costs to keep him alive, we may quite rationally compel him to abstain from idling by whatever means we employ to compel him to abstain from murder, arson, forgery, or any other crime. The one supremely foolish thing to do with him is to do nothing: that is, to be as idle, lazy, and heartless in dealing with him as he is in dealing with us. Even if we provided work for him instead of basing, as we do, our whole industrial system on successive competitive waves of overwork with their ensuing troughs of unemployment, we should still sternly deny him the alternative of not doing it; for the result must be that he will become poor and make his children poor if he has any; and poor people are cancers in the commonwealth, costing far more than if they were handsomely pensioned off as incurables. Jesus had more sense than to propose anything of the sort. He said to his disciples, in effect, "Do your work for love; and let the other people lodge and feed and clothe you for love." Or, as we should put it nowadays, "for nothing." All human experience and all natural uncommercialized human aspiration point to this as the right path. The Greeks said, "First secure an independent income; and then practise virtue." We all strive towards an independent income. We all know as well as Jesus did that if we have to take thought for the morrow as to whether there shall be anything to eat or drink it will be impossible for us to think of nobler things, or live a higher life than that of a mole, whose life is from beginning to end a frenzied pursuit of food. Until the community is organized in such a way that the fear of bodily want is forgotten as completely as the fear of wolves already is in civilized capitals, we shall never have a decent social life. Indeed the whole attraction of our present arrangements lies in the fact that they do relieve a handful of us from this fear; but as the relief is effected stupidly and wickedly by making the favored handful parasitic on the rest, they are smitten with the degeneracy which seems to be the inevitable biological penalty of complete parasitism, and corrupt culture and statecraft instead of contributing to them, their excessive leisure being as mischievous as the excessive toil of the laborers. Anyhow, the moral is clear. The two main problems of organized society, how to secure the subsistence of all its members, and how to prevent the theft of that subsistence by idlers, should be entirely dissociated; and the practical failure of one of them to automatically achieve the other recognized and acted on. We may not all have Jesus's psychological power of seeing, without any enlightenment from more modern economic phenomena, that they must fail; but we have the hard fact before us that they do fail. The only people who cling to the lazy delusion that it is possible to find a just distribution that will work automatically are those who postulate some revolutionary change like land nationalization, which by itself would obviously only force into greater urgency the problem of how to distribute the product of the land among all the individuals in the community.

Equal Distribution.

When that problem is at last faced, the question of the proportion in which the national income shall be distributed can have only one answer. All our shares must be equal. It has always been so; it always will be so. It is true that the incomes of robbers vary considerably from individual to individual; and the variation is reflected in the incomes of their parasites. The commercialization of certain exceptional talents has also produced exceptional incomes, direct and derivative. Persons who live on rent of land and capital are economically, though not legally, in the category of robbers, and have grotesquely different incomes. But in the huge mass of mankind variation of income from individual to individual is unknown, because it is ridiculously impracticable. As a device for persuading a carpenter that a judge is a creature of superior nature to himself, to be deferred and submitted to even to the death, we may give a carpenter a hundred pounds a year and a judge five thousand; but the wage for one carpenter is the wage for all the carpenters: the salary for one judge is the salary for all the judges.

The Captain and the Cabin Boy.

Nothing, therefore, is really in question, or ever has been, but the differences between class incomes. Already there is economic equality between captains, and economic equality between cabin boys. What is at issue still is whether there shall be economic equality between captains and cabin boys. What would Jesus have said? Presumably he would have said that if your only object is to produce a captain and a cabin boy for the purpose of transferring you from Liverpool to New York, or to manœuvre a fleet and carry powder from the magazine to the gun, then you need give no more than a shilling to the cabin boy for every pound you give to the more expensively trained captain. But if in addition to this you desire to allow the two human souls which are inseparable from the captain and the cabin boy, and which alone differentiate them from the donkey-engine, to develop all their possibilities, then you may find the cabin boy costing rather more than the captain, because cabin boy's work does not do so much for the soul as captain's work. Consequently you will have to give him at least as much as the captain unless you definitely wish him to be a lower creature, in which case the sooner you are hanged as an abortionist the better. That is the fundamental argument.

The Political and Biological Objections to Inequality.

But there are other reasons for objecting to class strati-fication of income which have heaped themselves up since the time of Jesus. In politics it defeats every form of government except that of a necessarily corrupt oli-garchy. Democracy in the most democratic modern re-publics: France and the United States for example, is an imposture and a delusion. It reduces justice and law to a farce: law becomes merely an instrument for keeping the poor in subjection; and accused workmen are tried, not by a jury of their peers, but by conspiracies of their exploiters. The press is the press of the rich and the curse of the poor: it becomes dangerous to teach men to read. The priest becomes the mere complement of the policeman in the machinery by which the countryhouse oppresses the village. Worst of all, marriage becomes a class affair: the infinite variety of choice which nature offers to the young in search of a mate is narrowed to a handful of persons of similar income; and beauty and health become the dreams of artists and the advertise-ments of quacks instead of the normal conditions of life. Society is not only divided but actually destroyed in all directions by inequality of income between classes: such stability as it has is due to the huge blocks of people be-tween whom there is equality of income.

Jesus as Economist.

It seems therefore that we must begin by holding the right to an income as sacred and equal, just as we now begin by holding the right to life as sacred and equal. Indeed the one right is only a restatement of the other. To hang me for cutting a dock laborer's throat after making much of me for leaving him to starve when I do

not happen to have a ship for him to unload is idiotic;
for as he does far less mischief with his throat cut than
when he is starving, a rational society would esteem the
cutthroat more highly than the capitalist. The thing has
become so obvious, and the evil so unendurable, that if our
attempt at civilization is not to perish like all the pre-
vious ones, we shall have to organize our society in such
a way as to be able to say to every person in the land,
"Take no thought, saying What shall we eat? or What
shall we drink? or Wherewithal shall we be clothed?"
We shall then no longer have a race of men whose hearts
are in their pockets and safes and at their bankers. As
Jesus said, where your treasure is, there will your heart
be also. That was why he recommended that money
should cease to be a treasure, and that we should take
steps to make ourselves utterly reckless of it, setting our
minds free for higher uses. In other words, that we
should all be gentlemen and take care of our country because our country takes care of us, instead of the com-
mercialized cads we are, doing everything and anything
for money, and selling our souls and bodies by the pound
and the inch after wasting half the day haggling over the
price. Decidedly, whether you think Jesus was God or
not, you must admit that he was a first-rate political
economist.

Jesus as Biologist.

He was also, as we now see, a first-rate biologist. It
took a century and a half of evolutionary preachers, from
Buffon and Goethe to Butler and Bergson, to convince us
that we and our father are one; that as the kingdom of
heaven is within us we need not go about looking for it
and crying Lo here! and Lo there!; that God is not a
picture of a pompous person in white robes in the family
Bible, but a spirit; that it is through this spirit that we

evolve towards greater abundance of life; that we are the lamps in which the light of the world burns: that, in short, we are gods though we die like men. All that is today sound biology and psychology; and the efforts of Natural Selectionists like Weismann to reduce evolution to mere automatism have not touched the doctrine of Jesus, though they have made short work of the theologians who conceived God as a magnate keeping men and angels as Lord Rothschild keeps buffaloes and emus at Tring.

Money the Midwife of Scientific Communism.

It may be asked here by some simple-minded reader why we should not resort to crude Communism as the disciples were told to do. This would be quite practicable in a village where production was limited to the supply of the primitive wants which nature imposes on all human beings alike. We know that people need bread and boots without waiting for them to come and ask for these things and offer to pay for them. But when civilization advances to the point at which articles are produced that no man absolutely needs and that only some men fancy or can use, it is necessary that individuals should be able to have things made to their order and at their own cost. It is safe to provide bread for everybody because everybody wants and eats bread; but it would be absurd to provide microscopes and trombones, pet snakes and polo mallets, alembics and test tubes for everybody, as nine-tenths of them would be wasted; and the nine-tenths of the population who do not use such things would object to their being provided at all. We have in the invaluable instrument called money a means of enabling every individual to order and pay for

the particular things he desires over and above the things
he must consume in order to remain alive, plus the things
the State insists on his having and using whether he wants
to or not; for example, clothes, sanitary arrangements,
armies and navies. In large communities, where even the
most eccentric demands for manufactured articles average themselves out until they can be foreseen within a
negligible margin of error, direct communism (Take what
you want without payment, as the people do in Morris's
News From Nowhere) will, after a little experience, be
found not only practicable but highly economical to an
extent that now seems impossible. The sportsmen, the
musicians, the physicists, the biologists will get their apparatus for the asking as easily as their bread, or, as at
present, their paving, street lighting, and bridges; and
the deaf man will not object to contribute to communal
flutes when the musician has to contribute to communal
ear trumpets. There are cases (for example, radium) in
which the demand may be limited to the merest handful
of laboratory workers, and in which nevertheless the
whole community must pay because the price is beyond
the means of any individual worker. But even when the
utmost allowance is made for extensions of communism
that now seem fabulous, there will still remain for a long
time to come regions of supply and demand in which men
will need and use money or individual credit, and for
which, therefore, they must have individual incomes.
Foreign travel is an obvious instance. We are so far
from even national communism still, that we shall probably have considerable developments of local communism
before it becomes possible for a Manchester man to go
up to London for a day without taking any money with
him. The modern practical form of the communism of
Jesus is therefore, for the present, equal distribution of
the surplus of the national income that is not absorbed by
simple communism.

Judge Not.

In dealing with crime and the family, modern thought and experience have thrown no fresh light on the views of Jesus. When Swift had occasion to illustrate the corruption of our civilization by making a catalogue of the types of scoundrels it produces, he always gave judges a conspicuous place alongside of them they judged. And he seems to have done this not as a restatement of the doctrine of Jesus, but as the outcome of his own observation and judgment. One of Mr. Gilbert Chesterton's stories has for its hero a judge who, whilst trying a criminal case, is so overwhelmed by the absurdity of his position and the wickedness of the things it forces him to do, that he throws off the ermine there and then, and goes out into the world to live the life of an honest man instead of that of a cruel idol. There has also been a propaganda of a soulless stupidity called Determinism, representing man as a dead object driven hither and thither by his environment, antecedents, circumstances, and so forth, which nevertheless does remind us that there are limits to the number of cubits an individual can add to his stature morally or physically, and that it is silly as well as cruel to torment a man five feet high for not being able to pluck fruit that is within the reach of men of average height. I have known a case of an unfortunate child being beaten for not being able to tell the time after receiving an elaborate explanation of the figures on a clock dial, the fact being that she was short-sighted and could not see them. This is a typical illustration of the absurdities and cruelties into which we are led by the counter-stupidity to Determinism: the doctrine of Free Will. The notion that people can be good if they like, and that you should give them a powerful additional motive for goodness by tormenting them when they do evil, would soon reduce itself to absurdity if its application were not kept within the limits which nature sets to the self-control of most of us. Nobody supposes that a man with no ear for music or no mathematical faculty could be compelled on pain of death, however cruelly inflicted, to hum all the themes of Beethoven's symphonies or to complete Newton's work on fluxions.

Limits to Free Will.

Consequently such of our laws as are not merely the intimidations by which tyrannies are maintained under pretext of law, can be obeyed through the exercise of a quite common degree of reasoning power and self-control. Most men and women can endure the ordinary annoyances and disappointments of life without committing murderous assaults. They conclude therefore that any person can refrain from such assaults if he or she chooses to, and proceed to reinforce self-control by threats of severe punishment. But in this they are mistaken. There are people, some of them possessing considerable powers of mind and body, who can no more restrain the fury into which a trifling mishap throws them than a dog can restrain himself from snapping if he is suddenly and painfully pinched. People fling knives and lighted paraffin lamps at one another in a dispute over a dinner-table. Men who have suffered several long sentences of penal servitude for murderous assaults will, the very day after they are released, seize their wives and cast them under drays at an irritating word. We have not only people who cannot resist an opportunity of stealing for the sake of satisfying their wants, but even people who have a specific mania for stealing, and do it when they are in no need of the things they steal. Burglary fascinates some men as sailoring fascinates some boys. Among respectable people how many are there who can be restrained by the warnings of their doctors and the lessons of experience from eating and drinking more than is good for them? It is true that between self-controlled people and ungovernable people there is a narrow margin of moral malingerers who can be made to behave themselves by the fear of consequences; but it is not worth while maintaining an abominable system of malicious, deliberate, costly and degrading ill-treatment of criminals for the sake of these marginal cases. For practical dealing with crime, Determinism or Predestination is quite a good working rule. People without self-control enough for social purposes may be killed, or may be kept in asylums with a view to studying their condition and ascertaining whether it is curable. To torture them and give ourselves virtuous airs at their expense is ridiculous and barbarous; and the desire to do it is vindictive and cruel. And though vindictiveness and cruelty are at least human qualities when they are frankly proclaimed and indulged, they are loathsome when they assume the robes of Justice. Which, I take it, is why Shakespear's Isabella gave such a dressing-down to Judge Angelo, and why Swift reserved the hottest corner of his hell for judges. Also, of course, why Jesus said "Judge not that ye be not judged" and "If any man hear my words and believe not, I judge him not" because "he hath one that judgeth him": namely, the Father who is one with him.

When we are robbed we generally appeal to the criminal law, not considering that if the criminal law were effective we should not have been robbed. That convicts us of vengeance.

I need not elaborate the argument further. I have dealt with it sufficiently elsewhere. I have only to point out that we have been judging and punishing ever since Jesus told us not to; and I defy anyone to make out a convincing case for believing that the world has been any better than it would have been if there had never been a judge, a prison, or a gallows in it all that time. We

have simply added the misery of punishment to the
misery of crime, and the cruelty of the judge to the
cruelty of the criminal. We have taken the bad man,
and made him worse by torture and degradation, incidentally making ourselves worse in the process. It does
not seem very sensible, does it? It would have been far
easier to kill him as kindly as possible, or to label him
and leave him to his conscience, or to treat him as an invalid or a lunatic is now treated (it is only of late years,
by the way, that madmen have been delivered from the
whip, the chain, and the cage); and this, I presume, is
the form in which the teaching of Jesus could have been
put into practice.

Jesus on Marriage and the Family.

When we come to marriage and the family, we find
Jesus making the same objection to that individual appropriation of human beings which is the essence of matri-
mony as to the individual appropriation of wealth. A
married man, he said, will try to please his wife, and a
married woman to please her husband, instead of doing
the work of God. This is another version of "Where your
treasure is, there will your heart be also." Eighteen hundred years later we find a very different person from
Jesus, Talleyrand to wit, saying the same thing. A married man with a family, said Talleyrand, will do anything
for money. Now this, though not a scientifically precise
statement, is true enough to be a moral objection to marriage. As long as a man has a right to risk his life or
his livelihood for his ideas he needs only courage and conviction to make his integrity unassailable. But he for-
feits that right when he marries. It took a revolution to
rescue Wagner from his Court appointment at Dresden;
and his wife never forgave him for being glad and feeling
free when he lost it and threw her back into poverty.

Millet might have gone on painting potboiling nudes to
the end of his life if his wife had not been of a heroic
turn herself. Women, for the sake of their children and
parents, submit to slaveries and prostitutions that no unattached woman would endure.

This was the beginning and the end of the objection of
Jesus to marriage and family ties, and the explanation
of his conception of heaven as a place where there should
be neither marrying nor giving in marriage. Now there
is no reason to suppose that when he said this he did not
mean it. He did not, as St. Paul did afterwards in his
name, propose celibacy as a rule of life; for he was not a
fool, nor, when he denounced marriage, had he yet come
to believe, as St. Paul did, that the end of the world was
at hand and there was therefore no more need to re-
plenish the earth. He must have meant that the race
should be continued without dividing with women and
men the allegiance the individual owes to God within
him. This raises the practical problem of how we are
to secure the spiritual freedom and integrity of the
priest and the nun without their barrenness and uncom-
pleted experience. Luther the priest did not solve the
problem by marrying a nun: he only testified in the most
convincing and practical way to the fact that celibacy was
a worse failure than marriage.

Why Jesus did not Marry.

To all appearance the problem oppresses only a few
exceptional people. Thoroughly conventional women
married to thoroughly conventional men should not be
conscious of any restriction: the chain not only leaves
them free to do whatever they want to do, but greatly
facilitates their doing it. To them an attack on marriage is not a blow struck in defence of their freedom
but at their rights and privileges. One would expect

that they would not only demur vehemently to the teachings of Jesus in this matter, but object strongly to his
not having been a married man himself. Even those who
regard him as a god descended from his throne in heaven
to take on humanity for a time might reasonably declare
that the assumption of humanity must have been incom-
plete at its most vital point if he were a celibate. But
the facts are flatly contrary. The mere thought of Jesus
as a married man is felt to be blasphemous by the most
conventional believers; and even those of us to whom
Jesus is no supernatural personage, but a prophet only
as Mahomet was a prophet, feel that there was something
more dignified in the bachelordom of Jesus than in the
spectacle of Mahomet lying distracted on the floor of his
harem whilst his wives stormed and squabbled and hen-
pecked round him. We are not surprised that when
Jesus called the sons of Zebedee to follow him, he did
not call their father, and that the disciples, like Jesus
himself, were all men without family entanglements. It
is evident from his impatience when people excused
themselves from following him because of their family
funerals, or when they assumed that his first duty was
to his mother, that he had found family ties and domestic
affections in his way at every turn, and had become persuaded at last that no man could follow his inner light
until he was free from their compulsion. The absence of
any protest against this tempts us to declare on this
question of marriage there are no conventional people;
and that everyone of us is at heart a good Christian
sexually.

Inconsistency of the Sex Instinct.

But the question is not so simple as that. Sex is an
exceedingly subtle and complicated instinct; and the
mass of mankind neither know nor care much about free-

dom of conscience, which is what Jesus was thinking about, and are concerned almost to obsession with sex, as to which Jesus said nothing. In our sexual natures we are torn by an irresistible attraction and an overwhelming repugnance and disgust. We have two tyrannous physical passions: concupiscence and chastity. We become mad in pursuit of sex: we become equally mad in the persecution of that pursuit. Unless we gratify our desire the race is lost: unless we restrain it we destroy ourselves. We are thus led to devise marriage institutions which will at the same time secure opportunities for the gratification of sex and raise up innumerable obstacles to it; which will sanctify it and brand it as infamous; which will identify it with virtue and with sin simultaneously. Obviously it is useless to look for any consistency in such institutions; and it is only by continual reform and readjustment, and by a considerable elasticity in their enforcement, that a tolerable result can be arrived at. I need not repeat here the long and elaborate examination of them that I prefixed to my play entitled Getting Married. Here I am concerned only with the views of Jesus on the question; and it is necessary, in order to understand the attitude of the world towards them, that we should not attribute the general approval of the decision of Jesus to remain unmarried as an endorsement of his views. We are simply in a state of confusion on the subject; but it is part of the confusion that we should conclude that Jesus was a celibate, and shrink even from the idea that his birth was a natural one, yet cling with ferocity to the sacredness of the institution which provides a refuge from celibacy.

For Better for Worse.

Jesus, however, did not express a complicated view of marriage. His objection to it was quite simple, as we have seen. He perceived that nobody could live the higher life unless money and sexual love were obtainable without sacrificing it; and he saw that the effect of marriage as it existed among the Jews (and as it still exists among ourselves) was to make the couples sacrifice every higher consideration until they had fed and pleased one another. The worst of it is that this dangerous preposterousness in marriage, instead of improving as the general conduct of married couples improves, becomes much worse. The selfish man to whom his wife is nothing but a slave, the selfish woman to whom her husband is nothing but a scapegoat and a breadwinner, are not held back from spiritual or any other adventures by fear of their effect on the welfare of their mates. Their wives do not make recreants and cowards of them: their husbands do not chain them to the cradle and the cooking range when their feet should be beautiful on the mountains. It is precisely as people become more kindly, more conscientious, more ready to shoulder the heavier part of the burden (which means that the strong shall give way to the weak and the slow hold back the swift), that marriage becomes an intolerable obstacle to individual evolution. And that is why the revolt against marriage of which Jesus was an exponent always recurs when civilization raises the standard of marital duty and affection, and at the same time produces a greater need for individual freedom in pursuit of a higher evolution.

The Remedy.

This, fortunately, is only one side of marriage; and the question arises, can it not be eliminated? The reply is reassuring: of course it can. There is no mortal reason in the nature of things why a married couple should be economically dependent on one another. The Communism advocated by Jesus, which we have seen to be entirely practicable, and indeed inevitable if our civilization is to be saved from collapse, gets rid of that difficulty completely. And with the economic dependence will go the force of the outrageous claims that derive their real sanction from the economic pressure behind them. When a man allows his wife to turn him from the best work he is capable of doing, and to sell his soul at the highest commercial prices obtainable; when he allows her to entangle him in a social routine that is wearisome and debilitating to him, or tie him to her apron strings when he needs that occasional solitude which is one of the most sacred of human rights, he does so because he has no right to impose eccentric standards of expenditure and unsocial habits on her, and because these conditions have produced by their pressure so general a custom of chaining wedded couples to one another that married people are coarsely derided when their partners break the chain. And when a woman is condemned by her parents to wait in genteel idleness and uselessness for a husband when all her healthy social instincts call her to acquire a profession and work, it is again her economic dependence on them that makes their tyranny effective.

The Case for Marriage.

Thus, though it would be too much to say that everything that is obnoxious in marriage and family life will be cured by Communism, yet it can be said that it will cure what Jesus objected to in these institutions. He made no comprehensive study of them: he only expressed his own grievance with an overwhelming sense that it is a grievance so deep that all the considerations on the other side are as dust in the balance. Obviously there are such considerations, and very weighty ones too. When Talleyrand said that a married man with a family is capable of anything, he meant anything evil; but an optimist may declare, with equal half truth, that a married man is capable of anything good; that marriage turns vagabonds into steady citizens; and that men and women will, for love of their mates and children, practise virtues that unattached individuals are incapable of. It is true that too much of this domestic virtue is self-denial, which is not a virtue at all; but then the following of the inner light at all costs is largely self-indulgence, which is just as suicidal, just as weak, just as cowardly as self-denial. Ibsen, who takes us into the matter far more resolutely than Jesus, is unable to find any golden rule: both Brand and Peer Gynt come to a bad end; and though Brand does not do as much mischief as Peer, the mischief he does do is of extraordinary intensity.

Celibacy no Remedy.

We must, I think, regard the protest of Jesus against marriage and family ties as the claim of a particular kind of individual to be free from them because they hamper his own work intolerably. When he said that if we are to follow him in the sense of taking up his work we must give up our family ties, he was simply stating a fact; and to this day the Roman Catholic priest, the Buddhist lama, and the fakirs of all the eastern denominations accept the saying. It is also accepted by the physically enterprising, the explorers, the restlessly energetic of all kinds: in short, by the adventurous. The greatest sacrifice in marriage is the sacrifice of the adventurous attitude towards life: the being settled. Those who are born tired may crave for settlement; but to fresher and stronger spirits it is a form of suicide.

Now to say of any institution that it is incompatible with both the contemplative and adventurous life is to disgrace it so vitally that all the moralizings of all the Deans and Chapters cannot reconcile our souls to its slavery. The unmarried Jesus and the unmarried Beethoven, the unmarried Joan of Arc, Clare, Teresa, Florence Nightingale seem as they should be; and the saying that there is always something ridiculous about a married philosopher becomes inevitable. And yet the celibate is still more ridiculous than the married man: the priest, in accepting the alternative of celibacy, disables himself; and the best priests are those who have been men of this world before they became men of the world to come. But as the taking of vows does not annul an existing marriage, and a married man cannot become a priest, we are again confronted with the absurdity that the best priest is a reformed rake. Thus does marriage, itself intolerable, thrust us upon intolerable alternatives. The practical solution is to make the individual economically independent of marriage and the family, and to make marriage as easily dissoluble as any other partnership: in other words, to accept the conclusions to which experience is slowly driving both our sociologists and our legislators. This will not instantly cure all the evils of marriage, nor root up at one stroke its detestable tradition of property in human bodies. But it will leave Nature free to effect a cure; and in free soil the root may wither and perish.

This disposes of all the opinions and teachings of Jesus which are still matters of controversy. They are all in line with the best modern thought. He told us what we have to do; and we have had to find the way to do it. Most of us are still, as most were in his own time, extremely recalcitrant, and are being forced along that way by painful pressure of circumstances, protesting at every step that nothing will induce us to go; that it is a ridiculous way, a disgraceful way, a socialistic way, an atheistic way, an immoral way, and that the vanguard ought to be ashamed of themselves and must be made to turn back at once. But they find that they have to follow the vanguard all the same if their lives are to be worth living.

After the Crucifixion.

Let us now return to the New Testament narrative; for what happened after the disappearance of Jesus is instructive. Unfortunately, the crucifixion was a complete political success. I remember that when I described it in these terms once before, I greatly shocked a most respectable newspaper in my native town, the Dublin Daily Express, because my journalistic phrase shewed that I was treating it as an ordinary event like Home Rule or the Insurance Act: that is (though this did not occur to the editor), as a real event which had really happened, instead of a portion of the Church service. I can only repeat, assuming as I am that it *was* a real event and did actually happen, that it was as complete a success as any in history. Christianity as a specific doctrine was slain with Jesus, suddenly and utterly. He was hardly cold in his grave, or high in his heaven (as you please), before the apostles dragged the tradition of him down to the level of the thing it has remained ever since. And that thing the intelligent heathen may study, if they would be instructed in it by modern books, in Samuel Butler's novel, The Way of All Flesh.

The Vindictive Miracles and the Stoning of Stephen.

Take, for example, the miracles. Of Jesus alone of all the Christian miracle workers there is no record, except in certain gospels that all men reject, of a malicious or destructive miracle. A barren fig-tree was the only victim of his anger. Every one of his miracles on sentient subjects was an act of kindness. John declares that he healed the wound of the man whose ear was cut off (by Peter, John says) at the arrest in the garden. One of the first things the apostles did with their miraculous power was to strike dead a wretched man and his wife who had defrauded them by holding back some money from the common stock. They struck people blind or dead without remorse, judging because they had been judged. They healed the sick and raised the dead apparently in a spirit of pure display and advertisement. Their doctrine did not contain a ray of that light which reveals Jesus as one of the redeemers of men from folly and error. They cancelled him, and went back straight to John the Baptist and his formula of securing remission of sins by repentance and the rite of baptism (being born again of water and the spirit). Peter's first harangue softens us by the human touch of its exordium, which was a quaint assurance to his hearers that they must believe him to be sober because it was too early in the day to get drunk; but of Jesus he had nothing to say except that he was the Christ foretold by the prophets as coming from the seed of David, and that they must believe this and be baptized. To this the other apostles added incessant denunciations of the Jews for having crucified him, and threats of the destruction that would overtake them if they did not repent: that is, if they did not join the sect which the apostles were now forming. A quite intolerable young speaker named Stephen delivered an oration to the council, in which he first inflicted on them a tedious sketch of the history of Israel, with which they were presumably as well acquainted as he, and then reviled them in the most insulting terms as "stiffnecked and uncircumcized." Finally, after boring and annoying them to the utmost bearable extremity, he looked up and declared that he saw the heavens open, and Christ standing on the right hand of God. This was

too much: they threw him out of the city and stoned him
to death.   It was a severe way of suppressing a tactless
and conceited bore; but it was pardonable and human
in comparison to the slaughter of poor Ananias and
Sapphira.

Paul.

Suddenly a man of genius, Paul, violently anti-Christian, enters on the scene, holding the clothes of the men
who are stoning Stephen. He persecutes the Christians
with great vigor, a sport which he combines with the
business of a tentmaker. This temperamental hatred of
Jesus, whom he has never seen, is a pathological symp-
tom of that particular sort of conscience and nervous constitution which brings its victims under the tyranny of
two delirious terrors: the terror of sin and the terror of
death, which may be called also the terror of sex and the
terror of life. Now Jesus, with his healthy conscience
on his higher plane, was free from these terrors. He con-
sorted freely with sinners, and was never concerned for
a moment, as far as we know, about whether his conduct
was sinful or not; so that he has forced us to accept him
as the man without sin. Even if we reckon his last days
as the days of his delusion, he none the less gave a
fairly convincing exhibition of superiority to the fear of
death. This must have both fascinated and horrified
Paul, or Saul, as he was first called. The horror accounts
for his fierce persecution of the Christians. The fascination accounts for the strangest of his fancies: the fancy
for attaching the name of Jesus Christ to the great idea
which flashed upon him on the road to Damascus, the idea
that he could not only make a religion of his two terrors,
but that the movement started by Jesus offered him the
nucleus for his new Church. It was a monstrous idea;
and the shocks of it, as he afterwards declared, struck
him blind for days. He heard Jesus calling to him from

the clouds, "Why persecute me?" His natural hatred of the teacher for whom Sin and Death had no terrors turned into a wild personal worship of him which has the ghastliness of a beautiful thing seen in a false light.

The chronicler of the Acts of the Apostles sees nothing of the significance of this. The great danger of conversion in all ages has been that when the religion of the high mind is offered to the lower mind, the lower mind, feeling its fascination without understanding it, and being incapable of rising to it, drags it down to its level by degrading it. Years ago I said that the conversion of a savage to Christianity is the conversion of Christianity to savagery. The conversion of Paul was no conversion at all: it was Paul who converted the religion that had raised one man above sin and death into a religion that delivered millions of men so completely into their dominion that their own common nature became a horror to them, and the religious life became a denial of life. Paul had no intention of surrendering either his Judaism or his Roman citizenship to the new moral world (as Robert Owen called it) of Communism and Jesuism. Just as in the XIX century Karl Marx, not content to take political economy as he found it, insisted on rebuilding it from the bottom upwards in his own way, and thereby gave a new lease of life to the errors it was just outgrowing, so Paul reconstructed the old Salvationism from which Jesus had vainly tried to redeem him, and produced a fantastic theology which is still the most amazing thing of the kind known to us. Being intellectually an inveterate Roman Rationalist, always discarding the irrational real thing for the unreal but ratiocinable postulate, he began by discarding Man as he is, and substituted a postulate which he called Adam. And when he was asked, as he surely must have been in a world not wholly mad, what had become of the natural man, he replied "Adam *is* the natural man." This was confusing to sim-

7

pletons, because according to tradition Adam was certainly the name of the natural man as created in the garden of Eden. It was as if a preacher of our own time had described as typically British Frankenstein's monster, and called him Smith, and somebody, on demanding what about the man in the street, had been told "Smith *is* the man in the street." The thing happens often enough; for indeed the world is full of these Adams and Smiths and men in the street and average sensual men and economic men and womanly women and what not, all of them imaginary Atlases carrying imaginary worlds on their unsubstantial shoulders.

The Eden story provided Adam with a sin: the "original sin" for which we are all damned. Baldly stated, this seems ridiculous; nevertheless it corresponds to something actually existent not only in Paul's consciousness but in our own. The original sin was not the eating of the forbidden fruit, but the consciousness of sin which the fruit produced. The moment Adam and Eve tasted the apple they found themselves ashamed of their sexual relation, which until then had seemed quite innocent to them; and there is no getting over the hard fact that this shame, or state of sin, has persisted to this day, and is one of the strongest of our instincts. Thus Paul's postulate of Adam as the natural man was pragmatically true: it worked. But the weakness of Pragmatism is that most theories will work if you put your back into making them work, provided they have some point of contact with human nature. Hedonism will pass the pragmatic test as well as Stoicism. Up to a certain point every social principle that is not absolutely idiotic works: Autocracy works in Russia and Democracy in America; Atheism works in France, Polytheism in India, Monotheism throughout Islam, and Pragmatism, or No-ism, in England. Paul's fantastic conception of the damned Adam, represented by Bunyan as a pilgrim with a great burden of sins on his back, corresponded to the fundamental condition of evolution, which is, that life, including human life, is continually evolving, and must therefore be continually ashamed of itself and its present and past. Bunyan's pilgrim wants to get rid of his bundle of sins; but he also wants to reach "yonder shining light;" and when at last his bundle falls off him into the sepulchre of Christ, his pilgrimage is still unfinished and his hardest trials still ahead of him. His conscience remains uneasy; "original sin" still torments him; and his adventure with Giant Despair, who throws him into the dungeon of Doubting Castle, from which he escapes by the use of a skeleton key, is more terrible than any he met whilst the bundle was still on his back. Thus Bunyan's allegory of human nature breaks through the Pauline theology at a hundred points. His theological allegory, The Holy War, with its troops of Election Doubters, and its cavalry of "those that rode Reformadoes," is, as a whole, absurd, impossible, and, except in passages where the artistic old Adam momentarily got the better of the Salvationist theologian, hardly readable.

Paul's theory of original sin was to some extent idiosyncratic. He tells us definitely that he finds himself quite well able to avoid the sinfulness of sex by practising celibacy; but he recognizes, rather contemptuously, that in this respect he is not as other men are, and says that they had better marry than burn, thus admitting that though marriage may lead to placing the desire to please wife or husband before the desire to please God, yet preoccupation with unsatisfied desire may be even more ungodly than preoccupation with domestic affection. This view of the case inevitably led him to insist that a wife should be rather a slave than a partner, her real function being, not to engage a man's love and loyalty, but on the contrary to release them for God by relieving the man of all preoccupation with sex just as in her capacity of housekeeper and cook she relieves his preoccupation with hunger by the simple expedient of satisfying his appetite. This slavery also justifies itself pragmatically by working effectively; but it has made Paul the eternal enemy of Woman. Incidentally it has led to many foolish surmises about Paul's personal character and circumstances, by people so enslaved by sex that a celibate appears to them a sort of monster. They forget that not only whole priesthoods, official and unofficial, from Paul to Carlyle and Ruskin, have defied the tyranny of sex, but immense numbers of ordinary citizens of both sexes have, either voluntarily or under pressure of circumstances easily surmountable, saved their energies for less primitive activities.

Howbeit, Paul succeeded in stealing the image of Christ crucified for the figure-head of his Salvationist vessel, with its Adam posing as the natural man, its doctrine of original sin, and its damnation avoidable only by faith in the sacrifice of the cross. In fact, no sooner had Jesus knocked over the dragon of superstition than Paul boldly set it on its legs again in the name of Jesus.

The Confusion of Christendom.

Now it is evident that two religions having such contrary effects on mankind should not be confused as they are under a common name. There is not one word of Pauline Christianity in the characteristic utterances of Jesus. When Saul watched the clothes of the men who stoned Stephen, he was not acting upon beliefs which Paul renounced. There is no record of Christ's having ever said to any man: "Go and sin as much as you like: you can put it all on me." He said "Sin no more," and insisted that he was putting up the standard of conduct, not debasing it, and that the righteousness of the Christian must exceed that of the Scribe and Pharisee. The notion that he was shedding his blood in order that every petty cheat and adulterator and libertine might wallow in it and come out whiter than snow, cannot be imputed to him on his own authority. "I come as an infallible patent medicine for bad consciences" is not one of the sayings in the gospels. If Jesus could have been consulted on Bunyan's allegory as to that business of the burden of sin dropping from the pilgrim's back when he caught sight of the cross, we must infer from his teaching that he would have told Bunyan in forcible terms that he had never made a greater mistake in his life, and that the business of a Christ was to make self-satisfied sinners feel the burden of their sins and stop committing them instead of assuring them that they could not help it, as it was all Adam's fault, but that it did not matter as long as they were credulous and friendly about himself. Even when he believed himself to be a god, he did not regard himself as a scapegoat. He was to take away the sins of the world by good government, by justice and mercy, by setting the welfare of little children above the pride of princes, by casting all the quackeries and idolatries which now usurp and malversate the power of God into what our local authorities quaintly call the dust destructor, and by riding on the clouds of heaven in glory instead of in a thousand-guinea motor car. That was delirious, if you like; but it was the delirium of a free soul, not of a shamebound one like Paul's. There has really never been a more monstrous imposition perpetrated than the imposition of the limitations of Paul's soul upon the soul of Jesus.

The Secret of Paul's Success.

Paul must soon have found that his followers had gained peace of mind and victory over death and sin at the cost of all moral responsibility; for he did his best to reintroduce it by making good conduct the test of sincere belief, and insisting that sincere belief was necessary to salvation. But as his system was rooted in the plain fact that as what he called sin includes sex and is therefore an ineradicable part of human nature (why else should Christ have had to atone for the sin of all future generations?) it was impossible for him to declare that sin, even in its wickedest extremity, could forfeit the sinner's salvation if he repented and believed. And to this day Pauline Christianity is, and owes its enormous vogue to being, a premium on sin. Its consequences have had to be held in check by the worldlywise majority through a violently anti-Christian system of criminal law and stern morality. But of course the main restraint is human nature, which has good impulses as well as bad ones, and refrains from theft and murder and cruelty, even when it is taught that it can commit them all at the expense of Christ and go happily to heaven afterwards, simply because it does not always want to murder or rob or torture.

It is now easy to understand why the Christianity of Jesus failed completely to establish itself politically and socially, and was easily suppressed by the police and the Church, whilst Paulinism overran the whole western civilized world, which was at that time the Roman Empire, and was adopted by it as its official faith, the old avenging gods falling helplessly before the new Redeemer. It still retains, as we may see in Africa, its power of bringing to simple people a message of hope and consolation that no other religion offers. But this enchantment is produced by its spurious association with the personal charm of Jesus, and exists only for untrained minds. In the hands of a logical Frenchman like Calvin, pushing it to its utmost conclusions, and devising "institutes" for hardheaded adult Scots and literal Swiss, it becomes the most infernal of fatalisms; and the lives of civilized children are blighted by its logic whilst negro piccaninnies are rejoicing in its legends.

Paul's Qualities.

Paul, however, did not get his great reputation by mere imposition and reaction. It is only in comparison with Jesus (to whom many prefer him) that he appears common and conceited. Though in The Acts he is only a vulgar revivalist, he comes out in his own epistles as a genuine poet, though by flashes only. He is no more a Christian than Jesus was a Baptist: he is a disciple of Jesus only as Jesus was a disciple of John. He does nothing that Jesus would have done, and says nothing that Jesus would have said, though much, like the famous ode to charity, that he would have admired. He is more Jewish than the Jews, more Roman than the Romans, proud both ways, full of startling confessions and self-revelations that would not surprise us if they were slipped into the pages of Nietzsche, tormented by an intellectual conscience that demanded an argued case even at the cost of sophistry, with all sorts of fine qualities and occasional illuminations, but always hopelessly in the toils of Sin, Death, and Logic, which had no power over Jesus. As we have seen, it was by introducing this bondage and terror of his into the Christian doctrine that he adapted it to the Church and State systems which Jesus transcended, and made it practicable by destroying the specifically Jesuist side of it. He would have been quite in his place in any modern Protestant State; and he, not Jesus, is the true head and founder of our Reformed Church, as Peter is of the Roman Church. The followers of Paul and Peter made Christendom, whilst the Nazarenes were wiped out.

The Acts of the Apostles.

Here we may return to the narrative called The Acts of the Apostles, which we left at the point where the stoning of Stephen was followed by the introduction of Paul. The author of The Acts, though a good story-teller, like Luke, was (herein also like Luke) much weaker in power of thought than in imaginative literary art. Hence we find Luke credited with the authorship of The Acts by people who like stories and have no aptitude for theology, whilst the book itself is denounced as spurious by Pauline theologians because Paul, and indeed all the apostles, are represented in it as very commonplace revivalists, interesting us by their adventures more than by any qualities of mind or character. Indeed, but for the epistles, we should have a very poor opinion of the apostles. Paul in particular is described as setting a fashion which has remained in continual use to this day. Whenever he addresses an audience, he dwells with great zest on his misdeeds before his pseudo conversion, with the effect of throwing into stronger relief his present state of blessedness; and he tells the story of that conversion over and over again, ending with exhortations to the hearers to come and be saved, and threats of the wrath that will overtake them if they refuse. At any revival meeting today the same thing may be heard, followed by the same conversions. This is natural enough; but it is totally unlike the preaching of Jesus, who never talked about his personal history, and never "worked up" an audience to hysteria. It aims at a purely nervous effect; it brings no enlightenment; the most ignorant man has only to become intoxicated with his own vanity, and mistake his self-satisfaction for the Holy Ghost, to become qualified as an apostle; and it has absolutely nothing to do with the characteristic doctrines of Jesus. The Holy Ghost may be at work all round producing wonders of art and

science, and strengthening men to endure all sorts of
martyrdoms for the enlargement of knowledge, and the
enrichment and intensification of life ("that ye may have
life more abundantly"); but the apostles, as described in
The Acts, take no part in the struggle except as persecutors and revilers. To this day, when their successors get
the upper hand, as in Geneva (Knox's "perfect city of
Christ") and in Scotland and Ulster, every spiritual ac-
tivity but moneymaking and churchgoing is stamped out;
heretics are ruthlessly persecuted; and such pleasures as
money can purchase are suppressed so that its possessors
are compelled to go on making money because there is
nothing else to do. And the compensation for all this
privation is partly an insane conceit of being the elect of
God, with a reserved seat in heaven, and partly, since
even the most infatuated idiot cannot spend his life admiring himself, the less innocent excitement of punishing other people for not admiring him, and the nosing
out of the sins of the people who, being intelligent enough
to be incapable of mere dull self-righteousness, and highly susceptible to the beauty and interest of the real work-
ings of the Holy Ghost, try to live more rational and
abundant lives. The abominable amusement of terrifying
children with threats of hell is another of these diver-
sions, and perhaps the vilest and most mischievous of
them. The net result is that the imitators of the apostles,
whether they are called Holy Willies or Stigginses in
derision, or, in admiration, Puritans or saints, are, outside their own congregations, and to a considerable extent inside them, heartily detested. Now nobody detests
Jesus, though many who have been tormented in their
childhood in his name include him in their general loathing of everything connected with the word religion;
whilst others, who know him only by misrepresentation
as a sentimental pacifist and an ascetic, include him in
their general dislike of that type of character. In the

same way a student who has had to "get up" Shakespear
as a college subject may hate Shakespear; and people
who dislike the theatre may include Molière in that dislike without ever having read a line of his or witnessed
one of his plays; but nobody with any knowledge of
Shakespear or Molière could possibly detest them, or
read without pity and horror a description of their being
insulted, tortured, and killed. And the same is true of
Jesus. But it requires the most strenuous effort of conscience to refrain from crying "Serve him right" when
we read of the stoning of Stephen; and nobody has ever
cared twopence about the martyrdom of Peter: many
better men have died worse deaths: for example, honest
Hugh Latimer, who was burned by us, was worth fifty
Stephens and a dozen Peters. One feels at last that
when Jesus called Peter from his boat, he spoiled an
honest fisherman, and made nothing better out of the
wreck than a salvation monger.

The Controversies on Baptism and Transubstantiation.

Meanwhile the inevitable effect of dropping the peculiar doctrines of Jesus and going back to John the Baptist, was to make it much easier to convert Gentiles than
Jews; and it was by following the line of least resistance
that Paul became the apostle to the Gentiles. The Jews
had their own rite of initiation: the rite of circumcision;
and they were fiercely jealous for it, because it marked
them as the chosen people of God, and set them apart
from the Gentiles, who were simply the uncircumcized.
When Paul, finding that baptism made way faster among
the Gentiles than among the Jews, as it enabled them to
plead that they too were sanctified by a rite of later and
higher authority than the Mosaic rite, he was compelled

to admit that circumcision did not matter; and this, to
the Jews, was an intolerable blasphemy. To Gentiles like
ourselves, a good deal of the Epistle to the Romans is
now tedious to unreadableness because it consists of a
hopeless attempt by Paul to evade the conclusion that if
a man were baptized it did not matter a rap whether he
was circumcized or not. Paul claims circumcision as an
excellent thing in its way for a Jew; but if it has no
efficacy towards salvation, and if salvation is the one
thing needful—and Paul was committed to both propositions—his pleas in mitigation only made the Jews more
determined to stone him.

Thus from the very beginning of apostolic Christianity, it was hampered by a dispute as to whether sal
vation was to be attained by a surgical operation or by
a sprinkling of water: mere rites on which Jesus would
not have wasted twenty words. Later on, when the new
sect conquered the Gentile west, where the dispute had
no practical application, the other ceremony—that of eating the god—produced a still more disastrous dispute, in
which a difference of belief, not as to the obligation to
perform the ceremony, but as to whether it was a symbolic
or a real ingestion of divine substance, produced persecution, slaughter, hatred, and everything that Jesus
loathed, on a monstrous scale.

But long before that, the superstitions which had fast-
ened on the new faith made trouble. The parthenogenetic birth of Christ, simple enough at first as a popular miracle, was not left so simple by the theologians.
They began to ask of what substance Christ was made in
the womb of the virgin. When the Trinity was added to
the faith the question arose, was the virgin the mother of
God or only the mother of Jesus? Arian schisms and
Nestorian schisms arose on these questions; and the leaders of the resultant agitations rancorously deposed one
another and excommunicated one another according to

their luck in enlisting the emperors on their side. In the IV century they began to burn one another for differences of opinion in such matters. In the VIII century Charlemagne made Christianity compulsory by killing those who refused to embrace it; and though this made an end of the voluntary character of conversion, Charlemagne may claim to be the first Christian who put men to death for any point of doctrine that really mattered. From his time onward the history of Christian controversy reeks with blood and fire, torture and warfare. The Crusades, the persecutions in Albi and elsewhere, the Inquisition, the "wars of religion" which followed the Reformation, all presented themselves as Christian phenomena; but who can doubt that they would have been repudiated with horror by Jesus? Our own notion that the massacre of St. Bartholomew's was an outrage on Christianity, whilst the campaigns of Gustavus Adolphus, and even of Frederick the Great, were a defence of it, is as absurd as the opposite notion that Frederick was Antichrist and Torquemada and Ignatius Loyola men after the very heart of Jesus. Neither they nor their exploits had anything to do with him. It is probable that Archbishop Laud and John Wesley died equally persuaded that he in whose name they had made themselves famous on earth would receive them in Heaven with open arms. Poor Fox the Quaker would have had ten times their chance; and yet Fox made rather a miserable business of life.

Nevertheless all these perversions of the doctrine of Jesus derived their moral force from his credit, and so had to keep his gospel alive. When the Protestants translated the Bible into the vernacular and let it loose among the people, they did an extremely dangerous thing, as the mischief which followed proves; but they incidentally let loose the sayings of Jesus in open competition with the sayings of Paul and Koheleth and David and

Solomon and the authors of Job and the Pentateuch; and, as we have seen, Jesus seems to be the winning name. The glaring contradiction between his teaching and the practice of all the States and all the Churches is no longer hidden. And it may be that though nineteen centuries have passed since Jesus was born (the date of his birth is now quaintly given as 7 B.C., though some contend for 100 B.C.), and though his Church has not yet been founded nor his political system tried, the bankruptcy of all the other systems when audited by our vital statistics, which give us a final test for all political systems, is driving us hard into accepting him, not as a scapegoat, but as one who was much less of a fool in practical matters than we have hitherto all thought him.

The Alternative Christs.

Let us now clear up the situation a little. The New Testament tells two stories for two different sorts of readers. One is the old story of the achievement of our salvation by the sacrifice and atonement of a divine personage who was barbarously slain and rose again on the third day: the story as it was accepted by the apostles. And in this story the political, economic, and moral views of the Christ have no importance: the atonement is everything; and we are saved by our faith in it, and not by works or opinions (other than that particular opinion) bearing on practical affairs.

The other is the story of a prophet who, after expressing several very interesting opinions as to practical conduct, both personal and political, which are now of pressing importance, and instructing his disciples to carry them out in their daily life, lost his head; believed himself to be a crude legendary form of god; and under that delusion courted and suffered a cruel execution in the belief that he would rise from the dead and come in glory

to reign over a regenerated world. In this form, the
political, economic and moral opinions of Jesus, as guides
to conduct, are interesting and important: the rest is mere
psychopathy and superstition. The accounts of the
resurrection, the parthenogenetic birth, and the more incredible miracles are rejected as inventions; and such
episodes as the conversation with the devil are classed
with similar conversations recorded of St. Dunstan,
Luther, Bunyan, Swedenborg, and Blake.

Credulity no Criterion.

This arbitrary acceptance and rejection of parts of the
gospel is not peculiar to the Secularist view. We have
seen Luke and John reject Matthew's story of the massacre of the innocents and the flight into Egypt without
ceremony. The notion that Matthew's manuscript is a
literal and infallible record of facts, not subject to the
errors that beset all earthly chroniclers, would have made
John stare, being as it is a comparatively modern fancy
of intellectually untrained people who keep the Bible
on the same shelf with Napoleon's Book of Fate, Old
Moore's Almanack, and handbooks of therapeutic herb-
alism. You may be a fanatical Salvationist and reject
more miracle stories than Huxley did; and you may
utterly repudiate Jesus as the Savior and yet cite him as
a historical witness to the possession by men of the most
marvellous thaumaturgical powers. "Christ Scientist"
and Jesus the Mahatma are preached by people whom
Peter would have struck dead as worse infidels than
Simon Magus; and the Atonement is preached by Baptist
and Congregationalist ministers whose views of the miracles are those of Ingersoll and Bradlaugh. Luther, who
made a clean sweep of all the saints with their million
miracles, and reduced the Blessed Virgin herself to the
status of an idol, concentrated Salvationism to a point

at which the most execrable murderer who believes in it
when the rope is round his neck, flies straight to the arms
of Jesus, whilst Tom Paine and Shelley fall into the bot-
tomless pit to burn there to all eternity. And sceptical
physicists like Sir William Crookes demonstrate by
laboratory experiments that "mediums" like Dunglas
Home can make the pointer of a spring-balance go round
without touching the weight suspended from it.

Belief in Personal Immortality no Criterion.

Nor is belief in individual immortality any criterion.
Theosophists, rejecting vicarious atonement so sternly
that they insist that the smallest of our sins brings its
Karma, also insist on individual immortality and metem-
psychosis in order to provide an unlimited field for
Karma to be worked out by the unredeemed sinner. The
belief in the prolongation of individual life beyond the
grave is far more real and vivid among table-rapping
Spiritualists than among conventional Christians. The
notion that those who reject the Christian (or any other)
scheme of salvation by atonement must reject also belief
in personal immortality and in miracles is as baseless as
the notion that if a man is an atheist he will steal your
watch.

I could multiply these instances to weariness. The
main difference that set Gladstone and Huxley by the
ears is not one between belief in supernatural persons
or miraculous events and the sternest view of such belief
as a breach of intellectual integrity: it is the difference
between belief in the efficacy of the crucifixion as an infallible cure for guilt, and a congenital incapacity for
believing this, or (the same thing) desiring to believe it.

The Secular View Natural, not Rational, therefore Inevitable.

It must therefore be taken as a flat fundamental modern fact, whether we like it or not, that whilst many of us cannot believe that Jesus got his curious grip of our souls by mere sentimentality, neither can we believe that he was John Barleycorn. The more our reason and study lead us to believe that Jesus was talking the most penetrating good sense when he preached Communism; when he declared that the reality behind the popular belief in God was a creative spirit in ourselves, called by him the Heavenly Father and by us Evolution, Élan Vital, Life Force and other names; when he protested against the claims of marriage and the family to appropriate that high part of our energy that was meant for the service of his Father, the more impossible it becomes for us to believe that he was talking equally good sense when he so suddenly announced that he was himself a visible concrete God; that his flesh and blood were miraculous food for us; that he must be tortured and slain in the traditional manner and would rise from the dead after three days; and that at his second coming the stars would fall from heaven and he become king of an earthly paradise. But it is easy and reasonable to believe that an overwrought preacher at last went mad as Swift and Ruskin and Nietzsche went mad. Every asylum has in it a patient suffering from the delusion that he is a god, yet otherwise sane enough. These patients do not nowadays declare that they will be barbarously slain and will rise from the dead, because they have lost that tradition of the destiny of godhead; but they claim everything appertaining to divinity that is within their knowledge.

Thus the gospels as memoirs and suggestive statements of sociological and biological doctrine, highly relevant to modern civilization, though ending in the history of a psycopathic delusion, are quite credible, intelligible, and interesting to modern thinkers. In any other light they are neither credible, intelligible, nor interesting except to people upon whom the delusion imposes.

"The Higher Criticism."

Historical research and paleographic criticism will no doubt continue their demonstrations that the New Testament, like the Old, seldom tells a single story or expounds a single doctrine, and gives us often an accretion and conglomeration of widely discrete and even unrelated traditions and doctrines. But these disintegrations, though technically interesting to scholars, and gratifying or exasperating, as the case may be, to people who are merely defending or attacking the paper fortifications of the infallibility of the Bible, have hardly anything to do with the purpose of these pages. I have mentioned the fact that most of the authorities are now agreed (for the moment) that the date of the birth of Jesus may be placed at about 7 B.C.; but they do not therefore date their letters 1923, nor, I presume, do they expect me to do so. What I am engaged in is a criticism (in the Kantian sense) of an established body of belief which has become an actual part of the mental fabric of my readers; and I should be the most exasperating of triflers and pedants if I were to digress into a criticism of some other belief or no-belief which my readers might conceivably profess if they were erudite Scriptural paleographers and historians, in which case, by the way, they would have to change their views so frequently that the gospel they received in their childhood would dominate them after all by its superior persistency. The chaos of mere facts in which the Sermon on the Mount and the Ode to Charity suggest nothing but disputes as to whether they are inter-

polations or not, in which Jesus becomes nothing but a
name suspected of belonging to ten different prophets or
executed persons, in which Paul is only the man who
could not possibly have written the epistles attributed to
him, in which Chinese sages, Greek philosophers, Latin
authors, and writers of ancient anonymous inscriptions
are thrown at our heads as the sources of this or that
scrap of the Bible, is neither a religion nor a criticism
of religion: one does not offer the fact that a good deal
of the medieval building in Peterborough Cathedral was
found to be flagrant jerry-building as a criticism of the
Dean's sermons. For good or evil, we have made a synthesis out of the literature we call the Bible; and though
the discovery that there is a good deal of jerry-building
in the Bible is interesting in its way, because everything
about the Bible is interesting, it does not alter the synthesis very materially even for the paleographers, and
does not alter it at all for those who know no more about
modern paleography than Archbishop Ussher did. I have
therefore indicated little more of the discoveries than
Archbishop Ussher might have guessed for himself if
he had read the Bible without prepossessions.

For the rest, I have taken the synthesis as it really
lives and works in men. After all, a synthesis is what
you want: it is the case you have to judge brought to an
apprehensible issue for you. Even if you have little more
respect for synthetic biography than for synthetic rubber,
synthetic milk, and the still unachieved synthetic proto-
plasm which is to enable us to make different sorts of
men as a pastry cook makes different sorts of tarts, the
practical issue still lies as plainly before you as before
the most credulous votaries of what pontificates as the
Higher Criticism.

The Perils of Salvationism.

The secular view of Jesus is powerfully reinforced by the increase in our day of the number of people who have had the means of educating and training themselves to the point at which they are not afraid to look facts in the face, even such terrifying facts as sin and death. The result is greater sternness in modern thought. The conviction is spreading that to encourage a man to believe that though his sins be as scarlet he can be made whiter than snow by an easy exercise of self-conceit, is to encourage him to be a rascal. It did not work so badly when you could also conscientiously assure him that if he let himself be caught napping in the matter of faith by death, a red-hot hell would roast him alive to all eternity. In those days a sudden death—the most enviable of all deaths—was regarded as the most frightful calamity. It was classed with plague, pestilence, and famine, battle and murder, in our prayers. But belief in that hell is fast vanishing. All the leaders of thought have lost it; and even for the rank and file it has fled to those parts of Ireland and Scotland which are still in the XVII century. Even there, it is tacitly reserved for the other fellow.

The Importance of Hell in the Salvation Scheme.

The seriousness of throwing over hell whilst still clinging to the Atonement is obvious. If there is no punishment for sin there can be no self-forgiveness for it. If Christ paid our score, and if there is no hell and therefore no chance of our getting into trouble by forgetting the obligation, then we can be as wicked as we like with impunity inside the secular law, even from self-reproach, which becomes mere ingratitude to the Savior. On the other hand, if Christ did not pay our score, it still stands against us; and such debts make us extremely uncomfortable. The drive of evolution, which we call conscience and honor, seizes on such slips, and shames us to the dust for being so low in the scale as to be capable of them. The "saved" thief experiences an ecstatic happiness which can never come to the honest atheist: he is tempted to steal again to repeat the glorious sensation. But if the atheist steals he has no such happiness. He is a thief and knows that he is a thief. Nothing can rub that off him. He may try to sooth his shame by some sort of restitution or equivalent act of benevolence; but that does not alter the fact that he did steal; and his conscience will not be easy until he has conquered his will to steal and changed himself into an honest man by developing that divine spark within him which Jesus insisted on as the everyday reality of what the atheist denies.

Now though the state of the believers in the atonement may thus be the happier, it is most certainly not more desirable from the point of view of the community. The fact that a believer is happier than a sceptic is no more to the point than the fact that a drunken man is happier than a sober one. The happiness of credulity is a cheap and dangerous quality of happiness, and by no means a necessity of life. Whether Socrates got as much happiness out of life as Wesley is an unanswerable question; but a nation of Socrateses would be much safer and happier than a nation of Wesleys; and its individuals would be higher in the evolutionary scale. At all events it is in the Socratic man and not in the Wesleyan that our hope lies now.

The Right to refuse Atonement.

Consequently, even if it were mentally possible for all of us to believe in the Atonement, we should have to cry

off it, as we evidently have a right to do. Every man to
whom salvation is offered has an inalienable natural right
to say "No, thank you: I prefer to retain my full moral
responsibility: it is not good for me to be able to load a
scapegoat with my sins: I should be less careful how I
committed them if I knew they would cost me nothing."
Then, too, there is the attitude of Ibsen: that iron moralist to whom the whole scheme of salvation was only an
ignoble attempt to cheat God; to get into heaven without
paying the price. To be let off, to beg for and accept eternal life as a present instead of earning it, would be mean
enough even if we accepted the contempt of the Power on
whose pity we were trading; but to bargain for a crown of
glory as well! that was too much for Ibsen: it provoked
him to exclaim, "Your God is an old man whom you
cheat," and to lash the deadened conscience of the XIX
century back to life with a whip of scorpions.

The Teaching of Christianity.

And there I must leave the matter to such choice as
your nature allows you. The honest teacher who has to
make known to a novice the facts about Christianity cannot in any essential regard, I think, put the facts otherwise than as I have put them. If children are to be delivered from the proselytizing atheist on the one hand,
and the proselytizing nun in the convent school on the
other, with all the other proselytizers that lie between
them, they must not be burdened with idle controversies
as to whether there was ever such a person as Jesus or
not. When Hume said that Joshua's campaigns were impossible, Whately did not wrangle about it: he proved,
on the same lines, that the campaigns of Napoleon were
impossible. Only fictitious characters will stand Hume's
sort of examination: nothing will ever make Edward the
Confessor and St. Louis as real to us as Don Quixote and

Mr. Pickwick. We must cut the controversy short by declaring that there is the same evidence for the existence of Jesus as for that of any other person of his time; and the fact that you may not believe everything Matthew tells you no more disproves the existence of Jesus than the fact that you do not believe everything Macaulay tells you disproves the existence of William III. The gospel narratives in the main give you a biography which is quite credible and accountable on purely secular grounds when you have trimmed off everything that Hume or Grimm or Rousseau or Huxley or any modern bishop could reject as fanciful. Without going further than this, you can become a follower of Jesus just as you can become a follower of Confucius or Lao Tse, and may therefore call yourself a Jesuist, or even a Christian, if you hold, as the strictest Secularist quite legitimately may, that all prophets are inspired, and all men with a mission, Christs.

The teacher of Christianity has then to make known to the child, first the song of John Barleycorn, with the fields and seasons as witness to its eternal truth. Then, as the child's mind matures, it can learn, as historical and psychological phenomena, the tradition of the scapegoat, the Redeemer, the Atonement, the Resurrection, the Second Coming, and how, in a world saturated with this tradition, Jesus has been largely accepted as the long expected and often prophesied Redeemer, the Messiah, *the* Christ. It is open to the child also to accept him. If the child is built like Gladstone, he will accept Jesus as his Savior, and Peter and John the Baptist as the Savior's revealer and forerunner respectively. If he is built like Huxley, he will take the secular view, in spite of all that a pious family can do to prevent him. The important thing now is that the Gladstones and Huxleys should no longer waste their time irrelevantly and ridiculously wrangling about the Gadarene swine, and that they should make up their minds as to the soundness of the secular doctrines of Jesus; for it is about these that they may come to blows in our own time.

Christianity and The Empire.

Finally, let us ask why it is that the old superstitions have so suddenly lost countenance that although, to the utter disgrace of the nation's leaders and rulers, the laws by which persecutors can destroy or gag all freedom of thought and speech in these matters are still unrepealed and ready to the hand of our bigots and fanatics (quite recently a respectable shopkeeper was convicted of "blasphemy" for saying that if a modern girl accounted for an illicit pregnancy by saying she had conceived of the Holy Ghost, we should know what to think: a remark which would never have occurred to him had he been properly taught how the story was grafted on the gospel), yet somehow they are used only against poor men, and that only in a half-hearted way. When we consider that from the time when the first scholar ventured to whisper as a professional secret that the Pentateuch could not possibly have been written by Moses to the time within my own recollection when Bishop Colenso, for saying the same thing openly, was inhibited from preaching and actually excommunicated, eight centuries elapsed (the point at issue, though technically interesting to paleographers and historians, having no more bearing on human welfare than the controversy as to whether uncial or cursive is the older form of writing); yet now, within fifty years of Colenso's heresy, there is not a Churchman of any authority living, or an educated layman, who could without ridicule declare that Moses wrote the Pentateuch as Pascal wrote his Thoughts or D'Aubigny his History of the Reformation, or that St. Jerome wrote the passage about the three witnesses in the Vulgate, or

that there are less than three different accounts of the
creation jumbled together in the book of Genesis. Now
the maddest Progressive will hardly contend that our
growth in wisdom and liberality has been greater in the
last half century than in the sixteen half centuries pre-
ceding: indeed it would be easier to sustain the thesis
that the last fifty years have witnessed a distinct reaction
from Victorian Liberalism to Collectivism which has per-
ceptibly strengthened the State Churches. Yet the fact
remains that whereas Byron's Cain, published a century
ago, is a leading case on the point that there is no copy-
right in a blasphemous book, the Salvation Army might
now include it among its publications without shocking
anyone.

I suggest that the causes which have produced this
sudden clearing of the air include the transformation of
many modern States, notably the old self-contained
French Republic and the tight little Island of Britain,
into empires which overflow the frontiers of all the
Churches. In India, for example, there are less than
four million Christians out of a population of three hundred and sixteen and a half millions. The King of England is the defender of the faith; but what faith is now
the faith? The inhabitants of this island would, within
the memory of persons still living, have claimed that their
faith is surely *the* faith of God, and that all others are
heathen. But we islanders are only forty-five millions;
and if we count ourselves all as Christians, there are still
seventy-seven and a quarter million Mahometans in the
Empire. Add to these the Hindoos and Buddhists, Sikhs
and Jains, whom I was taught in my childhood, by way
of religious instruction, to regard as gross idolators con-
signed to eternal perdition, but whose faith I can now
be punished for disparaging by a provocative word, and
you have a total of over three hundred and forty-two and
a quarter million heretics to swamp our forty-five million

Britons, of whom, by the way, only six thousand call themselves distinctively "disciples of Christ," the rest being members of the Church of England and other denominations whose discipleship is less emphatically affirmed. In short, the Englishman of today, instead of being, like the forefathers whose ideas he clings to, a subject of a State practically wholly Christian, is now crowded, and indeed considerably overcrowded, into a corner of an Empire in which the Christians are a mere eleven per cent of the population; so that the Nonconformist who allows his umbrella stand to be sold up rather than pay rates towards the support of a Church of England school, finds himself paying taxes not only to endow the Church of Rome in Malta, but to send Christians to prison for the blasphemy of offering Bibles for sale in the streets of Khartoum.

Turn to France, a country ten times more insular in its pre-occupation with its own language, its own history, its own character, than we, who have always been explorers and colonizers and grumblers. This once self-centred nation is forty millions strong. The total population of the French Republic is about one hundred and fourteen millions. The French are not in our hopeless Christian minority of eleven per cent; but they are in a minority of thirty-five per cent, which is fairly conclusive. And, being a more logical people than we, they have officially abandoned Christianity and declared that the French State has no specific religion.

Neither has the British State, though it does not say so. No doubt there are many innocent people in England who take Charlemagne's view, and would, as a matter of course, offer our eighty-nine per cent of "pagans, I regret to say" the alternative of death or Christianity but for a vague impression that these lost ones are all being converted gradually by the missionaries. But no statesman can entertain such ludicrously parochial delusions.

No English king or French president can possibly govern
on the assumption that the theology of Peter and Paul,
Luther and Calvin, has any objective validity, or that the
Christ is more than the Buddha, or Jehovah more than
Krishna, or Jesus more or less human than Mahomet or
Zoroaster or Confucius. He is actually compelled, in so
far as he makes laws against blasphemy at all, to treat
all the religions, including Christianity, as blasphemous
when paraded before people who are not accustomed to
them and do not want them. And even that is a conces-
sion to a mischievous intolerance which an empire should
use its control of education to eradicate.

On the other hand, Governments cannot really divest
themselves of religion, or even of dogma. When Jesus
said that people should not only live but live more abundantly, he was dogmatizing; and many Pessimist sages,
including Shakespear, whose hero begged his friend to
refrain from suicide in the words "Absent thee from
felicity awhile," would say dogmatizing very pernicious-
ly. Indeed many preachers and saints declare, some of
them in the name of Jesus himself, that this world is a
vale of tears, and that our lives had better be passed in
sorrow and even in torment, as a preparation for a better
life to come. Make these sad people comfortable; and
they baffle you by putting on hair shirts.

None the less, governments must proceed on dogmatic
assumptions, whether they call them dogmas or not; and
they must clearly be assumptions common enough to
stamp those who reject them as eccentrics or lunatics.
And the greater and more heterogeneous the population
the commoner the assumptions must be. A Trappist
monastery can be conducted on assumptions which would
in twenty-fours hours provoke the village at its gates to
insurrection. That is because the monastery selects its
people; and if a Trappist does not like it he can leave it.
But a subject of the British Empire or the French Re-

public is not selected; and if he does not like it he must lump it; for emigration is practicable only within narrow limits, and seldom provides an effective remedy, all civilizations being now much alike.

To anyone capable of comprehending government at all it must be evident without argument that the set of fundamental assumptions drawn up in the thirty-nine articles or in the Westminster Confession are wildly impossible as political constitutions for modern empires. A personal profession of them by any person disposed to take such professions seriously would practically disqualify him for high imperial office. A Calvinist Viceroy of India and a Particular Baptist Secretary of State for Foreign Affairs would wreck the empire. The Stuarts wrecked even the tight little island which was the nucleus of the empire by their Scottish logic and theological dogma; and it may be sustained very plausibly that the alleged aptitude of the English for self-government, which is contradicted by every chapter of their history, is really only an incurable inaptitude for theology, and indeed for co-ordinated thought in any direction, which makes them equally impatient of systematic despotism and systematic good government: their history being that of a badly governed and accidentally free people (comparatively). Thus our success in colonizing, as far as it has not been produced by exterminating the natives, has been due to our indifference to the salvation of our subjects. Ireland is the exception which proves the rule; for Ireland, the standing instance of the inability of the English to colonize without extermination of natives, is also the one country under British rule in which the conquerors and colonizers proceeded on the assumption that their business was to establish Protestantism as well as to make money and thereby secure at least the lives of the unfortunate inhabitants out of whose labor it could be made. At this moment Ulster is refusing to accept fellowcitizenship with the other Irish provinces because the south believes in St. Peter and Bossuet, and the north in St. Paul and Calvin. Imagine the effect of trying to govern India or Egypt from Belfast or from the Vatican!

The position is perhaps graver for France than for England, because the sixty-five per cent of French subjects who are neither French nor Christian nor Modernist includes some thirty millions of negroes who are susceptible, and indeed highly susceptible, of conversion to those salvationist forms of pseudo-Christianity which have produced all the persecutions and religious wars of the last fifteen hundred years. When the late explorer Sir Henry Stanley told me of the emotional grip which Christianity had over the Baganda tribes, and read me their letters, which were exactly like medieval letters in their literal faith and everpresent piety, I said "Can these men handle a rifle?" To which Stanley replied with some scorn "Of course they can, as well as any white man." Now at this moment (1915) a vast European war is being waged, in which the French are using Senegalese soldiers. I ask the French Government, which, like our own Government, is deliberately leaving the religious instruction of these negroes in the hands of missions of Petrine Catholics and Pauline Calvinists, whether they have considered the possibility of a new series of crusades, by ardent African Salvationists, to rescue Paris from the grip of the modern scientific "infidel," and to raise the cry of "Back to the Apostles: back to Charlemagne!"

We are more fortunate in that an overwhelming majority of our subjects are Hindoos, Mahometans and Buddhists: that is, they have, as a prophylactic against salvationist Christianity, highly civilized religions of their own. Mahometanism, which Napoleon at the end of his career classed as perhaps the best popular religion

for modern political use, might in some respects have
arisen as a reformed Christianity if Mahomet had had
to deal with a population of seventeenth-century Christians instead of Arabs who worshipped stones. As it is,
men do not reject Mahomet for Calvin; and to offer a
Hindoo so crude a theology as ours in exchange for his
own, or our Jewish canonical literature as an improve-
ment on Hindoo scripture, is to offer old lamps for older
ones in a market where the oldest lamps, like old furniture in England, are the most highly valued.

Yet, I repeat, government is impossible without a religion: that is, without a body of common assumptions.
The open mind never acts: when we have done our utmost to arrive at a reasonable conclusion, we still, when
we can reason and investigate no more, must close our
minds for the moment with a snap, and act dogmatically
on our conclusions. The man who waits to make an entirely reasonable will dies intestate. A man so reasonable
as to have an open mind about theft and murder, or about
the need for food and reproduction, might just as well be
a fool and a scoundrel for any use he could be as a legis-
lator or a State official. The modern pseudo-democratic
statesman, who says that he is only in power to carry out
the will of the people, and moves only as the cat jumps,
is clearly a political and intellectual brigand. The rule of
the negative man who has no convictions means in practice the rule of the positive mob. Freedom of conscience
as Cromwell used the phrase is an excellent thing; nevertheless if any man had proposed to give effect to freedom
of conscience as to cannibalism in England, Cromwell
would have laid him by the heels almost as promptly as
he would have laid a Roman Catholic, though in Fiji at
the same moment he would have supported heartily the
freedom of conscience of a vegetarian who disparaged the
sacred diet of Long Pig.

Here then come in the importance of the repudiation

by Jesus of proselytism. His rule "Dont pull up the
tares: sow the wheat: if you try to pull up the tares you
will pull up the wheat with it" is the only possible rule
for a statesman governing a modern empire, or a voter
supporting such a statesman. There is nothing in the
teaching of Jesus that cannot be assented to by a Brah-
man, a Mahometan, a Buddhist or a Jew, without any
question of their conversion to Christianity. In some
ways it is easier to reconcile a Mahometan to Jesus than
a British parson, because the idea of a professional priest
is unfamiliar and even monstrous to a Mahometan (the
tourist who persists in asking who is the dean of St.
Sophia puzzles beyond words the sacristan who lends
him a huge pair of slippers); and Jesus never suggested that his disciples should separate themselves from
the laity: he picked them up by the wayside, where any
man or woman might follow him. For priests he had not
a civil word; and they shewed their sense of his hostility
by getting him killed as soon as possible. He was, in
short, a thoroughgoing anti-Clerical. And though, as we
have seen, it is only by political means that his doctrine
can be put into practice, he not only never suggested a
sectarian theocracy as a form of Government, and would
certainly have prophesied the downfall of the late President Kruger if he had survived to his time, but, when
challenged, he refused to teach his disciples not to pay
tribute to Caesar, admitting that Caesar, who presumably
had the kingdom of heaven within him as much as any
disciple, had his place in the scheme of things. Indeed
the apostles made this an excuse for carrying subser-
vience to the State to a pitch of idolatry that ended in
the theory of the divine right of kings, and provoked men
to cut kings' heads off to restore some sense of proportion in the matter. Jesus certainly did not consider the
overthrow of the Roman empire or the substitution of a
new ecclesiastical organization for the Jewish Church

or for the priesthood of the Roman gods as part of his
program. He said that God was better than Mammon;
but he never said that Tweedledum was better than Tweedledee; and that is why it is now possible for British
citizens and statesmen to follow Jesus, though they cannot possibly follow either Tweedledum or Tweedledee
without bringing the empire down with a crash on their
heads. And at that I must leave it.

LONDON, *December* 1915.

ANDROCLES AND THE LION
XXIII
1912

9

1 Bagadera
2 Bardoules
3 Censodions
4 Cuporun
5 Luxtistun

6 Lessplus,

7 Burtolus,

8 Jespagions

9 Savobo

10 Reedtforsq

11 Cull flory

12 Rovkeer

13 Ceesef
14 /chossas
15 Secuter
16 Emper

PROLOGUE

Overture: forest sounds, roaring of lions, Christian hymn faintly.

A jungle path. A lion's roar, a melancholy suffering roar, comes from the jungle. It is repeated nearer. The lion limps from the jungle on three legs, holding up his right forepaw, in which a huge thorn sticks. He sits down and contemplates it. He licks it. He shakes it. He tries to extract it by scraping it along the ground, and hurts himself worse. He roars piteously. He licks it again. Tears drop from his eyes. He limps painfully off the path and lies down under the trees, exhausted with pain. Heaving a long sigh, like wind in a trombone, he goes to sleep.

Androcles and his wife Megaera come along the path. He is a small, thin, ridiculous little man who might be any age from thirty to fifty-five. He has sandy hair, watery compassionate blue eyes, sensitive nostrils, and a very presentable forehead; but his good points go no further: his arms and legs and back, though wiry of their kind, look shrivelled and starved. He carries a big bundle, is very poorly clad, and seems tired and hungry.

His wife is a rather handsome pampered slattern, well fed and in the prime of life. She has nothing to carry, and has a stout stick to help her along.

MEGAERA (*suddenly throwing down her stick*) I wont go another step.

ANDROCLES (*pleading wearily*) Oh, not again, dear.

3

whats the good of stopping every two miles and saying you wont go another step? We must get on to the next village before night. There are wild beasts in this wood: lions, they say.

MEGAERA. I dont believe a word of it. You are always threatening me with wild beasts to make me walk the very soul out of my body when I can hardly drag one foot before another. We havnt seen a single lion yet.

ANDROCLES. Well, dear, do you want to see one?

MEGAERA (*tearing the bundle from his back*) You cruel beast, you dont care how tired I am, or what becomes of me (*she throws the bundle on the ground*): always thinking of yourself. Self! self! self! always yourself! (*She sits down on the bundle*).

ANDROCLES (*sitting down sadly on the ground with his elbows on his knees and his head in his hands*) We all have to think of ourselves occasionally, dear.

MEGAERA. A man ought to think of his wife sometimes.

ANDROCLES. He cant always help it, dear. You make me think of you a good deal. Not that I blame you.

MEGAERA. Blame me! I should think not indeed. Is it my fault that I'm married to you?

ANDROCLES. No, dear: that is my fault.

MEGAERA. Thats a nice thing to say to me. Arnt you happy with me?

ANDROCLES. I dont complain, my love.

MEGAERA. You ought to be ashamed of yourself.

ANDROCLES. I am, my dear.

MEGAERA. Youre not: you glory in it.

ANDROCLES. In what, darling?

MEGAERA. In everything. In making me a slave, and making yourself a laughing-stock. Its not fair. You get me the name of being a shrew with your meek ways, always talking as if butter wouldnt melt in your mouth. And just because I look a big strong woman, and because I'm good-hearted and a bit hasty, and because youre always driving me to do things I'm sorry for afterwards, people say " Poor man: what a life his wife leads him!" Oh, if they only knew! And you think I dont know. But I do, I do, (*screaming*) I do.

ANDROCLES. Yes, my dear: I know you do.

MEGAERA. Then why dont you treat me properly and be a good husband to me?

ANDROCLES. What can I do, my dear?

MEGAERA. What can you do! You can return to your duty, and come back to your home and your friends, and sacrifice to the gods as all respectable people do, instead of having us hunted out of house and home for being dirty, disreputable, blaspheming atheists.

ANDROCLES. I'm not an atheist, dear: I am a Christian.

MEGAERA. Well, isnt that the same thing, only ten times worse? Everybody knows that the Christians are the very lowest of the low.

ANDROCLES. Just like us, dear.

MEGAERA. Speak for yourself. Dont you dare to compare me to common people. My father owned his own public-house; and sorrowful was the day for me when you first came drinking in our bar.

ANDROCLES. I confess I was addicted to it, dear. But I gave it up when I became a Christian.

MEGAERA. Youd much better have remained a drunkard. I can forgive a man being addicted to drink: its only natural; and I dont deny I like a drop myself sometimes. What I cant stand is your being addicted to Christianity. And whats worse again, your being addicted to animals. How is any woman to keep her house clean when you bring in every stray cat and lost cur and lame duck in the whole countryside? You took

the bread out of my mouth to feed them: you know you
did: dont attempt to deny it.

ANDROCLES.   Only when they were hungry and you
were getting too stout, dearie.

MEGAERA.   Yes, insult me, do. (*Rising*) Oh! I wont
bear it another moment.   You used to sit and talk to
those dumb brute beasts for hours, when you hadnt a
word for me.

ANDROCLES   They never answered back, darling. (*He
rises and again shoulders the bundle*).

MEGAERA.   Well, if youre fonder of animals than of
your own wife, you can live with them here in the jungle.
Ive had enough of them and enough of you.   I'm going
back.   I'm going home.

ANDROCLES (*barring the way back*) No, dearie: dont
take on like that.   We cant go back.   Weve sold everything: we should starve; and I should be sent to Rome
and thrown to the lions—

MEGAERA.   Serve you right!   I wish the lions joy of
you.   (*Screaming*) Are you going to get out of my way
and let me go home?

ANDROCLES.   No, dear—

MEGAERA.   Then Ill make my way through the forest;
and when I'm eaten by the wild beasts youll know what
a wife youve lost. (*She dashes into the jungle and nearly
falls over the sleeping lion*).   Oh! Oh! Andy! Andy!
(*She totters back and collapses into the arms of Androcles, who crushed by her weight, falls on his bundle*).

ANDROCLES (*extracting himself from beneath her and
slapping her hands in great anxiety*) What is it, my
precious, my pet?   Whats the matter? (*He raises her
head.   Speechless with terror, she points in the direction of the sleeping lion.   He steals cautiously towards
the spot indicated by Megaera.   She rises with an effort
and totters after him*).

MEGAERA.   No, Andy: youll be killed.   Come back.

*The lion utters a long snoring sign. Androcles sees
the lion and recoils fainting into the arms of Megaera,
who falls back on the bundle. They roll apart and lie
staring in terror at one another. The lion is heard groaning heavily in the jungle.*

ANDROCLES (*whispering*) Did you see? A lion.

MEGAERA (*despairing*) The gods have sent him to
punish us because youre a Christian. Take me away,
Andy. Save me.

ANDROCLES (*rising*) Meggy: theres one chance for
you. Itll take him pretty nigh twenty minutes to eat
me (I'm rather stringy and tough) and you can escape
in less time than that.

MEGAERA. Oh, dont talk about eating. (*The lion
rises with a great groan and limps towards them*). Oh!
(*She faints*).

ANDROCLES (*quaking, but keeping between the lion
and Megaera*) Dont you come near my wife, do you
hear? (*The lion groans. Androcles can hardly stand
for trembling*). Meggy: run. Run for your life. If
I take my eye off him, its all up. (*The lion holds up
his wounded paw and flaps it piteously before Androcles*). Oh, hes lame, poor old chap! Hes got a thorn
in his paw. A frightfully big thorn. (*Full of sympathy*) Oh, poor old man! Did um get an awful thorn
into um's tootsums wootsums? Has it made um too sick
to eat a nice little Christian man for um's breakfast?
Oh, a nice little Christian man will get um's thorn out
for um; and then um shall eat the nice Christian man
and the nice Christian man's nice big tender wifey pifey.
(*The lion responds by moans of self-pity*). Yes, yes,
yes, yes, yes. Now, now (*taking the paw in his hand*)
um is not to bite and not to scratch, not even if it hurts
a very, very little. Now make velvet paws. That right.
(*He pulls gingerly at the thorn. The lion, with an
angry yell of pain, jerks back his paw so abruptly that*

Androcles is thrown on his back). Steadeee! Oh, did the nasty cruel little Christian man hurt the sore paw? (*The lion moans assentingly but apologetically*). Well, one more little pull and it will be all over. Just one little, little, leetle pull; and then um will live happily ever after. (*He gives the thorn another pull. The lion roars and snaps his jaws with a terrifying clash*). Oh, mustnt frighten um's good kind doctor, um's affectionate nursey. That didnt hurt at all: not a bit. Just one more. Just to shew how the brave big lion can bear pain, not like the little crybaby Christian man. Oopsh! (*The thorn comes out. The lion yells with pain, and shakes his paw wildly*). Thats it! (*Holding up the thorn*). Now its out. Now lick um's paw to take away the nasty inflammation. See? (*He licks his own hand. The lion nods intelligently and licks his paw industriously*). Clever little liony-piony! Understands um's dear old friend Andy Wandy. (*The lion licks his face*). Yes, kissums Andy Wandy. (*The lion, wagging his tail violently, rises on his hind legs and embraces Androcles, who makes a wry face and cries*) Velvet paws! Velvet paws! (*The lion draws in his claws*). Thats right. (*He embraces the lion, who finally takes the end of his tail in one paw, places that tight around Androcles' waist, resting it on his hip. Androcles takes the other paw in his hand, stretches out his arm, and the two waltz rapturously round and round and finally away through the jungle*).

MEGAERA (*who has revived during the waltz*) Oh, you coward, you havnt danced with me for years; and now you go off dancing with a great brute beast that you havnt known for ten minutes and that wants to eat your own wife. Coward! Coward! Coward! (*She ruhes off after them into the jungle*).

ACT I

Evening. The end of three converging roads to Rome. Three triumphal arches span them where they debouch on a square at the gate of the city. Looking north through the arches one can see the campagna threaded by the three long dusty tracks. On the east and west sides of the square are long stone benches. An old beggar sits on the east side of the square, his bowl at his feet.

Through the eastern arch a squad of Roman soldiers tramps along escorting a batch of Christian prisoners of both sexes and all ages, among them one Lavinia, a good-looking resolute young woman, apparently of higher social standing than her fellow-prisoners. A centurion, carrying his vinewood cudgel, trudges alongside the squad, on its right, in command of it. All are tired and dusty; but the soldiers are dogged and indifferent, the Christians light-hearted and determined to treat their hardships as a joke and encourage one another.

A bugle is heard far behind on the road, where the rest of the cohort is following.

CENTURION (*stopping*) Halt! Orders from the Captain. (*They halt and wait*). Now then, you Christians, none of your larks. The captain's coming. Mind you behave yourselves. No singing. Look respectful. Look serious, if youre capable of it. See that big building over there? That's the Coliseum. That's where youll be thrown to the lions or set to fight the gladiators presently. Think of that; and itll help you to behave properly before the captain. (*The Captain arrives*). Attention! Salute! (*The soldiers salute*).

9

A CHRISTIAN (*cheerfully*) God bless you, Captain.

THE CENTURION (*scandalized*) Silence!

The Captain, a patrician, handsome, about thirty-five, very cold and distinguished, very superior and authoritative, steps up on a stone seat at the west side of the square, behind the centurion, so as to dominate the others more effectually.

THE CAPTAIN. Centurion.

THE CENTURION (*standing at attention and saluting*) Sir?

THE CAPTAIN (*speaking stiffly and officially*) You will remind your men, Centurion, that we are now entering Rome. You will instruct them that once inside the gates of Rome they are in the presence of the Emperor. You will make them understand that the lax discipline of the march cannot be permitted here. You will instruct them to shave every day, not every week. You will impress on them particularly that there must be an end to the profanity and blasphemy of singing Christian hymns on the march. I have to reprimand you, Centurion, for not only allowing this, but actually doing it yourself.

THE CENTURION (*apologetic*) The men march better, Captain.

THE CAPTAIN. No doubt. For that reason an exception is made in the case of the march called Onward Christian Soldiers. This may be sung, except when marching through the forum or within hearing of the Emperor's palace; but the words must be altered to "Throw them to the Lions."

The Christians burst into shrieks of uncontrollable laughter, to the great scandal of the Centurion.

CENTURION. Silence! Silen-n-n-n-nce! Wheres your behavior? Is that the way to listen to an officer? (*To the Captain*) Thats what we have to put up with from these Christians every day, sir. Theyre always laughing and joking something scandalous. Theyve no religion: thats how it is.

LAVINIA. But I think the Captain meant us to laugh, Centurion. It was so funny.

CENTURION. Youll find out how funny it is when youre thrown to the lions to-morrow. (*To the Captain, who looks displeased*) Beg pardon, Sir. (*To the Christians*) Silennnnce!

THE CAPTAIN. You are to instruct your men that all intimacy with Christian prisoners must now cease. The men have fallen into habits of dependence upon the prisoners, especially the female prisoners, for cooking, repairs to uniforms, writing letters, and advice in their private affairs. In a Roman soldier such dependence is inadmissible. Let me see no more of it whilst we are in the city. Further, your orders are that in addressing Christian prisoners, the manners and tone of your men must express abhorrence and contempt. Any shortcoming in this respect will be regarded as a breach of discipline. (*He turns to the prisoners*) Prisoners.

CENTURION (*fiercely*) Prisonerrrrrs! Tention! Silence!

THE CAPTAIN. I call your attention, prisoners, to the fact that you may be called on to appear in the Imperial Circus at any time from tomorrow onwards according to the requirements of the managers. I may inform you that as there is a shortage of Christians just now, you may expect to be called on very soon.

LAVINIA. What will they do to us, Captain?

CENTURION. Silence!

THE CAPTAIN. The women will be conducted into the arena with the wild beasts of the Imperial Menagerie, and will suffer the consequences. The men, if of an age to bear arms, will be given weapons to defend themselves, if they choose, against the Imperial Gladiators.

LAVINIA. Captain: is there no hope that this cruel persecution—

CENTURION (*shocked*) Silence! Hold your tongue, there. Persecution, indeed!

THE CAPTAIN (*unmoved and somewhat sardonic*) Persecution is not a term applicable to the acts of the Emperor. The Emperor is the Defender of the Faith. In throwing you to the lions he will be upholding the interests of religion in Rome. If you were to throw him to the lions, that would no doubt be persecution.

The Christians again laugh heartily.

CENTURION (*horrified*) Silence, I tell you! Keep silence there. Did anyone ever hear the like of this?

LAVINIA. Captain: there will be nobody to appreciate your jokes when we are gone.

THE CAPTAIN (*unshaken in his official delivery*) I call the attention of the female prisoner Lavinia to the fact that as the Emperor is a divine personage, her imputation of cruelty is not only treason, but sacrilege. I point out to her further that there is no foundation for the charge, as the Emperor does not desire that any prisoner should suffer; nor can any Christian be harmed save through his or her own obstinacy. All that is necessary is to sacrifice to the gods: a simple and convenient ceremony effected by dropping a pinch of incense on the altar, after which the prisoner is at once set free. Under such circumstances you have only your own perverse folly to blame if you suffer. I suggest to you that if you cannot burn a morsel of incense as a matter of conviction, you might at least do so as a matter of good taste, to avoid shocking the religious convictions of your fellow citizens. I am aware that these considerations do not weigh with Christians; but it is my duty to call your attention to them in order that you may have no ground for complaining of your treatment, or of accusing the Emperor of cruelty when he is shewing you the most signal clemency.

Looked at from this point of view, every Christian who has perished in the arena has really committed suicide.

LAVINIA. Captain: your jokes are too grim. Do not think it is easy for us to die. Our faith makes life far stronger and more wonderful in us than when we walked in darkness and had nothing to live for. Death is harder for us than for you: the martyr's agony is as bitter as his triumph is glorious.

THE CAPTAIN (*rather troubled, addressing her personally and gravely*) A martyr, Lavinia, is a fool. Your death will prove nothing.

LAVINIA. Then why kill me?

THE CAPTAIN. I mean that truth, if there be any truth, needs no martyrs.

LAVINIA. No; but my faith, like your sword, needs testing. Can you test your sword except by staking your life on it?

THE CAPTAIN (*suddenly resuming his official tone*) I call the attention of the female prisoner to the fact that Christians are not allowed to draw the Emperor's officers into arguments and put questions to them for which the military regulations provide no answer. (*The Christians titter*).

LAVINIA. Captain: how *c a n* you?

THE CAPTAIN. I call the female prisoner's attention specially to the fact that four comfortable homes have been offered her by officers of this regiment, of which she can have her choice the moment she chooses to sacrifice as all well-bred Roman ladies do. I have no more to say to the prisoners.

CENTURION. Dismiss! But stay where you are.

THE CAPTAIN. Centurion: you will remain here with your men in charge of the prisoners until the arrival of three Christian prisoners in the custody of a cohort of the tenth legion. Among these prisoners you will particularly identify an armorer named Ferrovius, of dangerous character and great personal strength, and a Greek tailor reputed to be a sorcerer, by name Androcles. You will add the three to your charge here and march them all to the Coliseum, where you will deliver them into the custody of the master of the gladiators and take his receipt, countersigned by the keeper of the beasts and the acting manager. You understand your instructions?

CENTURION. Yes, sir.

THE CAPTAIN. Dismiss. (*He throws off his air of parade, and descends down from the perch. The Centurion seats on it and prepares for a nap, whilst his men stand at ease. The Christians sit down on the west side of the square, glad to rest. Lavinia alone remains standing to speak to the Captain*).

LAVINIA. Captain: is this man who is to join us the famous Ferrovius, who has made such wonderful conversions in the northern cities?

THE CAPTAIN. Yes. We are warned that he has the strength of an elephant and the temper of a mad bull. Also that he is stark mad. Not a model Christian, it would seem.

LAVINIA. You need not fear him if he is a Christian, Captain.

THE CAPTAIN (*coldly*) I shall not fear him in any case, Lavinia.

LAVINIA (*her eyes dancing*) How brave of you, Captain!

THE CAPTAIN. You are right: it was silly thing to say. (*In a lower tone, humane and urgent*) Lavinia: do Christians know how to love?

LAVINIA (*composedly*) Yes, Captain: they love even their enemies.

THE CAPTAIN. Is that easy?

LAVINIA. Very easy, Captain, when their enemies are as handsome as you.

THE CAPTAIN. Lavinia: you are laughing at me.

LAVINIA. At you, Captain! Impossible.

THE CAPTAIN. Then you are flirting with me, which is worse. Don't be foolish.

LAVINIA. But such a very handsome captain.

THE CAPTAIN. Incorrigible! (*Urgently*) Listen to me. The men in that audience tomorrow will be the vilest of voluptuaries: men in whom the only passion excited by a beautiful woman is a lust to see her tortured and torn shrieking limb from limb. It is a crime to gratify that passion. It is offering yourself for violation by the whole rabble of the streets and the riff-raff of the court at the same time. Why will you not choose rather a kindly love and an honorable alliance?

LAVINIA. They cannot violate my soul. I alone can do that by sacrificing to false gods.

THE CAPTAIN. Sacrifice then to the true God. What does his name matter? We call him Jupiter. The Greeks call him Zeus. Call him what you will as you drop the incense on the altar flame: He will understand.

LAVINIA. No. I couldnt. That is the strange thing, Captain, that a little pinch of incense should make all that difference. Religion is such a great thing that when I meet really religious people we are friends at once, no matter what name we give to the divine will that made us and moves us. Oh, do you think that I, a woman, would quarrel with you for sacrificing to a woman god like Diana, if Diana meant to you what Christ means to me? No: we should kneel side by side before her altar like two children. But when men who believe neither in my god nor in their own—men who do not know the meaning of the word religion—when these men drag me to the foot of an iron statue that has become the symbol of the terror and darkness through which they walk, of their cruelty and greed, of their hatred of God and their oppression of man—when they ask me to pledge my soul before the people that this hideous idol is God, and that all this wickedness and falsehood is divine truth, I cannot do it, not if they could put a thousand cruel deaths on me. I tell you, it is physically impossible. Listen, Captain: did you ever try to catch a mouse in your hand? Once there was a dear little mouse that used to come out and play on my table as I was reading. I wanted to take him in my hand and caress him; and sometimes he got among my books so that he could not escape me when I stretched out my hand. And I did stretch out my hand; but it always came back in spite of me. I was not afraid of him in my heart; but my hand refused: it is not in the nature of my hand to touch a mouse. Well, Captain, if I took a pinch of incense in my hand and stretched it out over the altar fire, my hand would come back. My body would be true to my faith even if you could corrupt my mind. And all the time I should believe more in Diana than my persecutors have ever believed in anything. Can you understand that?

THE CAPTAIN (*simply*) Yes: I understand that. But my hand would not come back. The hand that holds the sword has been trained not to come back from anything but victory.

LAVINIA. Not even from death?

THE CAPTAIN. Least of all from death.

LAVINIA. Then I must not come back from death either. A woman has to be braver than a soldier.

THE CAPTAIN. Prouder, you mean.

LAVINIA (*startled*) Prouder! You call our courage pride!

THE CAPTAIN. There is no such thing as courage: there is only pride. You Christians are the proudest devils on earth.

LAVINIA (*hurt*) Pray God then my pride may never become a false pride. (*She turns away as if she did not wish to continue the conversation, but softens and says to him with a smile*) Thank you for trying to save me.

THE CAPTAIN. I knew it was no use; but one tries in spite of one's knowledge.

LAVINIA. Something stirs, even in the iron breast of a Roman soldier!

THE CAPTAIN. It will soon be iron again. I have seen many women die, and forgotten them in a week.

LAVINIA. Remember me for a fortnight, handsome Captain. I shall be watching you, perhaps.

THE CAPTAIN. From the skies? Do not deceive yourself, Lavinia. There is no future for you beyond the grave.

LAVINIA. What does that matter? Do you think I am only running away from the terrors of life into the comfort of heaven? If there were no future, or if the future were one of torment, I should have to go just the same. The hand of God is upon me.

THE CAPTAIN. Yes: when all is said, we are both patricians, Lavinia, and must die for our beliefs. Farewell. (*He offers her his hand. She takes it and presses it. He walks away, trim and calm. She looks after him for a moment, and cries a little as he disappears through the eastern arch. A trumpet-call is heard from the road through the western arch*).

CENTURION (*waking up and rising*) Cohort of the tenth with prisoners. Two file out with me to receive them. (*He goes out through the western arch, followed by four soldiers in two files*).

Lentulus and Metellus come into the square from the west side with a little retinue of servants. Both are young courtiers, dressed in the extremity of fashion. Lentulus is slender, fair-haired, epicene. Metellus is manly, compactly built, olive skinned, not a talker.

LENTULUS. Christians, by Jove! Lets chaff them.

METELLUS. Awful brutes. If you knew as much about them as I do you wouldnt want to chaff them. Leave them to the lions.

10

LENTULUS (*indicating Lavinia, who is still looking towards the arches after the captain*). That woman's got a figure. (*He walks past her, staring at her invitingly; but she is preoccupied and is not conscious of him*). Do you turn the other cheek when they kiss you?

LAVINIA (*starting*) What?

LENTULUS. Do you turn the other cheek when they kiss you, fascinating Christian?

LAVINIA. Don't be foolish. (*To Metellus, who has remained on her right, so that she is between them*) Please dont let your friend behave like a cad before the soldiers. How are they to respect and obey patricians if they see them behaving like street boys? (*Sharply to Lentulus*) Pull yourself together, man. Hold your head up. Keep the corners of your mouth firm; and treat me respectfully. What do you take me for?

LENTULUS (*irresolutely*) Look here, you know: I—you—I—

LAVINIA. Stuff! Go about your business. (*She turns decisively away and sits down with her comrades, leaving him disconcerted*).

METELLUS. You didnt get much out of that. I told you they were brutes.

LENTULUS. Plucky little filly! I suppose she thinks I care. (*With an air of indifference he strolls with Lentulus to the east side of the square, where they stand watching the return of the Centurion through the western arch with his men, escorting three prisoners: Ferrovius, Androcles, and Spintho. Ferrovius is a powerful, choleric man in the prime of life, with large nostrils, staring eyes, and a thick neck: a man whose sensibilities are keen and violent to the verge of madness. Spintho is a debauchee, the wreck of a good-looking man gone hopelessly to the bad. Androcles is overwhelmed with grief, and is restraining his tears with great difficulty*).

THE CENTURION (*to Lavinia*) Here are some pals

for you. This little bit is Ferrovius that you talk so much about. (*Ferrovius turns on him threateningly. The Centurion holds up his left forefinger in admonition*). Now remember that youre a Christian, and that you've got to return good for evil. (*Ferrovius controls himself convulsively; moves away from temptation to the east side near Lentulus; clasps his hands in silent prayer; and throws himself on his knees*). Thats the way to manage them, eh! This fine fellow (*indicating Androcles, who comes to his left, and makes Lavinia a heartbroken salutation*) is a sorcerer. A Greek tailor, he is. A real sorcerer, too: no mistake about it. The tenth marches with a leopard at the head of the column. He made a pet of the leopard; and now he's crying at being parted from it. (*Androcles sniffs lamentably*). Aint you, old chap? Well, cheer up, we march with a Billy goat (*Androcles brightens up*) thats killed two leopards and ate a turkey-cock. You can have him for a pet if you like. (*Androcles, quite consoled, goes past the Centurion to Lavinia, and sits down contentedly on the ground on her left*). This dirty dog (*collaring Spintho*) is a real Christian. He mobs the temples, he does (*at each accusation he gives the neck of Spintho's tunic a twist*); he goes smashing things mad drunk, he does; he steals the gold vessels, he does; he assaults the priestesses, he does—yah! (*He flings Spintho into the middle of the group of prisoners*). Youre the sort that makes duty a pleasure, you are.

Spintho (*gasping*) Thats it: strangle me. Kick me. Beat me. Revile me. Our Lord was beaten and reviled. Thats my way to heaven. Every martyr goes to heaven, no matter what hes done. That is so, isnt it, brother?

Centurion. Well, if youre going to heaven, *I* dont want to go there. I wouldnt be seen with you.

Lentulus. Haw! Good! (*Indicating the kneeling*

Ferrovius). Is this one of the turn-the-other-cheek gentlemen, Centurion?

CENTURION. Yes, sir. Lucky for you too, sir, if you want to take any liberties with. him.

LENTULUS (*to Ferrovius*) You turn the other cheek when youre struck, I'm told.

FERROVIUS (*slowly turning his great eyes on him*) Yes, by the grace of God, I do, n o w.

LENTULUS. Not that youre a coward, of course; but out of pure piety.

FERROVIUS. I fear God more than man; at least I try to.

LENTULUS. Lets see. (*He strikes him on the cheek. Androcles makes a wild movement to rise and interfere; but Lavinia holds him down, watching Ferrovius intently. Ferrovius, without flinching, turns the other cheek. Lentulus, rather out of countenance, titters foolishly, and strikes him again feebly*). You know, I should feel ashamed if I let myself be struck like that, and took it lying down. But then I'm not a Christian: I'm a man. (*Ferrovius rises impressively and towers over him. Lentulus becomes white with terror; and a shade of green flickers in his cheek for a moment*).

FERROVIUS (*with the calm of a steam hammer*) I have not always been faithful. The first man who struck me as you have just struck me was a stronger man than you: he hit me harder than I expected. I was tempted and fell; and it was then that I first tasted bitter shame. I never had a happy moment after that until I had knelt and asked his forgiveness by his bedside in the hospital. (*Putting his hands on Lentulus's shoulders with paternal weight*). But now I have learnt to resist with a strength that is not my own. I am not ashamed now, nor angry.

LENTULUS (*uneasily*) Er—good evening. (*He tries to move away*).

FERROVIUS (*gripping his shoulders*) Oh, do not

harden your heart, young man. Come: try for yourself whether our way is not better than yours. I will now strike you on one cheek; and you will turn the other and learn how much better you will feel than if you gave way to the promptings of anger. (*He holds him with one hand and clenches the other fist*).

LENTULUS. Centurion: I call on you to protect me.

CENTURION. You asked for it, sir. Its no business of ours. Youve had two whacks at him. Better pay him a trifle and square it that way.

LENTULUS. Yes, of course. (*To Ferrovius*) It was only a bit of fun, I assure you: I meant no harm. Here. (*He proffers a gold coin*).

FERROVIUS (*taking it and throwing it to the old beggar, who snatches it up eagerly, and hobbles off to spend it*) Give all thou hast to the poor. Come, friend: courage! I may hurt your body for a moment; but your soul will rejoice in the victory of the spirit over the flesh. (*He prepares to strike*).

ANDROCLES. Easy, Ferrovius, easy: you broke the last man's jaw.

Lentulus, with a moan of terror, attempts to fly; but Ferrovius holds him ruthlessly.

FERROVIUS. Yes; but I saved his soul. What matters a broken jaw?

LENTULUS. Don't touch me, do you hear? The law—

FERROVIUS. The law will throw me to the lions tomorrow: what worse could it do were I to slay you? Pray for strength; and it shall be given to you.

LENTULUS. Let me go. Your religion forbids you to strike me.

FERROVIUS. On the contrary, it commands me to strike you. How can you turn the other cheek, if you are not first struck on the one cheek?

LENTULUS (*almost in tears*) But I'm convinced already that what you said is quite right. I apologize for striking you.

FERROVIUS (*greatly pleased*) My son: have I softened your heart? Has the good seed fallen in a fruitful place? Are your feet turning towards a better path?

LENTULUS (*abjectly*) Yes, yes. Theres a great deal in what you say.

FERROVIUS (*radiant*) Join us. Come to the lions. Come to suffering and death.

LENTULUS (*falling on his knees and bursting into tears*) Oh, help me. Mother! mother!

FERROVIUS. These tears will water your soul and make it bring forth good fruit, my son. God has greatly blessed my efforts at conversion. Shall I tell you a miracle—yes, a miracle—wrought by me in Cappadocia? A young man—just such a one as you, with golden hair like yours—scoffed at and struck me as you scoffed at and struck me. I sat up all night with that youth wrestling for his soul; and in the morning not only was he a Christian, but his hair was as white as snow. (*Lentulus falls in a dead faint*). There, there: take him away. The spirit has overwrought him, poor lad. Carry him gently to his house; and leave the rest to heaven.

CENTURION. Take him home. (*The servants, intimidated, hastily carry him out. Metellus is about to follow when Ferrovius lays his hand on his shoulder*).

FERROVIUS. You are his friend, young man. You will see that he is taken safely home.

METELLUS (*with awestruck civility*) Certainly, sir. I shall do whatever you think best. Most happy to have made your acquaintance, I'm sure. You may depend on me. Good evening, sir.

FERROVIUS (*with unction*) The blessing of heaven upon you and him.

Metellus follows Lentulus. The Centurion returns to

his seat to resume his interrupted nap. The deepest awe has settled on the spectators. Ferrovius, with a long sigh of happiness, goes to Lavinia, and offers her his hand.

LAVINIA (*taking it*) So that is how you convert people, Ferrovius.

FERROVIUS. Yes: there has been a blessing on my work in spite of my unworthiness and my backslidings—all through my wicked, devilish temper. This man—

ANDROCLES (*hastily*) Dont slap me on the back, brother. She knows you mean me.

FERROVIUS. How I wish I were weak like our brother here! for then I should perhaps be meek and gentle like him. And yet there seems to be a special providence that makes my trials less than his. I hear tales of the crowd scoffing and casting stones and reviling the brethren; but when I come, all this stops: my influence calms the passions of the mob: they listen to me in silence; and infidels are often converted by a straight heart-to-heart talk with me. Every day I feel happier, more confident. Every day lightens the load of the great terror.

LAVINIA. The great terror? What is that?

Ferrovius shakes his head and does not answer. He sits down beside her on her left, and buries his face in his hands in gloomy meditation.

ANDROCLES. Well, you see, sister, hes never quite sure of himself. Suppose at the last moment in the arena, with the gladiators there to fight him, one of them was to say anything to annoy him, he might forget himself and lay that gladiator out.

LAVINIA. That would be splendid.

FERROVIUS (*springing up in horror*) What!

ANDROCLES. Oh, sister!

FERROVIUS. Splendid to betray my master, like Peter! Splendid to act like any common blackguard in the day of my proving! Woman: you are no Christian. (*He moves away from her to the middle of the square, as if her neighborhood contaminated him*).

LAVINIA (*laughing*) You know, Ferrovius, I am not always a Christian. I dont think anybody is. There are moments when I forget all about it, and something comes out quite naturally, as it did then.

SPINTHO. What does it matter? If you die in the arena, youll be a martyr; and all martyrs go to heaven, no matter what they have done. Thats so, isnt it, Ferrovius?

FERROVIUS. Yes: that is so, if we are faithful to the end.

LAVINIA. I'm not so sure.

SPINTHO. Dont say that. Thats blasphemy. Dont say that, I tell you. We shall be saved, no matter WHAT we do.

LAVINIA. Perhaps you men will all go into heaven bravely and in triumph, with your heads erect and golden trumpets sounding for you. But I am sure shall only be allowed to squeeze myself in through a little crack in the gate after a great deal of begging. I am not good always: I have moments only.

SPINTHO. Youre talking nonsense, woman. I tell you, martyrdom pays all scores.

ANDROCLES. Well, let us hope so, brother, for your sake. Youve had a gay time, havent you? with your raids on the temples. I cant help thinking that heaven will be very dull for a man of your temperament. (*Spintho snarls*). Dont be angry: I say it only to console you in case you should die in your bed tonight in the natural way. Theres a lot of plague about.

SPINTHO (*rising and running about in abject terror*) I never thought of that. O Lord, spare me to be martyred. Oh, what a thought to put into the mind of a brother! Oh, let me be martyred today, now. I shall die in the night and go to hell. Youre a sorcerer: youve put death into my mind. Oh, curse you, curse you! (*He tries to seize Androcles by the throat*).

FERROVIUS (*holding him in a grip of iron*) Whats this, brother? Anger! Violence! Raising your hand to a brother Christian!

SPINTHO. It's easy for you. Youre strong. Your nerves are all right. But I'm full of disease. (*Ferrovius takes his hand from him with instinctive disgust*). Ive drunk all my nerves away. I shall have the horrors all night.

ANDROCLES (*sympathetic*) Oh, dont take on so, brother. We're all sinners.

SPINTHO (*snivelling, trying to feel consoled*). Yes: I daresay if the truth were known, youre all as bad as I am.

LAVINIA (*contemptuously*) Does t h a t comfort you?

FERROVIUS (*sternly*) Pray, man, pray.

SPINTHO. Whats the good of praying? If we're martyred we shall go to heaven, shant we, whether we pray or not?

FERROVIUS. Whats that? Not pray! (*Seizing him again*) Pray this instant, you dog, you rotten hound, you slimy snake, you beastly goat, or—

SPINTHO. Yes: beat me: kick me. I forgive you: mind that.

FERROVIUS (*spurning him with loathing*) Yah! (*Spintho reels away and falls in front of Ferrovius*).

ANDROCLES (*reaching out and catching the skirt of Ferrovius's tunic*) Dear brother: if you wouldnt mind —just for my sake—

FERROVIUS. Well?

ANDROCLES. Dont call him by the names of the animals. Weve no right to. Ive had such friends in dogs. A pet snake is the best of company. I was nursed on goat's milk. Is it fair to them to call the like of him a dog or a snake or a goat?

FERROVIUS. I only meant that they have no souls.

ANDROCLES (*anxiously protesting*) Oh, believe me,
they have. Just the same as you and me. I really dont
think I could consent to go to heaven if I thought there
were to be no animals there. Think of what they suffer
here.

FERROVIUS. Thats true. Yes: that is just. They
will have their share in heaven.

SPINTHO (*who has picked himself up and is sneaking
past Ferrovius on his left, sneers derisively*)!!

FERROVIUS (*turning on him fiercely*) Whats that
you say?

SPINTHO (*cowering*). Nothing.

FERROVIUS (*clenching his fist*) Do animals go to
heaven or not?

SPINTHO. I never said they didnt.

FERROVIUS (*implacable*) Do they or do they not?

SPINTHO. They do: they do. (*Scrambling out of
Ferrovius's reach*). Oh, curse you for frightening me!

A bugle call is heard.

CENTURION (*waking up*) Tention! Form as before.
Now then, prisoners, up with you and trot along spry.
(*The soldiers fall in. The Christians rise*).

*A man with an ox goad comes running through the
central arch.*

THE OX DRIVER. Here, you soldiers! clear out of the
way for the Emperor.

THE CENTURION. Emperor! Wheres the Emperor?
You aint the Emperor, are you?

THE OX DRIVER. It's the menagerie service. My team
of oxen is drawing the new lion to the Coliseum. You
clear the road.

CENTURION. What! Go in after you in your dust,
with half the town at the heels of you and your lion!
Not likely. We go first.

THE OX DRIVER. The menagerie service is the Emperor's personal retinue. You clear out, I tell you.

CENTURION. You tell me, do you? Well, Ill tell you something. If the lion is menagerie service, the lion's dinner is menagerie service too. This (*pointing to the Christians*) is the lion's dinner. So back with you to your bullocks double quick; and learn your place. March. (*The soldiers start*). Now then, you Christians, step out there.

LAVINIA (*marching*) Come along, the rest of the dinner. I shall be the olives and anchovies.

ANOTHER CHRISTIAN (*laughing*) I shall be the soup.

ANOTHER. I shall be the fish.

ANOTHER. Ferrovius shall be the roast boar.

FERROVIUS (*heavily*) I see the joke. Yes, yes: I shall be the roast boar. Ha! ha! (*He laughs conscientiously and marches out with them*).

ANDROCLES. I shall be the mince pie. (*Each announcement is received with a louder laugh by all the rest as the joke catches on*).

CENTURION (*scandalized*) Silence! Have some sense of your situation. Is this the way for martyrs to behave? (*To Spintho, who is quaking and loitering*) I know what you 11 be at that dinner. Youll be the emetic. (*He shoves him rudely along*).

SPINTHO. Its too dreadful: I'm not fit to die.

CENTURION. Fitter than you are to live, you swine.

They pass from the square westward. The oxen, drawing a waggon with a great wooden cage and the lion in it, arrive through the central arch.

ACT II

Behind the Emperor's box at the Coliseum, where the performers assemble before entering the arena. In the middle a wide passage leading to the arena descends from the floor level under the imperial box. On both sides of this passage steps ascend to a landing at the back entrance to the box. The landing forms a bridge across the passage. At the entrance to the passage are two bronze mirrors, one on each side.

On the west side of this passage, on the right hand of any one coming from the box and standing on the bridge, the martyrs are sitting on the steps. Lavinia is seated half-way up, thoughtful, trying to look death in the face. On her left Androcles consoles himself by nursing a cat. Ferrovius stands behind them, his eyes blazing, his figure stiff with intense resolution. At the foot of the steps crouches Spintho, with his head clutched in his hands, full of horror at the approach of martyrdom.

On the east side of the passage the gladiators are standing and sitting at ease, waiting, like the Christians, for their turn in the arena. One (Retiarius) is a nearly naked man with a net and a trident. Another (Secutor) is in armor with a sword. He carries a helmet with a barred visor. The editor of the gladiators sits on a chair a little apart from them.

The Call Boy enters from the passage.

THE CALL BOY. Number six. Retiarius versus Secutor.

The gladiator with the net picks it up. The gladiator with the helmet puts it on; and the two go into the arena, the net thrower taking out a little brush and arranging his hair as he goes, the other tightening his straps and shaking his shoulders loose. Both look at themselves in the mirrors before they enter the passage.

LAVINIA. Will they really kill one another?

SPINTHO. Yes, if the people turn down their thumbs.

THE EDITOR. You know nothing about it. The people indeed! Do you suppose we would kill a man worth perhaps fifty talents to please the riffraff? I should like to catch any of my men at it.

SPINTHO. I thought—

THE EDITOR (*contemptuously*) You thought! Who cares what you think? You ll be killed all right enough.

SPINTHO (*groans and again hides his face*) ! ! !

LAVINIA. Then is nobody ever killed except us poor Christians?

THE EDITOR. If the vestal virgins turn down their thumbs, thats another matter. Theyre ladies of rank.

LAVINIA. Docs the Emperor ever interfere?

THE EDITOR. Oh, yes: he turns his thumbs up fast enough if the vestal virgins want to have one of his pet fighting men killed.

ANDROCLES. But dont they ever just only pretend to kill one another? Why shouldnt you pretend to die, and get dragged out as if you were dead; and then get up and go home, likc an actor?

THE EDITOR. See here: you want to know too much. Therc will be no pretending about the new lion: let that be enough for you. He's hungry.

SPINTHO (*groaning with horror*) Oh, Lord! cant you stop talking about it? Isnt it bad enough for us without that?

ANDROCLES. I'm glad he's hungry. Not that I want him to suffer, poor chap! but then he ll enjoy eating me so much more. Theres a cheerful side to everything.

THE EDITOR (*rising and striding over to Androcles*)

Here: dont you be obstinate. Come with me and drop
the pinch of incense on the altar. Thats all you need
do to be let off.

ANDROCLES. No: thank you very much indeed; but I
really mustnt.

THE EDITOR. What! Not to save your life?

ANDROCLES. Id rather not. I couldnt sacrifice to
Diana: shes a huntress, you know, and kills things.

THE EDITOR. That dont matter. You can choose
your own altar. Sacrifice to Jupiter: he likes animals:
he turns himself into an animal when he goes off duty.

ANDROCLES. No: its very kind of you; but I feel I
cant save myself that way.

THE EDITOR. But I dont ask you to do it to save yourself: I ask you to do it to oblige me personally.

ANDROCLES (*scrambling up in the greatest agitation*)
Oh, please dont say that. That is dreadful. You mean
so kindly by me that it seems quite horrible to disoblige
you. If you could arrange for me to sacrifice when
theres nobody looking, I shouldnt mind. But I must go
into the arena with the rest. My honor, you know.

THE EDITOR. Honor! The honor of a tailor?

ANDROCLES (*apologetically*) Well, perhaps honor is
too strong an expression. Still, you know, I couldnt allow the tailors to get a bad name through me.

THE EDITOR. How much will you remember of all
that when you smell the beast's breath and see his jaws
opening to tear out your throat?

SPINTHO (*rising with a yell of terror*) I cant bear it.
Wheres the altar? I'll sacrifice.

FERROVIUS. Dog of an apostate. Iscariot!

SPINTHO. I'll repent afterwards. I fully mean to die
in the arena: I'll die a martyr and go to heaven; but not
this time, not now, not until my nerves are better. Besides, I'm too young: I want to have just one more good
time. (*The gladiators laugh at him*). Oh, will no one

tell me where the altar is? (*He dashes into the passage and vanishes*).

ANDROCLES (*to the Editor, pointing after Spintho*) Brother: I cant do that, not even to oblige you. Dont ask me.

THE EDITOR. Well, if youre determined to die, I cant help you. But I wouldnt be put off by a swine like that.

FERROVIUS. Peace, peace: tempt him not. Get thee behind him, Satan.

THE EDITOR (*flushing with rage*) For two pins Id take a turn in the arena myself to-day, and pay you out for daring to talk to me like that.

Ferrovius springs forward.

LAVINIA (*rising quickly and interposing*) Brother, brother: you forget.

FERROVIUS (*curbing himself by a mighty effort*) Oh, my temper, my wicked temper! (*To the Editor, as Lavinia sits down again, reassured*). Forgive me, brother. My heart was full of wrath: I should have been thinking of your dear precious soul.

THE EDITOR. Yah! (*He turns his back on Ferrovius contemptuously, and goes back to his seat*).

FERROVIUS (*continuing*) And I forgot it all: I thought of nothing but offering to fight you with one hand tied behind me.

THE EDITOR (*turning pugnaciously*) What!

FERROVIUS (*on the border line between zeal and ferocity*) Oh, dont give way to pride and wrath, brother. I could do it so easily. I could—

They are separated by the Menagerie Keeper, who rushes in from the passage, furious.

THE KEEPER. Heres a nice business! Who let that Christian out of here down to the dens when we were changing the lion into the cage next the arena?

THE EDITOR. Nobody let him. He let himself.

THE KEEPER. Well, the lion's ate him.

Consternation. The Christians rise, greatly agitated. The gladiators sit callously, but are highly amused. All speak or cry out or laugh at once. Tumult.

LAVINIA. Oh, poor wretch! FERROVIUS. The apostate has perished. Praise be to God's justice! ANDROCLES. The poor beast was straving. It couldnt help itself. THE CHRISTIANS. What! Ate him! How frightful! How terrible! Without a moment to repent! God be merciful to him, a sinner! Oh, I cant bear to think of it! In the midst of his sin! Horrible, horrible! THE EDITOR. Serve the rotter right! THE GLADIATORS. Just walked into it, he did. Hes martyred all right enough. Good old lion! Old Jock doesnt like that: look at his face. Devil a better! The Emperor will laugh when he hears of it. I cant help smiling. Ha ha ha ! ! ! ! !

THE KEEPER. Now his appetite's taken off, he wont as much as look at another Christian for a week.

ANDROCLES. Couldnt you have saved him brother?

THE KEEPER. Saved him! Saved him from a lion that Id just got mad with hunger! a wild one that came out of the forest not four weeks ago! He bolted him before you could say Balbus.

LAVINIA (*sitting down again*) Poor Spintho! And it wont even count as martyrdom!

THE KEEPER. Serve him right! What call had he to walk down the throat of one of my lions before he was asked?

ANDROCLES. Perhaps the lion wont eat me now.

THE KEEPER. Yes: thats just like a Christian: think only of yourself! What am *I* to do? What am I to say to the Emperor when he sees one of my lions coming into the arena half asleep?

THE EDITOR. Say nothing. Give your old lion some bitters and a morsel of fried fish to wake up his appetite. (*Laughter*).

THE KEEPER. Yes: it's easy for you to talk; but—

THE EDITOR (*scrambling to his feet*) Sh! Attention there! The Emperor. (*The Keeper bolts precipitately into the passage. The gladiators rise smartly and form into line*).

The Emperor enters on the Christians' side, conversing with Metellus, and followed by his suite.

THE GLADIATORS. Hail, Caesar! those about to die salute thee.

CAESAR. Good morrow, friends.

Metellus shakes hands with the Editor, who accepts his condescension with bluff respect.

LAVINIA. Blessing, Caesar, and forgiveness!

CAESAR (*turning in some surprise at the salutation*) There is no forgiveness for Christianity.

LAVINIA. I did not mean that, Caesar. I mean that w e forgive y o u.

METELLUS. An inconceivable liberty! Do you not know, woman, that the Emperor can do no wrong and therefore cannot be forgiven?

LAVINIA. I expect the Emperor knows better. Anyhow, we forgive him.

THE CHRISTIANS. Amen!

CAESAR. Metellus: you see now the disadvantage of too much severity. These people have no hope; therefore they have nothing to restrain them from saying what they like to me. They are almost as impertinent as the gladiators. Which is the Greek sorcerer?

ANDROCLES (*humbly touching his forelock*) Me, your Worship.

CAESAR. My Worship! Good! A new title. Well, what miracles can you perform?

ANDROCLES. I can cure warts by rubbing them with my tailor's chalk; and I can live with my wife without beating her.

CAESAR. Is that all?

11

ANDROCLES. You dont know her, Caesar, or you wouldnt say that.

CAESAR. Ah, well, my friend, we shall no doubt contrive a happy release for you. Which is Ferrovius?

FERROVIUS. I am he.

CAESAR. They tell me you can fight.

FERROVIUS. It is easy to fight. *I* can die, Caesar.

CAESAR. That is still easier, is it not?

FERROVIUS. Not to me, Caesar. Death comes hard to my flesh; and fighting comes very easily to my spirit (*beating his breast and lamenting*) O sinner that I am! (*He throws himself down on the steps, deeply discouraged*).

CAESAR. Metellus: I should like to have this man in the Pretorian Guard.

METELLUS. *I* should not, Caesar. He looks a spoilsport. There are men in whose presence it is impossible to have any fun: men who are a sort of walking conscience. He would make us all uncomfortable.

CAESAR. For that reason, perhaps, it might be well to have him. An Emperor can hardly have too many consciences. (*To Ferrovius*) Listen, Ferrovius. (*Ferrovius shakes his head and will not look up*). You and your friends shall not be outnumbered to-day in the arena. You shall have arms; and there will be no more than one gladiator to each Christian. If you come out of the arena alive, I will consider favorably any request of yours, and give you a place in the Pretorian Guard. Even if the request be that no questions be asked about your faith I shall perhaps not refuse it.

FERROVIUS. I will not fight. I will die. Better stand with the archangels than with the Pretorian Guard.

CAESAR. I cannot believe that the archangels—whoever they may be—would not prefer to be recruited from the Pretorian Guard. However, as you please. Come: let us see the show.

As the Court ascends the steps, Secutor and Retiarius return from the arena through the passage: Secutor covered with dust and very angry: Retiarius grinning.

SECUTOR.   Ha, the Emperor.   Now we shall see. Caesar: I ask you whether it is fair for the Retiarius, instead of making a fair throw of his net at me, to swish it along the ground and throw the dust in my eyes, and then catch me when I'm blinded.   If the vestals had not turned up their thumbs I should have been a dead man.

CAESAR (*halting on the stair*) There is nothing in the rules against it.

SECUTOR (*indignantly*) Caesar: is it a dirty trick or is it not?

CAESAR.   It is a dusty one, my friend.   (*Obsequious laughter*).   Be on your guard next time.

SECUTOR.   Let h i m be on his guard.   Next time I'll throw my sword at his heels and strangle him with his own net before he can hop off.   (*To the Retiarius*) You see if I dont.   (*He goes out past the gladiators, sulky and furious*).

CAESAR (*to the chuckling Retiarius*).   These tricks are not wise, my friend.   The audience likes to see a dead man in all his beauty and splendor.   If you smudge his face and spoil his armor they will shew their displeasure by not letting you kill him.   And when your turn comes, they will remember it against you and turn their thumbs down.

THE RETIARIUS.   Perhaps that is why I did it, Caesar. He bet me ten sesterces that he would vanquish me.   If I had had to kill him I should not have had the money.

CAESAR (*indulgent, laughing*) You rogues: there is no end to your tricks.   I'll dismiss you all and have elephants to fight.   T h e y fight fairly.   (*He goes up to his box, and knocks at it.   It is opened from within by the Captain, who stands as on parade to let him pass*).

The Call Boy comes from the passage, followed by

three attendants carrying respectively a bundle of swords, some helmets, and some breastplates and pieces of armor which they throw down in a heap.

THE CALL BOY. By your leave, Caesar. Number eleven! Gladiators and Christians!

Ferrovius springs up, ready for martyrdom. The other Christians take the summons as best they can, some joyful and brave, some patient and dignified, some tearful and helpless, some embracing one another with emotion. The Call Boy goes back into the passage.

CAESAR (*turning at the door of the box*) The hour has come, Ferrovius. I shall go into my box and see you killed, since you scorn the Pretorian Guard. (*He goes into the box. The Captain shuts the door, remaining inside with the Emperor. Metellus and the rest of the suite disperse to their seats. The Christians, led by Ferrovius, move towards the passage*).

LAVINIA (*to Ferrovius*) Farewell.

THE EDITOR. Steady there. You Christians have got to fight. Here! arm yourselves.

FERROVIUS (*picking up a sword*) I'll die sword in hand to shew people that I could fight if it were my Master's will, and that I could kill the man who kills me if I chose.

THE EDITOR. Put on that armor.

FERROVIUS. No armor.

THE EDITOR (*bullying him*) Do what youre told. Put on that armor.

FERROVIUS (*gripping the sword and looking dangerous*) I said, No armor.

THE EDITOR. And what am I to say when I am accused of sending a naked man in to fight my men in armor?

FERROVIUS. Say your prayers, brother; and have no fear of the princes of this world.

THE EDITOR. Tsha! You obstinate fool! (*He bites his lips irresolutely, not knowing exactly what to do*).

ANDROCLES (*to Ferrovius*) Farewell, brother, till we meet in the sweet by-and-by.

THE EDITOR (*to Androcles*) You are going too. Take a sword there; and put on any armor you can find to fit you.

ANDROCLES. No, really: I cant fight: I never could: I cant bring myself to dislike anyone enough. I'm to be thrown to the lions with the lady.

THE EDITOR. Then get out of the way and hold your noise. (*Androcles steps aside with cheerful docility*). Now then! Are you all ready there?

A trumpet is heard from the arena.

FERROVIUS (*starting convulsively*) Heaven give me strength!

THE EDITOR. Aha! That frightens you, does it?

FERROVIUS. Man: there is no terror like the terror of that sound to me. When I hear a trumpet or a drum or the clash of steel or the hum of the catapult as the great stone flies, fire runs through my veins: I feel my blood surge up hot behind my eyes: I must charge: I must strike: I must conquer: Caesar himself will not be safe in his imperial seat if once that spirit gets loose in me. Oh, brothers, pray! exhort me! remind me that if I raise my sword my honor falls and my Master is crucified afresh.

ANDROCLES. Just keep thinking how cruelly you might hurt the poor gladiators.

FERROVIUS. It does not hurt a man to kill him.

LAVINIA. Nothing but faith can save you.

FERROVIUS. Faith! Which faith? There are two faiths. There is our faith. And there is the warrior's faith, the faith in fighting, the faith that sees God in the sword. How if that faith should overwhelm me?

LAVINIA. You will find your real faith in the hour of trial.

FERROVIUS. That is what I fear. I know that I am a fighter. How can I feel sure that I am a Christian?

realizes his faults

ANDROCLES. Throw away the sword, brother.

FERROVIUS. I cannot. It cleaves to my hand. I could as easily throw a woman I loved from my arms. (*Starting*) Who spoke that blasphemy? Not I.

LAVINIA. I cant help you, friend. I cant tell you not to save your own life. Something wilful in me wants to see you fight your way into heaven.

FERROVIUS. Ha!

ANDROCLES. But if you are going to give up our faith, brother, why not do it without hurting anybody? Dont fight them. Burn the incense.

FERROVIUS. Burn the incense! Never.

LAVINIA. That is only pride, Ferrovius.

FERROVIUS. O n l y pride! What is nobler than pride? (*Conscience stricken*) Oh, I'm steeped in sin. I'm proud of my pride.

LAVINIA. They say we Christians are the proudest devils on earth—that only the weak are meek. Oh, I am worse than you. I ought to send you to death; and I am tempting you.

ANDROCLES. Brother, brother: let t h e m rage and kill: let u s be brave and suffer. You must go as a lamb to the slaughter.

FERROVIUS. Aye, aye: that is right. Not as a lamb is slain by the butcher; but as a butcher might let himself be slain by a (*looking at the Editor*) by a silly ram whose head he could fetch off in one twist.

Before the Editor can retort, the Call Boy rushes up through the passage; and the Captain comes from the Emperor's box and descends the steps.

THE CALL BOY. In with you: into the arena. The stage is waiting.

THE CAPTAIN. The Emperor is waiting. (*To the Editor*) What are you dreaming of, man? Send your men in at once.

THE EDITOR. Yes, sir: it's these Christians hanging back.

FERROVIUS (*in a voice of thunder*) Liar!

THE EDITOR (*not heeding him*) March. (*The gladiators told off to fight with the Christians march down the passage*) Follow up there, you.

THE CHRISTIAN MEN AND WOMEN (*as they part*) Be steadfast, brother. Farewell. Hold up the faith, brother. Farewell. Go to glory, dearest. Farewell. Remember: we are praying for you. Farewell. Be strong, brother. Farewell. Dont forget that the divine love and our love surround you. Farewell. Nothing can hurt you: remember that, brother. Farewell. Eternal glory, dearest. Farewell.

THE EDITOR (*out of patience*) Shove them in, there.

The remaining gladiators and the Call Boy make a movement towards them.

FERROVIUS (*interposing*) Touch them, dogs; and we die here, and cheat the heathen of their spectacle. (*To his fellow Christians*) Brothers: the great moment has come. That passage is your hill to Calvary. Mount it bravely, but meekly; and remember! not a word of reproach, not a blow nor a struggle. Go. (*They go out through the passage. He turns to Lavinia*) Farewell.

LAVINIA. You forget: I must follow before you are cold.

FERROVIUS. It is true. Do not envy me because I pass before you to glory. (*He goes through the passage*).

THE EDITOR (*to the Call Boy*) Sickening work, this. Why cant they all be thrown to the lions? It's not a man's job. (*He throws himself moodily into his chair*).

The remaining gladiators go back to their former places indifferently. The Call Boy shrugs his shoulders and squats down at the entrance to the passage, near the Editor.

Lavinia and the Christian women sit down again, wrung with grief, some weeping silently, some praying, some calm and steadfast. Androcles sits down at Lavinia's feet. The Captain stands on the stairs, watching her curiously.

ANDROCLES. I'm glad I havnt to fight. That would really be an awful martyrdom. I a m lucky.

LAVINIA (*looking at him with a pang of remorse*). Androcles: burn the incense: youll be forgiven. Let my death atone for both. I feel as if I were killing you.

ANDROCLES. Dont think of me, sister. Think of yourself. That will keep your heart up.

The Captain laughs sardonically.

LAVINIA (*startled: she had forgotten his presence*) Are you there, handsome Captain? Have you come to see me die?

THE CAPTAIN (*coming to her side*) I am on duty with the Emperor, Lavinia.

LAVINIA. Is it part of your duty to laugh at us?

THE CAPTAIN. No: that is part of my private pleasure. Your friend here is a humorist. I laughed at his telling you to think of yourself to keep up your heart. *I* say, think of yourself and burn the incense.

LAVINIA. He is not a humorist: he was right. You ought to know that, Captain: you have been face to face with death.

THE CAPTAIN. Not with certain death, Lavinia. Only death in battle, which spares more men than death in bed. What you are facing is certain death. You have nothing left now but your faith in this craze of yours: this Christianity. Are your Christian fairy stories any truer than our stories about Jupiter and Diana, in which, I may tell

you, I believe no more than the Emperor does, or any
educated man in Rome?

LAVINIA. Captain: all that seems nothing to me now.
I'll not say that death is a terrible thing; but I will say
that it is so real a thing that when it comes close, all the
imaginary things—all the stories, as you call them—fade
into mere dreams beside that inexorable reality. I know
now that I am not dying for stories or dreams. Did you
hear of the dreadful thing that happened here while we
were waiting?

THE CAPTAIN. I heard that one of your fellows bolted,
and ran right into the jaws of the lion. I laughed. I
still laugh.

LAVINIA. Then you dont understand what that meant?

THE CAPTAIN. It meant that the lion had a cur for his
breakfast.

LAVINIA. It meant more than that, Captain. It meant
that a man cannot die for a story and a dream. None of
us believed the stories and the dreams more devoutly
than poor Spintho; but he could not face the great reality.
What he would have called my faith has been oozing
away minute by minute whilst Ive been sitting here, with
death coming nearer and nearer, with reality becoming
realler and realler, with stories and dreams fading away
into nothing.

THE CAPTAIN. Are you then going to die for nothing?

LAVINIA. Yes: that is the wonderful thing. It is since
all the stories and dreams have gone that I have now no
doubt at all that I must die for something greater than
dreams or stories.

THE CAPTAIN. But for what?

LAVINIA. I dont know. If it were for anything small
enough to know, it would be too small to die for. I think
I'm going to die for God. Nothing else is real enough
to die for.

THE CAPTAIN. What is God?

LAVINIA. When we know that, Captain, we shall be gods ourselves.

THE CAPTAIN. Lavinia; come down to earth. Burn the incense and marry me.

LAVINIA. Handsome Captain: would you marry me if I hauled down the flag in the day of battle and burnt the incense? Sons take after their mothers, you know. Do you want your son to be a coward?

THE CAPTAIN (*strongly moved*). By great Diana, I think I would strangle you if you gave in now.

LAVINIA (*putting her hand on the head of Androcles*) The hand of God is on us three, Captain.

THE CAPTAIN. What nonsense it all is! And what a monstrous thing that you should die for such nonsense, and that I should look on helplessly when my whole soul cries out against it! Die then if you must; but at least I can cut the Emperor's throat and then my own when I see your blood.

The Emperor throws open the door of his box angrily, and appears in wrath on the threshold. The Editor, the Call Boy, and the gladiators spring to their feet.

THE EMPEROR. The Christians will not fight; and your curs cannot get their blood up to attack them. It's all that fellow with the blazing eyes. Send for the whip. (*The Call Boy rushes out on the east side for the whip*). If that will not move them, bring the hot irons. The man is like a mountain. (*He returns angrily into the box and slams the door*).

The Call Boy returns with a man in a hideous Etruscan mask, carrying a whip. They both rush down the passage into the arena.

LAVINIA (*rising*) Oh, that is unworthy. Can they not kill him without dishonoring him?

ANDROCLES (*scrambling to his feet and running into*

the middle of the space between the staircases) It's
dreadful. Now *I* want to fight. I cant bear the sight of
a whip. The only time I ever hit a man was when he
lashed an old horse with a whip. It was terrible: I
danced on his face when he was on the ground. He mustnt
strike Ferrovius: I'll go into the arena and kill him first.
(*He makes a wild dash into the passage. As he does so
a great clamor is heard from the arena, ending in wild
applause. The gladiators listen and look inquiringly at
one another*).

THE EDITOR. Whats up now?

LAVINIA (*to the Captain*) What has happened, do you
think?

THE CAPTAIN. What c a n happen? They are killing
them, I suppose.

ANDROCLES (*running in through the passage, screaming with horror and hiding his eyes*)!!!

LAVINIA. Androcles, Androcles: whats the matter?

ANDROCLES. Oh, dont ask me, dont ask me. Something too dreadful. Oh! (*He crouches by her and hides
his face in her robe, sobbing*).

THE CALL BOY (*rushing through from the passage as
before*) Ropes and hooks there! Ropes and hooks.

THE EDITOR. Well, need you excite yourself about
it? (*Another burst of applause*).

*Two slaves in Etruscan masks, with ropes and drag
hooks, hurry in.*

ONE OF THE SLAVES. How many dead?

THE CALL BOY. Six. (*The slave blows a whistle
twice; and four more masked slaves rush through into
the arena with the same apparatus*) And the basket.
Bring the baskets. (*The slave whistles three times, and
runs through the passage with his companion*).

THE CAPTAIN. Who are the baskets for?

THE CALL BOY. For the whip. He's in pieces.

Theyre all in pieces, more or less. (*Lavinia hides her face*).

Two more masked slaves come in with a basket and follow the others into the arena, as the Call Boy turns to the gladiators and exclaims, exhausted) Boys, he's killed the lot.

THE EMPEROR (*again bursting from his box, this time in an ecstasy of delight*) Where is he? Magnificent! He shall have a laurel crown.

Ferrovius, madly waving his bloodstained sword, rushes through the passage in despair, followed by his coreligionists, and by the menagerie keeper, who goes to the gladiators. The gladiators draw their swords nervously.

FERROVIUS. Lost! lost forever! I have betrayed my Master. Cut off this right hand: it has offended. Ye have swords, my brethren: strike.

LAVINIA. No, no. What have you done, Ferrovius?

FERROVIUS. I know not; but there was blood behind my eyes; and theres blood on my sword. What does that mean?

THE EMPEROR (*enthusiastically, on the landing outside his box*) What does it mean? It means that you are the greatest man in Rome. It means that you shall have a laurel crown of gold. Superb fighter, I could almost yield you my throne. It is a record for my reign: I shall live in history. Once, in Domitian's time, a Gaul slew three men in the arena and gained his freedom. But when before has one naked man slain six armed men of the bravest and best? The persecution shall cease: if Christians can fight like this, I shall have none but Christians to fight for me. (*To the Gladiators*) You are ordered to become Christians, you there: do you hear?

RETIARIUS. It is all one to us, Caesar. Had I been there with my net, the story would have been different.

THE CAPTAIN (*suddenly seizing Lavinia by the wrist and dragging her up the steps to the Emperor*) Caesar: this woman is the sister of Ferrovius. If she is thrown to the lions he will fret. He will lose weight; get out of condition—

THE EMPEROR. The lions? Nonsense! (*To Lavinia*) Madam: I am proud to have the honor of making your acquaintance. Your brother is the glory of Rome.

LAVINIA. But my friends here. Must they die?

THE EMPEROR. Die! Certainly not. There has never been the slightest idea of harming them. Ladies and gentlemen: you are all free. Pray go into the front of the house and enjoy the spectacle to which your brother has so splendidly contributed. Captain: oblige me by conducting them to the seats reserved for my personal friends.

THE MENAGERIE KEEPER. Caesar: I must have one Christian for the lion. The people have been promised it; and they will tear the decorations to bits if they are disappointed.

THE EMPEROR. True, true: we must have somebody for the new lion.

FERROVIUS. Throw me to him. Let the apostate perish.

THE EMPEROR. No, no: you would tear him in pieces, my friend; and we cannot afford to throw away lions as if they were mere slaves. But we must have somebody. This is really extremely awkward.

THE MENAGERIE KEEPER. Why not that little Greek chap? Hes not a Christian: hes a sorcerer.

THE EMPEROR. The very thing: he will do very well.

THE CALL BOY (*issuing from the passage*) Number twelve. The Christian for the new lion.

ANDROCLES (*rising, and pulling himself sadly together*) Well, it was to be, after all.

LAVINIA. I'll go in his place, Caesar. Ask the Cap-

tain whether they do not like best to see a woman torn to
pieces. He told me so yesterday.

THE EMPEROR. There is something in that: there is
certainly something in that—if only I could feel sure that
your brother would not fret.

ANDROCLES. No: I should never have another happy
hour. No: on the faith of a Christian and the honor of a
tailor, I accept the lot that has fallen on me. If my wife
turns up, give her my love and say that my wish was
that she should be happy with her next, poor fellow!
Caesar: go to your box and see how a tailor can die. Make
way for number twelve there. (*He marches out along
the passage*).

*The vast audience in the amphitheatre now sees the
Emperor re-enter his box and take his place as Androcles,
desperately frightened, but still marching with piteous
devotion, emerges from the other end of the passage, and
finds himself at the focus of thousands of eager eyes. The
lion's cage, with a heavy portcullis grating, is on his left.
The Emperor gives a signal. A gong sounds. Androcles
shivers at the sound; then falls on his knees and prays.
The grating rises with a clash. The lion bounds into the
arena. He rushes round frisking in his freedom. He
sees Androcles. He stops; rises stiffly by straightening
his legs; stretches out his nose forward and his tail in a
horizontal line behind, like a pointer, and utters an ap-
palling roar. Androcles crouches and hides his face in
his hands. The lion gathers himself for a spring, swish-
ing his tail to and fro through the dust in an ecstasy of
anticipation. Androcles throws up his hands in suppli-
cation to heaven. The lion checks at the sight of Androcles's face. He then steals towards him; smells him;
arches his back; purrs like a motor car; finally rubs
himself against Androcles, knocking him over. Androcles,
supporting himself on his wrist, looks affrightedly at the*

lion. The lion limps on three paws, holding up the other as if it was wounded. A flash of recognition lights up the face of Androcles. He flaps his hand as if it had a thorn in it, and pretends to pull the thorn out and to hurt himself. The lion nods repeatedly. Androcles holds out his hands to the lion, who gives him both paws, which he shakes with enthusiasm. They embrace rapturously, finally waltz round the arena amid a sudden burst of deafening applause, and out through the passage, the Emperor watching them in breathless astonishment until they disappear, when he rushes from his box and descends the steps in frantic excitement.

THE EMPEROR. My friends, an incredible! an amazing thing! has happened. I can no longer doubt the truth of Christianity. (*The Christians press to him joyfully*) This Christian sorcerer—(*with a yell, he breaks off as he sees Androcles and the lion emerge from the passage, waltzing. He bolts wildly up the steps into his box, and slams the door. All, Christians and gladiators alike, fly for their lives, the gladiators bolting into the arena, the others in all directions. The place is emptied with magical suddenness*).

ANDROCLES (*naïvely*) Now I wonder why they all run away from us like that. (*The lion combining a series of yawns, purrs, and roars, achieves something very like a laugh*).

THE EMPEROR (*standing on a chair inside his box and looking over the wall*) Sorcerer: I command you to put that lion to death instantly. It is guilty of high treason. Your conduct is most disgra— (*the lion charges at him up the stairs*) help! (*He disappears. The lion rears against the box; looks over the partition at him, and roars. The Emperor darts out through the door and down to Androcles, pursued by the lion.*)

ANDROCLES. Dont run away, sir: he cant help spring

ing if you run. (*He seizes the Emperor and gets between him and the lion, who stops at once*). Dont be afraid of him.

THE EMPEROR. I am n o t afraid of him. (*The lion crouches, growling. The Emperor clutches Androcles*) Keep between us.

ANDROCLES. Never be afraid of animals, your Worship: thats the great secret. He'll be as gentle as a lamb when he knows that you are his friend. Stand quite still; and smile; and let him smell you all over just to reassure him; for, you see, hes afraid of you; and he must examine you thoroughly before he gives you his confidence. (*To the lion*) Come now, Tommy; and speak nicely to the Emperor, the great, good Emperor who has power to have all our heads cut off if we dont behave very, v e r y respectfully to him.

The lion utters a fearful roar. The Emperor dashes madly up the steps, across the landing, and down again on the other side, with the lion in hot pursuit. Androcles rushes after the lion; overtakes him as he is descending; and throws himself on his back, trying to use his toes as a brake. Before he can stop him the lion gets hold of the trailing end of the Emperor's robe.

ANDROCLES. Oh bad wicked Tommy, to chase the Emperor like that! Let go the Emperor's robe at once, sir: wheres your manners? (*The lion growls and worries the robe*). Dont pull it away from him, your worship. Hes only playing. Now I shall be really angry with you, Tommy, if you dont let go. (*The lion growls again*) I'll tell you what it is, sir: he thinks you and I are not friends.

THE EMPEROR (*trying to undo the clasp of his brooch*) Friends! You infernal scoundrel (*the lion growls*)— dont let him go. Curse this brooch! I cant get it loose.

ANDROCLES. We mustnt let him lash himself into a rage. You must shew him that you are my particular friend—if you will have the condescension. (*He seizes the Emperor's hands and shakes them cordially*). Look, Tommy: the nice Emperor is the dearest friend Andy Wandy has in the whole world: he loves him like a brother.

THE EMPEROR. You little brute, you damned filthy little dog of a Greek tailor: I'll have you burnt alive for daring to touch the divine person of the Emperor. (*The lion growls*).

ANDROCLES. Oh dont talk like that, sir. He understands every word you say: all animals do: they take it from the tone of your voice. (*The lion growls and lashes his tail*). I think hes going to spring at your worship. If you wouldnt mind saying something affectionate. (*The lion roars*).

THE EMPEROR (*shaking Androcles' hands frantically*) My dearest Mr. Androcles, my sweetest friend, my long lost brother, come to my arms. (*He embraces Androcles*). Oh, what an abominable smell of garlic!

The lion lets go the robe and rolls over on his back, clasping his forepaws over one another coquettishly above his nose.

ANDROCLES. There! You see, your worship, a child might play with him now. See! (*He tickles the lion's belly. The lion wriggles ecstatically*). Come and pet him.

THE EMPEROR. I must conquer these unkingly terrors. Mind you dont go away from him, though. (*He pats the lion's chest*).

ANDROCLES. Oh, sir, how few men would have the courage to do that!

THE EMPEROR. Yes: it takes a bit of nerve. Let us have the Court in and frighten them. Is he safe, do you think?

ANDROCLES. Quite safe now, sir.

THE EMPEROR (*majestically*) What ho, there! All

12

who are within hearing, return without fear. Caesar has tamed the lion. (*All the fugitives steal cautiously in. The menagerie keeper comes from the passage with other keepers armed with iron bars and tridents*). Take those things away. I have subdued the beast. (*He places his foot on it*).

FERROVIUS (*timidly approaching the Emperor and looking down with awe on the lion*) It is strange that I, who fear no man, should fear a lion.

THE CAPTAIN. Every man fears something, Ferrovius.

THE EMPEROR. How about the Pretorian Guard now?

FERROVIUS. In my youth I worshipped Mars, the God of War. I turned from him to serve the Christian god; but today the Christian god forsook me; and Mars overcame me and took back his own. The Christian god is not yet. He will come when Mars and I are dust; but meanwhile I must serve the gods that are, not the God that will be. Until then I accept service in the Guard, Caesar.

THE EMPEROR. Very wisely said. All really sensible men agree that the prudent course is to be neither bigoted in our attachment to the old nor rash and unpractical in keeping an open mind for the new, but to make the best of both dispensations.

THE CAPTAIN. What do you say, Lavinia? Will you too be prudent?

LAVINIA (*on the stair*) No: I'll strive for the coming of the God who is not yet.

THE CAPTAIN. May I come and argue with you occasionally?

LAVINIA. Yes, handsome Captain: you may. (*He kisses her hands*).

THE EMPEROR. And now, my friends, though I do not, as you see, fear this lion, yet the strain of his presence is considerable; for none of us can feel quite sure what he will do next.

THE MENAGERIE KEEPER. Caesar: give us this Greek sorcerer to be a slave in the menagerie. He has a way with the beasts.

ANDROCLES (*distressed*). Not if they are in cages. They should not be kept in cages. They must all be let out.

THE EMPEROR. I give this sorcerer to be a slave to the first man who lays hands on him. (*The menagerie keepers and the gladiators rush for Androcles. The lion starts up and faces them. They surge back*). You see how magnanimous we Romans are, Androcles. We suffer you to go in peace.

ANDROCLES. I thank your worship. I thank you all, ladies and gentlemen. Come, Tommy. Whilst we stand together, no cage for you: no slavery for me. (*He goes out with the lion, everybody crowding away to give him as wide a berth as possible*).

*   *   *   *   *   *

In this play I have represented one of the Roman persecutions of the early Christians, not as the conflict of a false theology with a true, but as what all such persecutions essentially are: an attempt to suppress a propaganda that seemed to threaten the interests involved in the established law and order, organized and maintained in the name of religion and justice by politicians who are pure opportunist Have-and-Holders. People who are shewn by their inner light the possibility of a better world based on the demand of the spirit for a nobler and more abundant life, not for themselves at the expense of others, but for everybody, are naturally dreaded and therefore hated by the Have-and-Holders, who keep always in reserve two sure weapons against them. The first is a persecution effected by the provocation, organization, and arming of that herd instinct which makes men abhor all departures from custom, and, by the most cruel punishments and the wildest calumnies, force eccentric people to behave and profess exactly as other people do. The second is by leading the herd to war, which immediately and infallibly makes them forget everything, even their most cherished and hardwon public liberties and private interests, in the irresistible surge of their pugnacity and the tense pre-occupation of their terror.

There is no reason to believe that there was anything more in the Roman persecutions than this. The attitude of the Roman Emperor and the officers of his staff towards the opinions at issue were much the same as those of a modern British Home Secretary towards members of the lower middle classes when some pious policeman charges them with Bad Taste, technically called blasphemy: Bad Taste being a violation of Good Taste, which in such matters practically means Hypocrisy. The Home Secretary and the judges who try the case are usually far more sceptical and blasphemous than the poor men whom they persecute; and their professions of horror at the blunt utterance of their own opinions are revolting to those behind the scenes who have any genuine religious sensibility; but the thing is done because the governing classes, provided only the law against blasphemy is not applied to themselves, strongly approve of such persecution because it enables them to represent their own privileges as part of the religion of the country.

Therefore my martyrs are the martyrs of all time, and my persecutors the persecutors of all time. My Emperor, who has no sense of the value of common people's lives, and amuses himself with killing as carelessly as with sparing, is the sort of monster you can make of any silly-clever gentleman by idolizing him. We are still so easily imposed on by such idols that one of the leading pastors of the Free Churches in London denounced my play on the ground that my persecuting Emperor is a very fine fellow, and the persecuted Christians ridiculous. From which I conclude that a popular pulpit may be as perilous to a man's soul as an imperial throne.

All my articulate Christians, the reader will notice, have different enthusiasms, which they accept as the same religion only because it involves them in a common opposition to the official religion and consequently in a common doom. Androcles is a humanitarian naturalist, whose views surprise everybody. Lavinia, a clever and fearless freethinker, shocks the Pauline Ferrovius, who is comparatively stupid and conscience ridden. Spintho, the blackguardly debauchee, is presented as one of the typical Christians of that period on the authority of St. Augustine, who seems to have come to the conclusion at one period of his development that most Christians were what we call wrong uns. No doubt he was to some extent right: I have had occasion often to point out that revolutionary movements attract those who are not good enough for established institutions as well as those who are too good for them.

But the most striking aspect of the play at this moment is the terrible topicality given it by the war. We were at peace when I pointed out, by the mouth of Ferrovius, the path of an honest man who finds out, when the trumpet sounds, that he cannot follow Jesus. Many years earlier, in The Devil's Disciple, I touched the same theme even more definitely, and shewed the minister throwing off his black coat for ever when he discovered, amid the thunder of the captains and the shouting, that he was a born fighter. Great numbers of our clergy have found themselves of late in the position of Ferrovius and Anthony Anderson. They have discovered that they hate not only their enemies but everyone who does not share their hatred, and that they want to fight and to force other people to fight. They have turned their churches into recruiting stations and their vestries into munition work-

shops. But it has never occurred to them to take off their
black coats and say quite simply, "I find in the hour of
trial that the Sermon on the Mount is tosh, and that I am
not a Christian. I apologize for all the unpatriotic nonsense I have been preaching all these years. Have the
goodness to give me a revolver and a commission in a
regiment which has for its chaplain a priest of the god
Mars: *my* God." Not a bit of it. They have stuck to
their livings and served Mars in the name of Christ, to
the scandal of all religious mankind. When the Archbishop of York behaved like a gentleman and the Head
Master of Eton preached a Christian sermon, and were
reviled by the rabble, the Martian parsons encouraged
the rabble. For this they made no apologies or excuses,
good or bad. They simple indulged their passions, just
as they had always indulged their class prejudices and
commercial interests, without troubling themselves for a
moment as to whether they were Christians or not. They
did not protest even when a body calling itself the Anti-
German League (not having noticed, apparently, that it
had been anticipated by the British Empire, the French
Republic, and the Kingdoms of Italy, Japan, and Serbia)
actually succeeded in closing a church at Forest Hill in
which God was worshipped in the German language.
One would have supposed that this grotesque outrage on
the commonest decencies of religion would have provoked
a remonstrance from even the worldliest bench of bishops.
But no: apparently it seemed to the bishops as natural
that the House of God should be looted when He allowed
German to be spoken in it as that a baker's shop with a
German name over the door should be pillaged. Their
verdict was, in effect, "Serve God right, for creating the
Germans!" The incident would have been impossible in
a country where the Church was as powerful as the
Church of England, had it had at the same time a spark
of catholic as distinguished from tribal religion in it.

As it is, the thing occurred; and as far as I have observed, the only people who gasped were the Freethinkers.

Thus we see that even among men who make a profession of religion the great majority are as Martian as the majority of their congregations. The average clergyman is an official who makes his living by christening babies, marrying adults, conducting a ritual, and making the best he can (when he has any conscience about it) of a certain routine of school superintendence, district visiting, and organization of almsgiving, which does not necessarily touch Christianity at any point except the point of the tongue. The exceptional or religious clergyman may be an ardent Pauline salvationist, in which case his more cultivated parishioners dislike him, and say that he ought to have joined the Methodists. Or he may be an artist expressing religious emotion without intellectual definition by means of poetry, music, vestments and architecture, also producing religious ecstacy by physical expedients, such as fasts and vigils, in which case he is denounced as a Ritualist. Or he may be either a Unitarian Deist like Voltaire or Tom Paine, or the more modern sort of Anglican Theosophist to whom the Holy Ghost is the Élan Vital of Bergson, and the Father and Son are an expression of the fact that our functions and aspects are manifold, and that we are all sons and all either potential or actual parents, in which case he is strongly suspected by the straiter Salvationists of being little better than an Atheist. All these varieties, you see, excite remark. They may be very popular with their congregations; but they are regarded by the average man as the freaks of the Church. The Church, like the society of which it is an organ, is balanced and steadied by the great central Philistine mass above whom theology looms as a highly spoken of and doubtless most important thing, like Greek Tragedy, or classical music, or the higher mathematics, but who are very glad when church is over and they can go home to lunch or dinner, having in fact, for all practical purposes, no reasoned convictions at all, and being equally ready to persecute a poor Free-thinker for saying that St. James was not infallible, and to send one of the Peculiar People to prison for being so very peculiar as to take St. James seriously.

In short, a Christian martyr was thrown to the lions not because he was a Christian, but because he was a crank: that is, an unusual sort of person. And multitudes of people, quite as civilized and amiable as we, crowded to see the lions eat him just as they now crowd the lion-house in the Zoo at feeding-time, not because they really cared two-pence about Diana or Christ, or could have given you any intelligent or correct account of the things Diana and Christ stood against one another for, but simply because they wanted to see a curious and exciting spectacle. You, dear reader, have probably run to see a fire; and if somebody came in now and told you that a lion was chasing a man down the street you would rush to the window. And if anyone were to say that you were as cruel as the people who let the lion loose on the man, you would be justly indignant. Now that we may no longer see a man hanged, we assemble outside the jail to see the black flag run up. That is our duller method of enjoying ourselves in the old Roman spirit. And if the Government decided to throw persons of unpopular or eccentric views to the lions in the Albert Hall or the Earl's Court stadium tomorrow, can you doubt that all the seats would be crammed, mostly by people who could not give you the most superficial account of the views in question. Much less unlikely things have happened. It is true that if such a revival does take place soon, the martyrs will not be members of heretical religious sects: they will be Peculiars, Anti-Vivisectionists, Flat-Earth men, scoffers at the laboratories, or infidels who refuse to kneel down when a procession of doctors goes by. But the lions will hurt them just as much, and the spectators will enjoy themselves just as much, as the Roman lions and spectators used to do.

It was currently reported in the Berlin newspapers that when Androcles was first performed in Berlin, the Crown Prince rose and left the house, unable to endure the (I hope) very clear and fair exposition of autocratic Imperialism given by the Roman captain to his Christian prisoners. No English Imperialist was intelligent and earnest enough to do the same in London. If the report is correct, I confirm the logic of the Crown Prince, and am glad to find myself so well understood. But I can assure him that the Empire which served for my model when I wrote Androcles was, as he is now finding to his cost, much nearer my home than the German one.

OVERRULED
XXIV

1912

PREFACE TO OVERRULED.

The Alleviations of Monogamy.

This piece is not an argument for or against polygamy. It is a clinical study of how the thing actually occurs among quite ordinary people, innocent of all unconventional views concerning it. The enormous majority of cases in real life are those of people in that position. Those who deliberately and conscientiously profess what are oddly called advanced views by those others who believe them to be retrograde, are often, and indeed mostly, the last people in the world to engage in unconventional adventures of any kind, not only because they have neither time nor disposition for them, but because the friction set up between the individual and the community by the expression of unusual views of any sort is quite enough hindrance to the heretic without being complicated by personal scandals. Thus the theoretic libertine is usually a person of blameless family life, whilst the practical libertine is mercilessly severe on all other libertines, and excessively conventional in professions of social principle.

What is more, these professions are not hypocritical: they are for the most part quite sincere. The common libertine, like the drunkard, succumbs to a temptation which he does not defend, and against which he warns others with an earnestness proportionate to the intensity of his own remorse. He (or she) may be a liar and a humbug, pretending to be better than the detected libertines, and clamoring for their condign punishment;

61

but this is mere self-defence. No reasonable person expects the burglar to confess his pursuits, or to refrain from joining in the cry of Stop Thief when the police get on the track of another burglar. If society chooses to penalize candor, it has itself to thank if its attack is countered by falsehood. The clamorous virtue of the libertine is therefore no more hypocritical than the plea of Not Guilty which is allowed to every criminal. But one result is that the theorists who write most sincerely and favorably about polygamy know least about it; and the practitioners who know most about it keep their knowledge very jealously to themselves. Which is hardly fair to the practice.

Inaccessibility of the Facts.

Also it is impossible to estimate its prevalence. A practice to which nobody confesses may be both universal and unsuspected, just as a virtue which everybody is expected, under heavy penalties, to claim, may have no existence. It is often assumed—indeed it is the official assumption of the Churches and the divorce courts—that a gentleman and a lady cannot be alone together innocently. And that is manifest blazing nonsense, though many women have been stoned to death in the east, and divorced in the west, on the strength of it. On the other hand, the innocent and conventional people who regard the gallant adventures as crimes of so horrible a nature that only the most depraved and desperate characters engage in them or would listen to advances in that direction without raising an alarm with the noisiest indignation, are clearly examples of the fact that most sections of society do not know how the other sections live. Industry is the most effective check on gallantry. Women may, as Napoleon said, be the occupation of the idle man just as men are the preoccupation of the idle woman; but the mass of mankind is too busy and too poor for the long and expensive sieges which the professed libertine lays to virtue. Still, wherever there is idleness or even a reasonable supply of elegant leisure there is a good deal of coquetry and philandering. It is so much pleasanter to dance on the edge of a precipice than to go over it that leisured society is full of people who spend a great part of their lives in flirtation, and conceal nothing but the humiliating secret that they have never gone any further. For there is no pleasing people in the matter of reputation in this department: every insult is a flattery; every testimonial is a disparagement: Joseph is despised and promoted, Potiphar's wife admired and condemned: in short, you are never on solid ground until you get away from the subject altogether. There is a continual and irreconcilable conflict between the natural and conventional sides of the case, between spontaneous human relations between independent men and women on the one hand and the property relation between husband and wife on the other, not to mention the confusion under the common name of love of a generous natural attraction and interest with the murderous jealousy that fastens on and clings to its mate (especially a hated mate) as a tiger fastens on a carcase. And the confusion is natural; for these extremes are extremes of the same passion; and most cases lie somewhere on the scale between them, and are so complicated by ordinary likes and dislikes, by incidental wounds to vanity or gratifications of it, and by class feeling, that A will be jealous of B and not of C, and will tolerate infidelities on the part of D whilst being furiously angry when they are committed by E.

The Convention of Jealousy.

That jealousy is independent of sex is shewn by its intensity in children, and by the fact that very jealous people are jealous of everybody without regard to relationship or sex, and cannot bear to hear the person they "love" speak favorably of anyone under any circumstances (many women, for instance, are much more jealous of their husbands' mothers and sisters than of unrelated women whom they suspect him of fancying); but it is seldom possible to disentangle the two passions in practice. Besides, jealousy is an inculcated passion, forced by society on people in whom it would not occur spontaneously. In Brieux's Bourgeois aux Champs, the benevolent hero finds himself detested by the neighboring peasants and farmers, not because he preserves game, and sets mantraps for poachers, and defends his legal rights over his land to the extremest point of unsocial savagery, but because, being an amiable and public-spirited person, he refuses to do all this, and thereby offends and disparages the sense of property in his neighbors. The same thing is true of matrimonial jealousy; the man who does not at least pretend to feel it and behave as badly as if he really felt it is despised and insulted; and many a man has shot or stabbed a friend or been shot or stabbed by him in a duel, or disgraced himself and ruined his own wife in a divorce scandal, against his conscience, against his instinct, and to the destruction of his home, solely because Society conspired to drive him to keep its own lower morality in countenance in this miserable and undignified manner.

Morality is confused in such matters. In an elegant plutocracy, a jealous husband is regarded as a boor. Among the tradesmen who supply that plutocracy with its meals, a husband who is not jealous, and refrains from assailing his rival with his fists, is regarded as a ridiculous, contemptible and cowardly cuckold. And the laboring class is divided into the respectable section which takes the tradesman's view, and the disreputable section which enjoys the license of the plutocracy without its money: creeping below the law as its exemplars prance above it; cutting down all expenses of respectability and even decency; and frankly accepting squalor and disrepute as the price of anarchic self-indulgence. The conflict between Malvolio and Sir Toby, between the marquis and the bourgeois, the cavalier and the puritan, the ascetic and the voluptuary, goes on continually, and goes on not only between class and class and individual and individual, but in the selfsame breast in a series of reactions and revulsions in which the irresistible becomes the unbearable, and the unbearable the irresistible, until none of us can say what our characters really are in this respect.

The Missing Data of a Scientific Natural History of Marriage.

Of one thing I am persuaded: we shall never attain to a reasonable healthy public opinion on sex questions until we offer, as the data for that opinion, our actual conduct and our real thoughts instead of a moral fiction which we agree to call virtuous conduct, and which we then— and here comes in the mischief—pretend is our conduct and our thoughts. If the result were that we all believed one another to be better than we really are, there would be something to be said for it; but the actual result appears to be a monstrous exaggeration of the power and continuity of sexual passion. The whole world shares the fate of Lucrezia Borgia, who, though she seems on investigation to have been quite a suitable wife for a modern British Bishop, has been invested by the popular historical imagination with all the extravagances of a Messalina or a Cenci. Writers of belles lettres who are rash enough to admit that their whole life is not one constant preoccupation with adored members of the opposite sex, and who even countenance La Rochefoucauld's remark that very few people would ever imagine themselves in love if

13

they had never read anything about it, are gravely declared to be abnormal or physically defective by critics
of crushing unadventurousness and domestication. French
authors of saintly temperament are forced to include
in their retinue countesses of ardent complexion with
whom they are supposed to live in sin. Sentimental controversies on the subject are endless; but they are useless,
because nobody tells the truth. Rousseau did it by an
extraordinary effort, aided by a superhuman faculty for
human natural history, but the result was curiously discon-
certing because, though the facts were so conventionally
shocking that people felt that they ought to matter a great
deal, they actually mattered very little. And even at that
everybody pretends not to believe him.

Artificial Retribution.

The worst of that is that busybodies with perhaps
rather more than a normal taste for mischief are continually trying to make negligible things matter as much in
fact as they do in convention by deliberately inflicting
injuries—sometimes atrocious injuries—on the parties
concerned. Few people have any knowledge of the savage punishments that are legally inflicted for aberrations
and absurdities to which no sanely instructed community
would call any attention. We create an artificial morality, and consequently an artificial conscience, by manu-
facturing disastrous consequences for events which, left
to themselves, would do very little harm (sometimes not
any) and be forgotten in a few days.

But the artificial morality is not therefore to be condemned offhand. In many cases it may save mischief
instead of making it: for example, though the hanging of
a murderer is the duplication of a murder, yet it may be
less murderous than leaving the matter to be settled by
blood feud or vendetta. As long as human nature insists

on revenge, the official organization and satisfaction of
revenge by the State may be also its minimization. The
mischief begins when the official revenge persists after the
passion it satisfies has died out of the race. Stoning a
woman to death in the east because she has ventured to
marry again after being deserted by her husband may be
more merciful than allowing her to be mobbed to death;
but the official stoning or burning of an adulteress in the
west would be an atrocity because few of us hate an
adulteress to the extent of desiring such a penalty, or of
being prepared to take the law into our own hands if it
were withheld. Now what applies to this extreme case
applies also in due degree to the other cases. Offences in
which sex is concerned are often needlessly magnified by
penalties, ranging from various forms of social ostracism
to long sentences of penal servitude, which would be seen
to be monstrously disproportionate to the real feeling
against them if the removal of both the penalties and the
taboo on their discussion made it possible for us to ascer-
tain their real prevalence and estimation. Fortunately
there is one outlet for the truth. We are permitted to
discuss in jest what we may not discuss in earnest. A
serious comedy about sex is taboo: a farcical comedy is
privileged.

The Favorite Subject of Farcical Comedy.

The little piece which follows this preface accordingly
takes the form of a farcical comedy, because it is a con-
tribution to the very extensive dramatic literature which
takes as its special department the gallantries of married
people. The stage has been preoccupied by such affairs
for centuries, not only in the jesting vein of Restoration
Comedy and Palais Royal farce, but in the more tragically
turned adulteries of the Parisian school which dominated
the stage until Ibsen put them out of countenance and

relegated them to their proper place as articles of commerce. Their continued vogue in that department maintains the tradition that adultery is the dramatic subject *par excellence*, and indeed that a play that is not about adultery is not a play at all. I was considered a heresiarch of the most extravagant kind when I expressed my opinion at the outset of my career as a playwright, that adultery is the dullest of themes on the stage, and that from Francesca and Paolo down to the latest guilty couple of the school of Dumas *fils*, the romantic adulterers have all been intolerable bores.

The Pseudo Sex Play.

Later on, I had occasion to point out to the defenders of sex as the proper theme of drama, that though they were right in ranking sex as an intensely interesting subject, they were wrong in assuming that sex is an indispensable motive in popular plays. The plays of Molière are, like the novels of the Victorian epoch or Don Quixote, as nearly sexless as anything not absolutely inhuman can be; and some of Shakespear's plays are sexually on a par with the census: they contain women as well as men, and that is all. This had to be admitted; but it was still assumed that the plays of the XIX century Parisian school are, in contrast with the sexless masterpieces, saturated with sex; and this I strenuously denied. A play about the convention that a man should fight a duel or come to fisticuffs with his wife's lover if she has one, or the convention that he should strangle her like Othello, or turn her out of the house and never see her or allow her to see her children again, or the convention that she should never be spoken to again by any decent person and should finally drown herself, or the convention that persons involved in scenes of recrimination or confession by these conventions should call each other certain abusive names

and describe their conduct as guilty and frail and so on:
all these may provide material for very effective plays;
but such plays are not dramatic studies of sex: one might
as well say that Romeo and Juliet is a dramatic study of
pharmacy because the catastrophe is brought about
through an apothecary. Duels are not sex; divorce cases
are not sex; the Trade Unionism of married women is not
sex. Only the most insignificant fraction of the gallantries of married people produce any of the conventional
results; and plays occupied wholly with the conventional
results are therefore utterly unsatisfying as sex plays,
however interesting they may be as plays of intrigue and
plot puzzles.

The world is finding this out rapidly. The Sunday
papers, which in the days when they appealed almost
exclusively to the lower middle class were crammed with
police intelligence, and more especially with divorce and
murder cases, now lay no stress on them; and police
papers which confined themselves entirely to such matters,
and were once eagerly read, have perished through the
essential dulness of their topics. And yet the interest
in sex is stronger than ever: in fact, the literature
that has driven out the journalism of the divorce courts
is a literature occupied with sex to an extent and with
an intimacy and frankness that would have seemed utterly
impossible to Thackeray or Dickens if they had been told
that the change would complete itself within fifty years
of their own time.

Art and Morality.

It is ridiculous to say, as inconsiderate amateurs of the
arts do, that art has nothing to do with morality. What is
true is that the artist's business is not that of the policeman; and that such factitious consequences and put-up
jobs as divorces and executions and the detective opera-

tions that lead up to them are no essential part of life,
though, like poisons and buttered slides and red-hot
pokers, they provide material for plenty of thrilling or
amusing stories suited to people who are incapable of any
interest in psychology. But the fine artists must keep the
policeman out of his studies of sex and studies of crime.
It is by clinging nervously to the policeman that most of
the pseudo sex plays convince me that the writers have
either never had any serious personal experience of their
ostensible subject, or else have never conceived it possible that the stage door present the phenomena of sex as
they appear in nature.

The Limits of Stage Presentation.

But the stage presents much more shocking phenomena
than those of sex. There is, of course, a sense in which
you cannot present sex on the stage, just as you cannot
present murder. Macbeth must no more really kill Dun-
can than he must himself be really slain by Macduff. But
the feelings of a murderer can be expressed in a certain
artistic convention; and a carefully prearranged sword
exercise can be gone through with sufficient pretence of
earnestness to be accepted by the willing imaginations
of the younger spectators as a desperate combat.

The tragedy of love has been presented on the stage in
the same way. In Tristan and Isolde, the curtain does
not, as in Romeo and Juliet, rise with the lark: the whole
night of love is played before the spectators. The lovers
do not discuss marriage in an elegantly sentimental way:
they utter the visions and feelings that come to lovers at
the supreme moments of their love, totally forgetting that
there are such things in the world as husbands and lawyers and duelling codes and theories of sin and notions of
propriety and all the other irrelevancies which provide

hackneyed and bloodless material for our so-called plays
of passion.

Pruderies of the French Stage.

To all stage presentations there are limits.   If Macduff
were to stab Macbeth, the spectacle would be intolerable;
and even the pretence which we allow on our stage is
ridiculously destructive to the illusion of the scene.   Yet
pugilists and gladiators will actually fight and kill in public without sham, even as a spectacle for money.   But no
sober couple of lovers of any delicacy could endure to be
watched.   We in England, accustomed to consider the
French stage much more licentious than the British, are
always surprised and puzzled when we learn, as we may
do any day if we come within reach of such information,
that French actors are often scandalized by what they consider the indecency of the English stage, and that French
actresses who desire a greater license in appealing to the
sexual instincts than the French stage allows them, learn
and establish themselves on the English stage.   The German and Russian stages are in the same relation to the
French and perhaps more or less all the Latin stages.   The
reason is that, partly from a want of respect for the
theatre, partly from a sort of respect for art in general
which moves them to accord moral privileges to artists,
partly from the very objectionable tradition that the
realm of art is Alsatia and the contemplation of works
of art a holiday from the burden of virtue, partly because French prudery does not attach itself to the same
points of behavior as British prudery, and has a different code of the mentionable and the unmentionable,
and for many other reasons the French tolerate plays
which are never performed in England until they have
been spoiled by a process of bowdlerization; yet French
taste is more fastidious than ours as to the exhibition and

treatment on the stage of the physical incidents of sex.
On the French stage a kiss is as obvious a convention as
the thrust under the arm by which Macduff runs Macbeth
through. It is even a purposely unconvincing convention: the actors rather insisting that it shall be impossible
for any spectator to mistake a stage kiss for a real one.
In England, on the contrary, realism is carried to the
point at which nobody except the two performers can per-
ceive that the caress is not genuine. And here the English stage is certainly in the right; for whatever question
there arises as to what incidents are proper for represen-
tation on the stage or not, my experience as a playgoer
leaves me in no doubt that once it is decided to represent
an incident, it will be offensive, no matter whether it be a
prayer or a kiss, unless it is presented with a convincing
appearance of sincerity.

Our Disillusive Scenery.

For example, the main objection to the use of illusive
scenery (in most modern plays scenery is not illusive;
everything visible is as real as in your drawing room at
home) is that it is unconvincing; whilst the imaginary
scenery with which the audience provides a platform or
tribune like the Elizabethan stage or the Greek stage used
by Sophocles, is quite convincing. In fact, the more
scenery you have the less illusion you produce. The wise
playwright, when he cannot get absolute reality of pres-
entation, goes to the other extreme, and aims at atmosphere and suggestion of mood rather than at direct simu-
lative illusion. The theatre, as I first knew it, was a place
of wings and flats which destroyed both atmosphere and
illusion. This was tolerated, and even intensely enjoyed,
but not in the least because nothing better was possible;
for all the devices employed in the productions of Mr.
Granville Barker or Max Reinhardt or the Moscow Art

Theatre were equally available for Colley Cibber and
Garrick, except the intensity of our artificial light. When
Garrick played Richard II in slashed trunk hose and
plumes, it was not because he believed that the Plantag-
enets dressed like that, or because the costumers could
not have made him a XV century dress as easily as a
nondescript combination of the state robes of George III
with such scraps of older fashions as seemed to playgoers
for some reason to be romantic. The charm of the theatre in those days was its makebelieve. It has that charm
still, not only for the amateurs, who are happiest when
they are most unnatural and impossible and absurd, but
for audiences as well. I have seen performances of my
own plays which were to me far wilder burlesques than
Sheridan's Critic or Buckingham's Rehearsal; yet they
have produced sincere laughter and tears such as the most
finished metropolitan productions have failed to elicit.
Fielding was entirely right when he represented Partridge
as enjoying intensely the performance of the king in
Hamlet because anybody could see that the king was an
actor, and resenting Garrick's Hamlet because it might
have been a real man. Yet we have only to look at the
portraits of Garrick to see that his performances would
nowadays seem almost as extravagantly stagey as his
costumes. In our day Calvé's intensely real Carmen
never pleased the mob as much as the obvious fancy
ball masquerading of suburban young ladies in the same
character.

Holding the Mirror up to Nature.

Theatrical art begins as the holding up to Nature of a
distorting mirror. In this phase it pleases people who
are childish enough to believe that they can see what they
look like and what they are when they look at a true
mirror. Naturally they think that a true mirror can teach

them nothing. Only by giving them back some monstrous image can the mirror amuse them or terrify them. It is not until they grow up to the point at which they learn that they know very little about themselves, and that they do not see themselves in a true mirror as other people see them, that they become consumed with curiosity as to what they really are like, and begin to demand that the stage shall be a mirror of such accuracy and intensity of illumination that they shall be able to get glimpses of their real selves in it, and also learn a little how they appear to other people.

For audiences of this highly developed class, sex can no longer be ignored or conventionalized or distorted by the playwright who makes the mirror. The old sentimental extravagances and the old grossnesses are of no further use to him. Don Giovanni and Zerlina are not gross: Tristan and Isolde are not extravagant or sentimental. They say and do nothing that you cannot bear to hear and see; and yet they give you, the one pair briefly and slightly, and the other fully and deeply, what passes in the minds of lovers. The love depicted may be that of a philosophic adventurer tempting an ignorant country girl, or of a tragically serious poet entangled with a woman of noble capacity in a passion which has become for them the reality of the whole universe. No matter: the thing is dramatized and dramatized directly, not talked about as something that happened before the curtain rose, or that will happean after it falls.

Farcical Comedy Shirking its Subject.

Now if all this can be done in the key of tragedy and philosophic comedy, it can, I have always contended, be done in the key of farcical comedy; and Overruled is a trifling experiment in that manner. Conventional farcical comedies are always finally tedious because the heart of

them, the inevitable conjugal infidelity, is always evaded.
Even its consequences are evaded. | Mr. Granville Barker
has pointed out rightly that if the third acts of our
farcical comedies dared to describe the consequences that
would follow from the first and second in real life, they
would end as squalid tragedies; and in my opinion they
would be greatly improved thereby even as entertain-
ments; for I have never seen a three-act farcical comedy
without being bored and tired by the third act, and
observing that the rest of the audience were in the same
condition, though they were not vigilantly introspective
enough to find that out, and were apt to blame one
another, especially the husbands and wives, for their
crossness. | But it is happily by no means true that con-
jugal infidelities always produce tragic consequences, or
that they need produce even the unhappiness which they
often do produce. Besides, the more momentous the consequences, the more interesting become the impulses and
imaginations and reasonings, if any, of the people who
disregard them. If I had an opportunity of conversing
with the ghost of an executed murderer, I have no doubt
he would begin to tell me eagerly about his trial, with the
names of the distinguished ladies and gentlemen who
honored him with them presence on that occasion, and
then about his execution. All of which would bore me
exceedingly. I should say, "My dear sir: such manufactured ceremonies do not interest me in the least. I
know how a man is tried, and how he is hanged. I should
have had you killed in a much less disgusting, hypocritical, and unfriendly manner if the matter had been in my
hands. What I want to know about is the murder. How
did you feel when you committed it? Why did you do it?
What did you say to yourself about it? If, like most
murderers, you had not been hanged, would you have committed other murders? Did you really dislike the victim, or did you want his money, or did you murder a per-

son whom you did not dislike, and from whose death you had nothing to gain, merely for the sake of murdering? If so, can you describe the charm to me? Does it come upon you periodically; or is it chronic? Has curiosity anything to do with it?" I would ply him with all manner of questions to find out what murder is really like; and I should not be satisfied until I had realized that I, too, might commit a murder, or else that there is some specific quality present in a murderer and lacking in me. And, if so, what that quality is.

In just the same way, I want the unfaithful husband or the unfaithful wife in a farcical comedy not to bother me with their divorce cases or the stratagems they employ to avoid a divorce case, but to tell me how and why married couples are unfaithful. I don't want to hear the lies they tell one another to conceal what they have done, but the truths they tell one another when they have to face what they have done without concealment or excuse. No doubt prudent and considerate people conceal such adventures, when they can, from those who are most likely to be wounded by them; but it is not to be presumed that, when found out, they necessarily disgrace themselves by irritating lies and transparent subterfuges.

My playlet, which I offer as a model to all future writers of farcical comedy, may now, I hope, be read without shock. I may just add that Mr. Sibthorpe Juno's view that morality demands, not that we should behave morally (an impossibility to our sinful nature) but that we shall not attempt to defend our immoralities, is a standard view in England, and was advanced in all seriousness by an earnest and distinguished British moralist shortly after the first performance of Overruled. My objection to that aspect of the doctrine of original sin is that no necessary and inevitable operation of human nature can reasonably be regarded as sinful at all, and that a morality which assumes the contrary is an absurd morality, and can be kept in countenance only by hypocrisy. When people were ashamed of sanitary problems, and refused to face them, leaving them to solve themselves clandestinely in dirt and secrecy, the solution arrived at was the Black Death. A similar policy as to sex problems has solved itself by an even worse plague than the Black Death; and the remedy for that is not salvarsan, but sound moral hygiene, the first foundation of which is the discontinuance of our habit of telling not only the comparatively harmless lies that we know we ought not to tell, but the ruinous lies that we foolishly think we ought to tell.

OVERRULED.

*A lady and gentleman are sitting together on a ches-
terfield in a retired corner of the lounge of a seaside hotel.
It is a summer night: the French window behind them
stands open. The terrace without overlooks a moonlit
harbor. The lounge is dark. The chesterfield, uphol-
stered in silver grey, and the two figures on it in evening
dress, catch the light from an arc lamp somewhere; but
the walls, covered with a dark green paper, are in gloom.
There are two stray chairs, one on each side. On the
gentleman's right, behind him up near the window, is an
unused fireplace. Opposite it on the lady's left is a door.
The gentleman is on the lady's right.*

*The lady is very attractive, with a musical voice and
soft appealing manners. She is young: that is, one feels
sure that she is under thirty-five and over twenty-four.
The gentleman does not look much older. He is rather
handsome, and has ventured as far in the direction of
poetic dandyism in the arrangement of his hair as any
man who is not a professional artist can afford to in England. He is obviously very much in love with the lady,
and is, in fact, yielding to an irresistible impulse to throw
his arms around her.*

THE LADY. Dont—oh dont be horrid. Please, Mr.
Lunn [*she rises from the lounge and retreats behind it*]!
Promise me you won't be horrid.

GREGORY LUNN. I'm not being horrid, Mrs. Juno.
I'm not going to be horrid. I love you: thats all. I'm
extraordinarily happy.

78

MRS. JUNO. You will really be good?

GREGORY. I'll be whatever you wish me to be. I tell you I love you. I love loving you. I dont want to be tired and sorry, as I should be if I were to be horrid. I dont want you to be tired and sorry. Do come and sit down again.

MRS. JUNO [*coming back to her seat*]. Youre sure you dont want anything you oughtnt to?

GREGORY. Quite sure. I only want you [*she recoils*]. Dont be alarmed. I like wanting you. As long as I have a want, I have a reason for living. Satisfaction is death.

MRS. JUNO. Yes; but the impulse to commit suicide is sometimes irresistible.

GREGORY. Not with you.

MRS. JUNO. What!

GREGORY. Oh, it sounds uncomplimentary; but it isnt really. Do you know why half the couples who find themselves situated as we are now behave horridly?

MRS. JUNO. Because they cant help it if they let things go too far.

GREGORY. Not a bit of it. It's because they have nothing else to do, and no other way of entertaining each other. You dont know what it is to be alone with a woman who has little beauty and less conversation. What is a man to do? She cant talk interestingly; and if he talks that way himself she doesnt understand him. He cant look at her: if he does, he only finds out that she isnt beautiful. Before the end of five minutes they are both hideously bored. Theres only one thing that can save the situation; and thats what you call being horrid. With a beautiful, witty, kind woman, theres no time for such follies. It's so delightful to look at her, to listen to her voice, to hear all she has to say, that nothing else happens. That is why the woman who is supposed to have a thousand lovers seldom has one; whilst the stupid, graceless animals of women have dozens.

MRS. JUNO. I wonder! It's quite true that when one feels in danger one talks like mad to stave it off, even when one doesnt quite want to stave it off.

GREGORY. One never does quite want to stave it off. Danger is delicious. But death isnt. We court the danger; but the real delight is in escaping, after all.

MRS. JUNO. I dont think we'll talk about it any more. Danger is all very well when you do escape; but sometimes one doesnt. I tell you franky I dont feel as safe as you do—if, you really do.

GREGORY. But surely you can do as you please without injuring anyone, Mrs. Juno. That is the whole secret of your extraordinary charm for me.

MRS. JUNO. I dont understand.

GREGORY. Well, I hardly know how to begin to explain. But the root of the matter is that I am what people call a good man.

MRS. JUNO. I thought so until you began making love to me.

GREGORY. But you knew I loved you all along.

MRS. JUNO. Yes, of course; but I depended on you not to tell me so; because I thought you were good. Your blurting it out spoilt it. And it was wicked besides.

GREGORY. Not at all. You see, it's a great many years since Ive been able to allow myself to fall in love. I know lots of charming women; but the worst of it is, theyre all married. Women dont become charming, to my taste, until theyre fully developed; and by that time, if theyre really nice, theyre snapped up and married. And then, because I am a good man, I have to place a limit to my regard for them. I may be fortunate enough to gain friendship and even very warm affection from them; but my loyalty to their husbands and their hearths and their happiness obliges me to draw a line and not overstep it. Of course I value such affectionate regard very highly indeed. I am surrounded with women who are most dear to me. But every one of them has a post sticking up, if I may put it that way, with the inscription: Trespassers Will Be Prosecuted. How we all loathe that notice! In every lovely garden, in every dell full of primroses, on every fair hillside, we meet that confounded board; and there is always a gamekeeper round the corner. But what is that to the horror of meeting it on every beautiful woman, and knowing that there is a husband round the corner? I have had this accursed board standing between me and every dear and desirable woman until I thought I had lost the power of letting myself fall really and wholeheartedly in love.

MRS. JUNO. Wasnt there a widow?

GREGORY. No. Widows are extraordinarily scarce in modern society. Husbands live longer than they used to; and even when they do die, their widows have a string of names down for their next.

MRS. JUNO. Well, what about the young girls?

GREGORY. Oh, who cares for young girls? Theyre sympathetic. Theyre beginners. They dont attract me. I'm afraid of them.

MRS. JUNO. Thats the correct thing to say to a woman of my age. But it doesnt explain why you seem to have put your scruples in your pocket when you met me.

GREGORY. Surely thats quite clear. I—

MRS. JUNO. No: please dont explain. I dont want to know. I take your word for it. Besides, it doesnt matter now. Our voyage is over; and to-morrow I start for the north to my poor father's place.

GREGORY [*surprised*]. Your poor father! I thought he was alive.

MRS. JUNO. So he is. What made you think he wasnt?

GREGORY. You said your p o o r father.

14

MRS. JUNO. Oh, thats a trick of mine. Rather a silly trick, I suppose; but theres something pathetic to me about men: I find myself calling them poor So-and-So when theres nothing whatever the matter with them.

GREGORY [*who has listened in growing alarm*]. But— I—is?—wa—? Oh, Lord!

MRS. JUNO. Whats the matter?

GREGORY. Nothing.

MRS. JUNO. Nothing! [*Rising anxiously*]. Nonsense: youre ill.

GREGORY. No. It was something about your late husband—

MRS. JUNO. My l a t e husband! What do you mean? [*clutching him, horror-stricken*]. Dont tell me he's dead.

GREGORY [*rising, equally appalled*]. Dont tell me he's alive.

MRS. JUNO. Oh, dont frighten me like this. Of course he's alive—unless youve heard anything.

GREGORY. The first day we met—on the boat—you spoke to me of your poor dear husband.

MRS. JUNO [*releasing him, quite reassured*]. Is that all?

GREGORY. Well, afterwards you called him poor Tops. Always poor Tops, or poor dear Tops. What could I think?

MRS. JUNO [*sitting down again*]. I wish you hadnt given me such a shock about him; for I havent been treating him at all well. Neither have you.

GREGORY [*relapsing into his seat, overwhelmed*]. And you mean to tell me youre not a widow!

MRS. JUNO. Gracious, no! I'm not in black.

GREGORY. Then I have been behaving like a blackguard. I have broken my promise to my mother. I shall never have an easy conscience again.

MRS. JUNO. I'm sorry. I thought you knew.

GREGORY. You thought I was a libertine?

MRS. JUNO. No: of course I shouldnt have spoken to you if I had thought that. I thought you liked me, but that you knew, and would be good.

GREGORY [*stretching his hands towards her breast*]. I thought the burden of being good had fallen from my soul at last. I saw nothing there but a bosom to rest on: the bosom of a lovely woman of whom I could dream without guilt. What do I see now?

MRS. JUNO. Just what you saw before.

GREGORY [*despairingly*]. No, no.

MRS. JUNO. What else?

GREGORY. Trespassers Will Be Prosecuted: Trespassers Will Be Prosecuted.

MRS. JUNO. They wont if they hold their tongues. Dont be such a coward. My husband wont eat you.

GREGORY. I'm not afraid of your husband. I'm afraid of my conscience.

MRS. JUNO [*losing patience*]. Well! I don't consider myself at all a badly behaved woman; for nothing has passed between us that was not perfectly nice and friendly; but really! to hear a grown-up man talking about promises to his mother!—

GREGORY [*interrupting her*]. Yes, yes: I know all about that. It's not romantic: it's not Don Juan: it's not advanced; but we feel it all the same. It's far deeper in our blood and bones than all the romantic stuff. My father got into a scandal once: that was why my mother made me promise never to make love to a married woman. And now Ive done it I cant feel honest. Dont pretend to despise me or laugh at me. You feel it too. You said just now that your own conscience was uneasy when you thought of your husband. What must it be when you think of my wife?

MRS. JUNO [*rising aghast*]. Your wife ! ! ! You

dont dare sit there and tell me coolly that youre a married man!

GREGORY. I never led you to believe I was unmarried.

MRS. JUNO. Oh! You never gave me the faintest hint that you had a wife.

GREGORY. I did indeed. I discussed things with you that only married people really understand.

MRS. JUNO. Oh!!

GREGORY. I thought it the most delicate way of letting you know.

MRS. JUNO. Well, you a r e a daisy, I must say. I suppose thats vulgar; but really! really!! You and your goodness! However, now weve found one another out theres only one thing to be done. Will you please go?

GREGORY [rising slowly]. I o u g h t to go.

MRS. JUNO. Well, go.

GREGORY. Yes. Er—[he tries to go]. I—I somehow cant. [He sits down again helplessly]. My conscience is active: my will is paralyzed. This is really dreadful. Would you mind ringing the bell and asking them to throw me out? You ought to, you know.

MRS. JUNO. What! make a scandal in the face of the whole hotel! Certainly not. Dont be a fool.

GREGORY. Yes; but I cant go.

MRS. JUNO. Then I can. Goodbye.

GREGORY [clinging to her hand]. Can you really?

MRS. JUNO. Of course I—[she wavers]. Oh, dear! [They contemplate one another helplessly]. I cant. [She sinks on the lounge, hand in hand with him].

GREGORY. For heaven's sake pull yourself together. It's a question of self-control.

MRS. JUNO [dragging her hand away and retreating to the end of the chesterfield]. No: it's a question of distance. Self-control is all very well two or three yards off, or on a ship, with everybody looking on. Dont come any nearer.

GREGORY. This is a ghastly business. I want to go away; and I cant.

MRS. JUNO. I think you ought to go [*he makes an effort; and she adds quickly*] but if you try I shall grab you round the neck and disgrace myself. I implore you to sit still and be nice.

GREGORY. I implore you to run away. I believe I can trust myself to let you go for your own sake. But it will break my heart.

MRS. JUNO. I dont want to break your heart. I can't bear to think of your sitting here alone. I cant bear to think of sitting alone myself somewhere else. It's so senseless—so ridiculous—when we might be so happy. I dont want to be wicked, or coarse. But I like you very much; and I do want to be affectionate and human.

GREGORY. I ought to draw a line.

MRS. JUNO. So you shall, dear. Tell me: do you really like me? I dont mean l o v e me: you might love the housemaid—

GREGORY [*vehemently*]. No!

MRS. JUNO. Oh, yes you might; and what does that matter, anyhow? Are you really fond of me? Are we friends—comrades? Would you be sorry if I died?

GREGORY [*shrinking*]. Oh, dont.

MRS. JUNO. Or was it the usual aimless man's lark, a mere shipboard flirtation?

GREGORY. .Oh, no, no: nothing half so bad, so vulgar, so wrong. I assure you I only meant to be agreeable. It grew on me before I noticed it.

MRS. JUNO. And you were glad to let it grow?

GREGORY. I let it grow because the board was not up.

MRS. JUNO. Bother the board! I am just as fond of Sibthorpe as—

GREGORY. Sibthorpe!

MRS. JUNO.   Sibthorpe is my husband's Christian name. I oughtnt to call him Tops to you now.

GREGORY [*chuckling*].   It sounded like something to drink. But I have no right to laugh at him. My Christian name is Gregory, which sounds like a powder.

MRS. JUNO [*chilled*].   That is so like a man! I offer you my heart's warmest friendliest feeling; and you think of nothing but a silly joke. A quip like that makes you forget me.

GREGORY.   Forget you! Oh, if I only could!

MRS. JUNO.   If you could, would you?

GREGORY [*burying his shamed face in his hands*].   No: I'd die first. Oh, I hate myself.

MRS. JUNO.   I glory in myself. It's so jolly to be reckless. C a n a man be reckless, I wonder.

GREGORY [*straightening himself desperately*].   No. I'm not reckless. I know what I'm doing: my conscience is awake. Oh, where is the intoxication of love? the delirium? the madness that makes a man think the world well lost for the woman he adores? I dont think anything of the sort: I see that it's not worth it: I know that it's wrong: I have never in my life been cooler, more businesslike.

MRS. JUNO [*opening her arms to him*] But you cant resist me.

GREGORY.   I must. I ought [*throwing himself into her arms*].   Oh, my darling, my treasure, we shall be sorry for this.

MRS. JUNO.   We can forgive ourselves. Could we forgive ourselves if we let this moment slip?

GREGORY.   I protest to the last. I'm against this. I have been pushed over a precipice. I'm innocent. This wild joy, this exquisite tenderness, this ascent into heaven can thrill me to the uttermost fibre of my heart [*with a gesture of ecstasy she hides her face on his shoulder*]; but it cant subdue my mind or corrupt my conscience,

which still shouts to the skies that I'm not a willing party
to this outrageous conduct. I repudiate the bliss with
which you are filling me.

MRS. JUNO. Never mind your conscience. Tell me
how happy you are.

GREGORY. No: I recall you to your duty. But oh, I
will give you my life with both hands if you can tell me
that you feel for me one millionth part of what I feel for
you now.

MRS. JUNO. Oh, yes, yes. Be satisfied with that.
Ask for no more. Let me go.

GREGORY. I cant. I have no will. Something stronger
than either of us is in command here. Nothing on earth
or in heaven can part us now. You know that, dont you?

MRS. JUNO. Oh, dont make me say it. Of course I
know. Nothing—not life nor death nor shame nor
a n y t h i n g can part us.

A MATTER-OF-FACT MALE VOICE IN THE CORRIDOR.
All right. This must be it.

*The two recover with a violent start; release one
another; and spring back to opposite sides of the lounge.*

GREGORY. That did it.

MRS. JUNO [*in a thrilling whisper*] Sh-sh-sh! That
was my husband's voice.

GREGORY. Impossible: it's only our guilty fancy.

A WOMAN'S VOICE. This is the way to the lounge. I
know it.

GREGORY. Great Heaven! were both mad. Thats my
wife's voice.

MRS. JUNO. Ridiculous! Oh! were dreaming it all.
We—[*the door opens; and Sibthorpe Juno appears in the
roseate glow of the corridor (which happens to be papered
in pink) with Mrs. Lunn, like Tannhäuser in the hill
of Venus. He is a fussily energetic little man, who gives
himself an air of gallantry by greasing the points of his
moustaches and dressing very carefully. She is a tall,*

*imposing, handsome, languid woman, with flashing dark
eyes and long lashes. They make for the chesterfield,
not noticing the two palpitating figures blotted against
the walls in the gloom on either side. The figures flit
away noiselessly through the window and disappear*].

JUNO [*officiously*] Ah: here we are. [*He leads the
way to the sofa*]. Sit down: I'm sure youre tired. [*She
sits*]. Thats right. [*He sits beside her on her left*].
Hullo! [*he rises*] this sofa's quite warm.

MRS. LUNN [*bored*] Is it? I dont notice it. I expect
the sun's been on it.

JUNO. I felt it quite distinctly: I'm more thinly clad
than you. [*He sits down again, and proceeds, with a sigh
of satisfaction*]. What a relief to get off the ship and
have a private room! Thats the worst of a ship. Youre
under observation all the time.

MRS. LUNN. But why not?

JUNO. Well, of course theres no reason: at least I suppose not. But, you know, part of the romance of a journey is that a man keeps imagining that something might
happen; and he cant do that if there are a lot of people
about and it simply cant happen.

MRS. LUNN. Mr. Juno: romance is all very well on
board ship; but when your foot touches the soil of England theres an end of it.

JUNO. No: believe me, thats a foreigner's mistake:
we are the most romantic people in the world, we English. Why, my very presence here is a romance.

MRS. LUNN [*faintly ironical*] Indeed?

JUNO. Yes. Youve guessed, of course, that I'm a
married man.

MRS. LUNN. Oh, thats all right. I'm a married woman.

JUNO. Thank Heaven for that! To my English
mind, passion is not real passion without guilt. I am a
red-blooded man, Mrs. Lunn: I cant help it. The tragedy
of my life is that I married, when quite young, a woman

whom I couldnt help being very fond of. I longed for a
guilty passion—for the real thing—the wicked thing; and
yet I couldnt care twopence for any other woman when
my wife was about. Year after year went by: I felt
my youth slipping away without ever having had a romance in my life; for marriage is all very well; but it isnt
romance. Theres nothing wrong in it, you see.

MRS. LUNN. Poor man! How you must have suffered!

JUNO. No: that was what was so tame about it. I
wanted to suffer. You get so sick of being happily married. It's always the happy marriages that break up.
At last my wife and I agreed that we ought to take a
holiday.

MRS. LUNN. Hadnt you holidays every year?

JUNO. Oh, the seaside and so on! Thats not what we
meant. We meant a holiday from one another.

MRS. LUNN. How very odd!

JUNO. She said it was an excellent idea; that domestic
felicity was making us perfectly idiotic; that she wanted
a holiday, too. So we agreed to go round the world in
opposite directions. I started for Suez on the day she
sailed for New York.

MRS. LUNN [*suddenly becoming attentive*] Thats precisely what Gregory and I did. Now I wonder did he
want a holiday from me! What he said was that he wanted the delight of meeting me after a long absence.

JUNO. Could anything be more romantic than that?
Would anyone else than an Englishman have thought of
it? I daresay my temperament seems tame to your boil-
ing southern blood—

MRS. LUNN. My what!

JUNO. Your southern blood. Dont you remember how
you told me, that night in the saloon when I sang "Farewell and adieu to you dear Spanish ladies," that you were
by birth a lady of Spain? Your splendid Andalusian
beauty speaks for itself.

MRS. LUNN. Stuff! I was born in Gibraltar. My father was Captain Jenkins. In the artillery.

JUNO [*ardently*] It is climate and not race that determines the temperament. The fiery sun of Spain blazed on your cradle; and it rocked to the roar of British cannon.

MRS. LUNN. What eloquence! It reminds me of my husband when he was in love—before we were married. Are you in love?

JUNO. Yes; and with the same woman.

MRS. LUNN. Well, of course, I didnt suppose you were in love with two women.

JUNO. I dont think you quite understand. I meant that I am in love with you.

MRS. LUNN [*relapsing into deepest boredom*] Oh, that! Men do fall in love with me. They all seem to think me a creature with volcanic passions: I'm sure I dont know why; for all the volcanic women I know are plain little creatures with sandy hair. I dont consider human volcanoes respectable. And I'm so tired of the subject! Our house is always full of women who are in love with my husband and men who are in love with me. We encourage it because it's pleasant to have company.

JUNO. And is your husband as insensible as yourself?

MRS. LUNN. Oh, Gregory's not insensible: very far from it; but I am the only woman in the world for him.

JUNO. But you? Are you really as insensible as you say you are?

MRS. LUNN. I never said anything of the kind. I'm not at all insensible by nature; but (I dont know whether youve noticed it) I am what people call rather a fine figure of a woman.

JUNO [*passionately*] Noticed it! Oh, Mrs. Lunn! Have I been able to notice anything else since we met?

MRS. LUNN. There you go, like all the rest of them!

I ask you, how do you expect a woman to keep up what you call her sensibility when this sort of thing has happened to her about three times a week ever since she was seventeen? It used to upset me and terrify me at first. Then I got rather a taste for it. It came to a climax with Gregory: that was why I married him. Then it became a mild lark, hardly worth the trouble. After that I found it valuable once or twice as a spinal tonic when I was run down; but now it's an unmitigated bore. I dont mind your declaration: I daresay it gives you a certain pleasure to make it. I quite understand that you adore me; but (if you dont mind) I'd rather you didnt keep on saying so.

JUNO. Is there then no hope for me?

MRS. LUNN. Oh, yes. Gregory has an idea that married women keep lists of the men theyll marry if they become widows. I'll put your name down, if that will satisfy you.

JUNO. Is the list a long one?

MRS. LUNN. Do you mean the real list? Not the one I shew to Gregory: there are hundreds of names on that; but the little private list that he'd better not see?

JUNO. Oh, will you really put me on that? Say you will.

MRS. LUNN. Well, perhaps I will. [*He kisses her hand*]. Now dont begin abusing the privilege.

JUNO. May I call you by your Christian name?

MRS. LUNN. No: it's too long. You cant go about calling a woman Seraphita.

JUNO [*ecstatically*] Seraphita!

MRS. LUNN. I used to be called Sally at home; but when I married a man named Lunn, of course that became ridiculous. Thats my one little pet joke. Call me Mrs. Lunn for short. And change the subject, or I shall go to sleep.

JUNO. I cant change the subject. For me there is no

other subject. Why else have you put me on your list?

MRS. LUNN. Because youre a solicitor. Gregory's a solicitor. I'm accustomed to my husband being a solicitor and telling me things he oughtnt to tell anybody.

JUNO [*ruefully*] Is that all? Oh, I cant believe that the voice of love has ever thoroughly awakened you.

MRS. LUNN. No: it sends me to sleep. [*Juno appeals against this by an amorous demonstration*]. It's no use, Mr. Juno: I'm hopelessly respectable: the Jenkinses always were. Dont you realize that unless most women were like that, the world couldnt go on as it does?

JUNO [*darkly*] You think it goes on respectably; but I can tell you as a solicitor——

MRS. LUNN. Stuff! of course all the disreputable people who get into trouble go to you, just as all the sick people go to the doctors; but most people never go to a solicitor.

JUNO [*rising, with a growing sense of injury*] Look here, Mrs. Lunn: do you think a man's heart is a potato? or a turnip? or a ball of knitting wool? that you can throw it away like this?

MRS. LUNN. I dont throw away balls of knitting wool. A man's heart seems to me much like a sponge: it sops up dirty water as well as clean.

JUNO. I have never been treated like this in my life. Here am I, a married man, with a most attractive wife: a wife I adore, and who adores me, and has never as much as looked at any other man since we were married. I come and throw all this at your feet. I! I, a solicitor! braving the risk of your husband putting me into the divorce court and making me a beggar and an outcast! I do this for your sake. And you go on as if I were making no sacrifice: as if I had told you it's a fine evening, or asked you to have a cup of tea. It's not human.

It's not right. Love has its rights as well as respectability [*he sits down again, aloof and sulky*].

MRS. LUNN. Nonsense! Here, heres a flower [*she gives him one*]. Go and dream over it until you feel hungry. Nothing brings people to their senses like hunger.

JUNO [*contemplating the flower without rapture*] What good's this?

MRS. LUNN [*snatching it from him*] Oh! you dont love me a bit.

JUNO. Yes I do. Or at least I did. But I'm an Englishman; and I think you ought to respect the conventions of English life.

MRS. JUNO. But I am respecting them; and youre not.

JUNO. Pardon me. I may be doing wrong; but I'm doing it in a proper and customary manner. You may be doing right; but youre doing it in an unusual and questionable manner. I am not prepared to put up with that. I can stand being badly treated: I'm no baby, and can take care of myself with anybody. And of course I can stand being well treated. But the thing I cant stand is being unexpectedly treated. It's outside my scheme of life. So come now! youve got to behave naturally and straightforwardly with me. You can leave husband and child, home, friends, and country, for my sake, and come with me to some southern isle—or say South America—where we can be all in all to one another. Or you can tell your husband and let him jolly well punch my head if he can. But I'm damned if I'm going to stand any eccentricity. It's not respectable.

GREGORY [*coming in from the terrace and advancing with dignity to his wife's end of the chesterfield*]. Will you have the goodness, sir, in addressing this lady, to keep your temper and refrain from using profane language?

MRS. LUNN [*rising, delighted*] Gregory! Darling [*she enfolds him in a copious embrace*]!

JUNO [*rising*] You make love to another man to my face!

MRS. LUNN. Why, he's my husband.

JUNO. That takes away the last rag of excuse for such conduct. A nice world it would be if married people were to carry on their endearments before everybody!

GREGORY. This is ridiculous. What the devil business is it of yours what passes between my wife and myself? Youre not her husband, are you?

JUNO. Not at present; but I'm on the list. I'm her prospective husband: youre only her actual one. I'm the anticipation: youre the disappointment.

MRS. LUNN. Oh, my Gregory is not a disappointment. [*Fondly*] Are you, dear?

GREGORY. You just wait, my pet. I'll settle this chap for you. [*He disengages himself from her embrace, and faces Juno. She sits down placidly*]. You call me a disappointment, do you? Well, I suppose every husband's a disappointment. What about yourself? Dont try to look like an unmarried man. I happen to know the lady you disappointed. I travelled in the same ship with her; and—

JUNO. And you fell in love with her.

GREGORY [*taken aback*] Who told you that?

JUNO. Aha! you confess it. Well, if you want to know, nobody told me. Everybody falls in love with my wife.

GREGORY. And do you fall in love with everybody's wife?

JUNO. Certainly not. Only with yours.

MRS. LUNN. But whats the good of saying that, Mr. Juno? I'm married to him; and theres an end of it.

JUNO. Not at all. You can get a divorce.

MRS. LUNN. What for?

Juno. For his misconduct with my wife.

Gregory [*deeply indignant*] How dare you, sir, asperse the character of that sweet lady? a lady whom I have taken under my protection.

Juno. Protection!

Mrs. Juno [*returning hastily*] Really you must be more careful what you say about me, Mr. Lunn.

Juno. My precious! [*He embraces her*]. Pardon this betrayal of my feeling; but Ive not seen my wife for several weeks; and she is very dear to me.

Gregory. I call this cheek. Who is making love to his own wife before people now, pray?

Mrs. Lunn. Wont you introduce me to your wife, Mr. Juno?

Mrs. Juno. How do you do? [*They shake hands; and Mrs. Juno sits down beside Mrs. Lunn, on her left*].

Mrs. Lunn. I'm so glad to find you do credit to Gregory's taste. I'm naturally rather particular about the women he falls in love with.

Juno [*sternly*] This is no way to take your husband's unfaithfulness. [*To Lunn*] You ought to teach your wife better. Wheres her feelings? It's scandalous.

Gregory. What about your own conduct, pray?

Juno. I dont defend it; and theres an end of the matter.

Gregory. Well, upon my soul! What difference does your not defending it make?

Juno. A fundamental difference. To serious people I may appear wicked. I dont defend myelf: I am wicked, though not bad at heart. To thoughtless people I may even appear comic. Well, laugh at me: I have given myself away. But Mrs. Lunn seems to have no opinion at all about me. She doesnt seem to know whether I'm wicked or comic. She doesnt seem to care. She has no more sense. I say it's not right. I repeat, I have sinned; and I'm prepared to suffer.

MRS. JUNO. Have you really sinned, Tops?

MRS. LUNN [*blandly*] I dont remember your sinning. I have a shocking bad memory for trifles; but I think I should remember that—if you mean me.

JUNO [*raging*] Trifles! I have fallen in love with a monster.

GREGORY. Dont you dare call my wife a monster.

MRS. JUNO [*rising quickly and coming between them*]. Please dont lose your temper, Mr. Lunn: I wont have my Tops bullied.

GREGORY. Well, then, let him not brag about sinning with my wife. [*He turns impulsively to his wife; makes her rise; and takes her proudly on his arm*]. What pretension has he to any such honor?

JUNO. I sinned in intention. [*Mrs. Juno abandons him and resumes her seat, chilled*]. I'm as guilty as if I had actually sinned. And I insist on being treated as a sinner, and not walked over as if I'd done nothing, by your wife or any other man.

MRS. LUNN. Tush! [*She sits down again contemptuously*].

JUNO [*furious*] I wont be belittled.

MRS. LUNN [*to Mrs. Juno*] I hope youll come and stay with us now that you and Gregory are such friends, Mrs. Juno.

JUNO. This insane magnanimity—

MRS. LUNN. Dont you think youve said enough, Mr. Juno? This is a matter for two women to settle. Wont you take a stroll on the beach with my Gregory while we talk it over. Gregory is a splendid listener.

JUNO. I dont think any good can come of a conversation between Mr. Lunn and myself. We can hardly be expected to improve one another's morals. [*He passes behind the chesterfield to Mrs. Lunn's end; seizes a chair; deliberately pushes it between Gregory and Mrs. Lunn; and sits down with folded arms, resolved not to budge*].

GREGORY. Oh! Indeed! Oh, all right. If you come
to that—[*he crosses to Mrs. Juno; plants a chair by her
side; and sits down with equal determination*].

JUNO. Now we are both equally guilty.

GREGORY. Pardon me. I'm not guilty.

JUNO. In intention. Dont quibble. You were guilty
in intention, as I was.

GREGORY. No. I should rather describe myself as being
guilty in fact, but not in intention.

JUNO   ⎫ *rising and*   ⎧ What!
MRS. JUNO ⎬ *exclaiming*   ⎨ No, really—
MRS. LUNN ⎭ *simultaneously* ⎩ Gregory!

GREGORY. Yes: I maintain that I am responsible for
my intentions only, and not for reflex actions over which
I have no control. [*Mrs. Juno sits down, ashamed*]. I
promised my mother that I would never tell a lie, and
that I would never make love to a married woman. I
never have told a lie—

MRS. LUNN [*remonstrating*] Gregory! [*She sits
down again*].

GREGORY. I say never. On many occasions I have re-
sorted to prevarication; but on great occasions I have always told the truth. I regard this as a great occasion; and
I wont be intimidated into breaking my promise. I
solemnly declare that I did not know until this evening
that Mrs. Juno was married. She will bear me out when
I say that from that moment my intentions were strictly
and resolutely honorable; though my conduct, which I
could not control and am therefore not responsible for,
was disgraceful—or would have been had this gentleman
not walked in and begun making love to my wife under
my very nose.

JUNO [*flinging himself back into his chair*] Well, I
like this!

MRS. LUNN. Really, darling, theres no use in the pot
calling the kettle black.

15

GREGORY. When you say darling, may I ask which of us you are addressing?

MRS. LUNN. I really dont know. I'm getting hopelessly confused.

JUNO. Why don't you let my wife say something? I dont think she ought to be thrust into the background like this.

MRS. LUNN. I'm sorry, I'm sure. Please excuse me, dear.

MRS. JUNO [*thoughtfully*] I dont know what to say. I must think over it. I have always been rather severe on this sort of thing; but when it came to the point I didnt behave as I thought I should behave. I didnt intend to be wicked; but somehow or other, Nature, or whatever you choose to call it, didnt take much notice of my intentions. [*Gregory instinctively seeks her hand and presses it*]. And I really did think, Tops, that I was the only woman in the world for you.

JUNO [*cheerfully*] Oh, thats all right, my precious. Mrs. Lunn thought she was the only woman in the world for him.

GREGORY [*reflectively*] So she is, in a sort of a way.

JUNO [*flaring up*] And so is my wife. Dont you set up to be a better husband than I am; for youre not. Ive owned I'm wrong. You havent.

MRS. LUNN. Are you sorry, Gregory?

GREGORY [*perplexed*] Sorry?

MRS. LUNN. Yes, sorry. I think it's time for you to say youre sorry, and to make friends with Mr. Juno before we all dine together.

GREGORY. Seraphita: I promised my mother—

MRS. JUNO [*involuntarily*] Oh, bother your mother! [*Recovering herself*] I beg your pardon.

GREGORY. A promise is a promise. I cant tell a deliberate lie. I know I ought to be sorry; but the flat fact is that I'm not sorry. I find that in this business, somehow or other, there is a disastrous separation between my moral principles and my conduct.

JUNO. Theres nothing disastrous about it. It doesnt matter about your conduct if your principles are all right.

GREGORY. Bosh! It doesn't matter about your principles if your conduct is all right.

JUNO. But your conduct isnt all right; and my principles are.

GREGORY. Whats the good of your principles being right if they wont work?

JUNO. They w i l l work, sir, if you exercise self-sacrifice.

GREGORY. Oh yes: if, if, if. You know jolly well that self-sacrifice doesnt work either when you really want a thing. How much have you sacrificed yourself, pray?

MRS. LUNN. Oh, a great deal, Gregory. Dont be rude. Mr. Juno is a very nice man: he has been most attentive to me on the voyage.

GREGORY. And Mrs. Juno's a very nice woman. She oughtnt to be; but she is.

JUNO. Why oughtnt she to be a nice woman, pray?

GREGORY. I mean she oughtnt to be nice to me. And you oughtnt to be nice to my wife. And your wife oughtnt to like me. And my wife oughtnt to like you. And if they do, they oughtnt to go on liking us. And I oughtnt to like your wife; and you oughtnt to like mine; and if we do we oughtnt to go on liking them. But we do, all of us. We oughtnt; but we do.

JUNO. But, my dear boy, if we admit we are in the wrong wheres the harm of it? Were not perfect; but as long as we keep the ideal before us—

GREGORY. How?

JUNO. By admitting were wrong.

MRS. LUNN [*springing up, out of patience, and pacing round the lounge intolerantly*] Well, really, I must have my dinner. These two men, with their morality, and their promises to their mothers, and their admissions that they were wrong, and their sinning and suffering, and their going on at one another as if it meant anything, or as if it mattered, are getting on my nerves. [*Stooping over the back of the chesterfield to address Mrs. Juno*] If you will be so very good, my dear, as to take my sentimental husband off my hands occasionally, I shall be more than obliged to you: I'm sure you can stand more male sentimentality than I can. [*Sweeping away to the fireplace*] I, on my part, will do my best to amuse your excellent husband when you find him tiresome.

JUNO. I call this polyandry.

MRS. LUNN. I wish you wouldnt call innocent things by offensive names, Mr. Juno. What do you call your own conduct?

JUNO [*rising*] I tell you I have admitted—

GREGORY		What's the good of keeping on at that?
MRS. JUNO	*together*	Oh, not that again, please.
MRS. LUNN		Tops: I'll scream if you say that again.

JUNO. Oh, well, if you wont listen to me—! [*He sits down again*].

MRS. JUNO. What is the position now exactly? [*Mrs. Lunn shrugs her shoulders and gives up the conundrum. Gregory looks at Juno. Juno turns away his head huffily*]. I mean, what are we going to do?

MRS. LUNN. What would you advise, Mr. Juno?

JUNO. I should advise you to divorce your husband.

MRS. LUNN. Do you want me to drag your wife into court and disgrace her?

JUNO. No: I forgot that. Excuse me; but for the moment I thought I was married to you.

GREGORY. I think we had better let bygones be bygones. [*To Mrs. Juno, very tenderly*] You will forgive me, wont you? Why should you let a moment's forget-fulness embitter all our future life?

MRS. JUNO. But it's Mrs. Lunn who has to forgive you.

GREGORY. Oh, dash it, I forgot. This is getting ridiculous.

MRS. LUNN. I'm getting hungry.

MRS. JUNO. Do you really mind, Mrs. Lunn?

MRS. LUNN. My dear Mrs. Juno, Gregory is one of those terribly uxorious men who ought to have ten wives. If any really nice woman will take him off my hands for a day or two occasionally, I shall be greatly obliged to her.

GREGORY. Seraphita: you cut me to the soul [*he weeps*].

MRS. LUNN. Serve you right! Youd think it quite proper if it cut me to the soul.

MRS. JUNO. Am I to take Sibthorpe off your hands too, Mrs. Lunn?

JUNO [*rising*] Do you suppose I'll allow this?

MRS. JUNO. Youve admitted that youve done wrong, Tops. Whats the use of your allowing or not allowing after that?

JUNO. I do not admit that I have done wrong. I admit that what I did was wrong.

GREGORY. Can you explain the distinction?

JUNO. It's quite plain to anyone but an imbecile. If you tell me Ive done something wrong you insult me. But if you say that something that I did is wrong you simply raise a question of morals. I tell you flatly if you say I did anything wrong you will have to fight me. In fact I think we ought to fight anyhow. I don't particularly want to; but I feel that England expects us to.

GREGORY. I wont fight. If you beat me my wife would

share my humiliation. If I beat you, she would sympathize with you and loathe me for my brutality.

MRS. LUNN. Not to mention that as we are human beings and not reindeer or barndoor fowl, if two men presumed to fight for us we couldnt decently ever speak to either of them again.

GREGORY. Besides, neither of us could beat the other, as we neither of us know how to fight. We should only blacken each others eyes and make fools of ourselves.

JUNO. I dont admit that. Every Englishman can use his fists.

GREGORY. Youre an Englishman. Can you use yours?

JUNO. I presume so: I never tried.

MRS. JUNO. You never told me you couldnt fight, Tops. I thought you were an accomplished boxer.

JUNO. My precious: I never gave you any ground for such a belief.

MRS. JUNO. You always talked as if it were a matter of course. You spoke with the greatest contempt of men who didnt kick other men downstairs.

JUNO. Well, I cant kick Mr. Lunn downstairs. Were on the ground floor.

MRS. JUNO. You could throw him into the harbor.

GREGORY. Do you want me to be thrown into the harbor?

MRS. JUNO. No: I only want to shew Tops that he's making a ghastly fool of himself.

GREGORY [*rising and prowling disgustedly between the chesterfield and the windows*] We're all making fools of ourselves.

JUNO [*following him*] Well, if we're not to fight, I must insist at least on your never speaking to my wife again.

GREGORY. Does my speaking to your wife do you any harm?

JUNO. No. But it's the proper course to take. [*Em-*

phatically]. We m u s t behave with some sort of decency.

MRS. LUNN. And are you never going to speak to me again, Mr. Juno?

JUNO. I'm prepared to promise never to do so. I think your husband has a right to demand that. Then if I speak to you after, it will not be his fault. It will be a breach of my promise; and I shall not attempt to defend my conduct.

GREGORY [*facing him*] I shall talk to your wife as often as she'll let me.

MRS. JUNO. I have no objection to your speaking to me, Mr. Lunn.

JUNO. Then I shall take steps.

GREGORY. What steps?

JUNO. Steps. Measures. Proceedings. Such steps as may seem advisable.

MRS. LUNN [*to Mrs. Juno*] Can your husband afford a scandal, Mrs. Juno?

MRS. JUNO. No.

MRS. LUNN. Neither can mine.

GREGORY. Mrs. Juno: I'm very sorry I let you in for all this. I dont know how it is that we contrive to make feelings like ours, which seems to me to be beautiful and sacred feelings, and which lead to such interesting and exciting adventures, end in vulgar squabbles and degrading scenes.

JUNO. I decline to admit that my conduct has been vulgar or degrading.

GREGORY. I promised—

JUNO. Look here, old chap: I dont say a word against your mother; and I'm sorry she's dead; but really, you know, most women are mothers; and they all die some time or other; yet that doesnt make them infallible authorities on morals, does it?

GREGORY. I was about to say so myself. Let me add

that if you do things merely because you think some other fool expects you to do them, and he expects you to do them because he thinks you expect him to expect you to do them, it will end in everybody doing what nobody wants to do, which is in my opinion a silly state of things.

JUNO. Lunn: I love your wife; and that's all about it.

GREGORY. Juno: I love yours. What then?

JUNO. Clearly she must never see you again.

MRS. JUNO. Why not?

JUNO. Why not! My love: I'm surprised at you.

MRS. JUNO. Am I to speak only to men who dislike me?

JUNO. Yes: I think that is, properly speaking, a married woman's duty.

MRS. JUNO. Then I wont do it: thats flat. I like to be liked. I like to be loved. I want everyone round me to love me. I dont want to meet or speak to anyone who doesnt like me.

JUNO. But, my precious, this is the most horrible immorality.

MRS. LUNN. I dont intend to give up meeting you, Mr. Juno. You amuse me very much. I dont like being loved: it bores me. But I do like to be amused.

JUNO. I hope we shall meet very often. But I hope also we shall not defend our conduct.

MRS. JUNO [rising] This is unendurable. Weve all been flirting. Need we go on footling about it?

JUNO [huffily] I dont know what you call footling—

MRS. JUNO [cutting him short] You do. Youre footling. Mr. Lunn is footling. Cant we admit that we're human and have done with it?

JUNO. I have admitted it all along. I—

MRS. JUNO [almost screaming] Then stop footling.

The dinner gong sounds.

MRS. LUNN [rising] Thank heaven! Lets go in to dinner. Gregory: take in Mrs. Juno.

GREGORY. But surely I ought to take in our guest, and not my own wife.

MRS. LUNN. Well, Mrs. Juno is not your wife, is she?

GREGORY. Oh, of course: I beg your pardon. I'm hopelessly confused. [*He offers his arm to Mrs. Juno, rather apprehensively*].

MRS. JUNO. You seem quite afraid of me [*she takes his arm*].

GREGORY. I am. I simply adore you. [*They go out together; and as they pass through the door he turns and says in a ringing voice to the other couple*] I have said to Mrs. Juno that I simply adore her. [*He takes her out defiantly*].

MRS. LUNN [*calling after him*] Yes, dear. Shes a darling. [*To Juno*] Now, Sibthorpe.

JUNO [*giving her his arm gallantly*] You have called me Sibthorpe! Thank you. I think Lunn's conduct fully justifies me in allowing you to do it.

MRS. LUNN. Yes: I think you may let yourself go now.

JUNO. Seraphita: I worship you beyond expression.

MRS. LUNN. Sibthorpe: you amuse me beyond description. Come. [*They go in to dinner together*].

PYGMALION
XXV
1912

PREFACE TO PYGMALION.

A Professor of Phonetics.

As will be seen later on, Pygmalion needs, not a preface, but a sequel, which I have supplied in its due place.

The English have no respect for their language, and will not teach their children to speak it. They spell it so abominably that no man can teach himself what it sounds like. It is impossible for an Englishman to open his mouth without making some other Englishman hate or despise him. German and Spanish are accessible to foreigners: English is not accessible even to Englishmen. The reformer England needs today is an energetic phonetic enthusiast: that is why I have made such a one the hero of a popular play. There have been heroes of that kind crying in the wilderness for many years past. When I became interested in the subject towards the end of the eighteen-seventies, Melville Bell was dead; but Alexander J. Ellis was still a living patriarch, with an impressive head always covered by a velvet skull cap, for which he would apologize to public meetings in a very courtly manner. He and Tito Pagliardini, another phonetic veteran, were men whom it was impossible to dislike. Henry Sweet, then a young man, lacked their sweetness of character: he was about as conciliatory to conventional mortals as Ibsen or Samuel Butler. His great ability as a phonetician (he was, I think, the best of them all at his job) would have entitled him to high official recognition, and perhaps enabled him to popularize his subject, but for his Satanic contempt for all academic dignitaries and persons in general who thought more of

Greek than of phonetics. Once, in the days when the Imperial Institute rose in South Kensington, and Joseph Chamberlain was booming the Empire, I induced the editor of a leading monthly review to commission an article from Sweet on the imperial importance of his subject. When it arrived, it contained nothing but a savagely derisive attack on a professor of language and literature whose chair Sweet regarded as proper to a phonetic expert only. The article, being libelous, had to be returned as impossible; and I had to renounce my dream of dragging its author into the limelight. When I met him afterwards, for the first time for many years, I found to my astonishment that he, who had been a quite tolerably presentable young man, had actually managed by sheer scorn to alter his personal appearance until he had become a sort of walking repudiation of Oxford and all its traditions. It must have been largely in his own despite that he was squeezed into something called a Readership of phonetics there. The future of phonetics rests probably with his pupils, who all swore by him; but nothing could bring the man himself into any sort of compliance with the university, to which he nevertheless clung by divine right in an intensely Oxonian way. I daresay his papers, if he has left any, include some satires that may be published without too destructive results fifty years hence. He was, I believe, not in the least an illnatured man: very much the opposite, I should say; but he would not suffer fools gladly.

Those who knew him will recognize in my third act the allusion to the patent shorthand in which he used to write postcards, and which may be acquired from a four and six-penny manual published by the Clarendon Press. The postcards which Mrs. Higgins describes are such as I have received from Sweet. I would decipher a sound which a cockney would represent by *zerr*, and a Frenchman by *seu*, and then write demanding with some heat what on earth it meant. Sweet, with boundless contempt for my stupidity, would reply that it not only meant but obviously was the word Result, as no other word containing that sound, and capable of making sense with the context, existed in any language spoken on earth. That less expert mortals should require fuller indications was beyond Sweet's patience. Therefore, though the whole point of his "Current Shorthand" is that it can express every sound in the language perfectly, vowels as well as consonants, and that your hand has to to make no stroke except the easy and current ones with which you write m, n, and u, l, p, and q, scribbling them at whatever angle comes easiest to you, his unfortunate determination to make this remarkable and quite legible script serve also as a shorthand reduced it in his own practice to the most inscrutable of cryptograms. His true objective was the provision of a full, accurate, legible script for our noble but ill-dressed language; but he was led past that by his contempt for the popular Pitman system of shorthand, which he called the Pitfall system. The triumph of Pitman was a triumph of business organization: there was a weekly paper to persuade you to learn Pitman: there were cheap textbooks and exercise books and transcripts of speeches for you to copy, and schools where experienced teachers coached you up to the necessary proficiency. Sweet could not organize his market in that fashion. He might as well have been the Sybil who tore up the leaves of prophecy that nobody would attend to. The four and six-penny manual, mostly in his lithographed handwriting, that was never vulgarly advertized, may perhaps some day be taken up by a syndicate and pushed upon the public as The Times pushed the Encyclopædia Britannica; but until then it will certainly not prevail against Pitman. I have bought three copies of it during my lifetime; and I am informed by the publishers that its cloistered existence is still a steady and healthy one. I actually learned the system two several times; and yet the shorthand in which I am writing these lines is Pitman's. And the reason is, that my secretary cannot transcribe Sweet, having been perforce taught in the schools of Pitman. Therefore, Sweet railed at Pitman as vainly as Thersites railed at Ajax: his raillery, however it may have eased his soul, gave no popular vogue to Current Shorthand.

Pygmalion Higgins is not a portrait of Sweet, to whom the adventure of Eliza Doolittle would have been impossible; still, as will be seen, there are touches of Sweet in the play. With Higgins's physique and temperament Sweet might have set the Thames on fire. As it was, he impressed himself professionally on Europe to an extent that made his comparative personal obscurity, and the failure of Oxford to do justice to his eminence, a puzzle to foreign specialists in his subject. I do not blame Oxford, because I think Oxford is quite right in demanding a certain social amenity from its nurslings (heaven knows it is not exorbitant in its requirements!); for although I well know how hard it is for a man of genius with a seriously underrated subject to maintain serene and kindly relations with the men who underrate it, and who keep all the best places for less important subjects which they profess without originality and sometimes without much capacity for them, still, if he overwhelms them with wrath and disdain, he cannot expect them to heap honors on him.

Of the later generations of phoneticians I know little. Among them towers the Poet Laureate, to whom perhaps Higgins may owe his Miltonic sympathies, though here again I must disclaim all portraiture. But if the play makes the public aware that there are such people as phoneticians, and that they are among the most important people in England at present, it will serve its turn.

I wish to boast that Pygmalion has been an extremely successful play all over Europe and North America as

well as at home. It is so intensely and deliberately
didactic, and its subject is esteemed so dry, that I delight
in throwing it at the heads of the wiseacres who repeat
the parrot cry that art should never be didactic. It goes
to prove my contention that art should never be anything
else.

Finally, and for the encouragement of people troubled
with accents that cut them off from all high employment,
I may add that the change wrought by Professor Higgins
in the flower girl is neither impossible nor uncommon.
The modern concierge's daughter who fulfils her ambition
by playing the Queen of Spain in Ruy Blas at the Théâtre
Français is only one of many thousands of men and
women who have sloughed off their native dialects and
acquired a new tongue. But the thing has to be done scientifically, or the last state of the aspirant may be worse
than the first. An honest and natural slum dialect is more
tolerable than the attempt of a phonetically untaught person to imitate the vulgar dialect of the golf club; and
I am sorry to say that in spite of the efforts of our
Academy of Dramatic Art, there is still too much sham
golfing English on our stage, and too little of the noble
English of Forbes Robertson.

16

ACT I

Covent Garden at 11.15 *p.m. Torrents of heavy summer rain. Cab whistles blowing frantically in all directions. Pedestrians running for shelter into the market and under the portico of St. Paul's Church, where there are already several people, among them a lady and her daughter in evening dress. They are all peering out gloomily at the rain, except one man with his back turned to the rest, who seems wholly preoccupied with a notebook in which he is writing busily.*

The church clock strikes the first quarter.

THE DAUGHTER [*in the space between the central pillars, close to the one on her left*] I'm getting chilled to the bone. What can Freddy be doing all this time? Hes been gone twenty minutes.

THE MOTHER [*on her daughter's right*] Not so long. But he ought to have got us a cab by this.

A BYSTANDER [*on the lady's right*] He wont get no cab not until half-past eleven, missus, when they come back after dropping their theatre fares.

THE MOTHER. But we must have a cab. We cant stand here until half-past eleven. It's too bad.

THE BYSTANDER. Well, it aint my fault, missus.

THE DAUGHTER. If Freddy had a bit of gumption, he would have got one at the theatre door.

THE MOTHER. What could he have done, poor boy?

THE DAUGHTER. Other people got cabs. Why couldnt he?

Freddy rushes in out of the rain from the Southamp-

114

*ton Street side, and comes between them closing a drip-
ping umbrella. He is a young man of twenty, in evening dress, very wet around the ankles.*

THE DAUGHTER. Well, havnt you got a cab?

FREDDY. Theres not one to be had for love or money.

THE MOTHER. Oh, Freddy, there must be one. You
cant have tried.

THE DAUGHTER. It's too tiresome. Do you expect us to
go and get one ourselves?

FREDDY. I tell you theyre all engaged. The rain was so
sudden: nobody was prepared; and everybody had to take
a cab. Ive been to Charing Cross one way and nearly
to Ludgate Circus the other; and they were all engaged.

THE MOTHER. Did you try Trafalgar Square?

FREDDY. There wasnt one at Trafalgar Square.

THE DAUGHTER. Did you try?

FREDDY. I tried as far as Charing Cross Station. Did
you expect me to walk to Hammersmith?

THE DAUGHTER. You havnt tried at all.

THE MOTHER. You really are very helpless, Freddy.
Go again; and dont come back until you have found a
cab.

FREDDY. I shall simply get soaked for nothing.

THE DAUGHTER. And what about us? Are we to stay
here all night in this draught, with next to nothing on.
You selfish pig—

FREDDY. Oh, very well: I'll go, I'll go. [*He opens his
umbrella and dashes off Strandwards, but comes into col-
lision with a flower girl, who is hurrying in for shelter,
knocking her basket out of her hands. A blinding flash
of lightning, followed instantly by a rattling peal of thunder, orchestrates the incident*].

THE FLOWER GIRL. Nah then, Freddy: look wh' y'
gowin, deah.

FREDDY. Sorry [*he rushes off*].

THE FLOWER GIRL [*picking up her scattered flowers*

and replacing them in the basket] Theres menners
f' yer! Te-oo banches o voylets trod into the mad.
[*She sits down on the plinth of the column, sorting her
flowers, on the lady's right. She is not at all an attractive
person. She is perhaps eighteen, perhaps twenty, hardly
older. She wears a little sailor hat of black straw that
has long been exposed to the dust and soot of London
and has seldom if ever been brushed. Her hair needs
washing rather badly: its mousy color can hardly be
natural. She wears a shoddy black coat that reaches
nearly to her knees and is shaped to her waist. She has
a brown skirt with a coarse apron. Her boots are much
the worse for wear. She is no doubt as clean as she can
afford to be; but compared to the ladies she is very dirty.
Her features are no worse than theirs; but their condition leaves something to be desired; and she needs the
services of a dentist*].

THE MOTHER. How do you know that my son's name
is Freddy, pray?

THE FLOWER GIRL. Ow, eez ye-ooa san, is e? Wal,
fewd dan y' de-ooty bawmz a mather should, eed now
bettern to spawl a pore gel's flahrzn than ran awy athaht
pyin. Will ye-oo py me f'them? [*Here, with apologies, this desperate attempt to represent her dialect
without a phonetic alphabet must be abandoned as unintelligible outside London.*]

THE DAUGHTER. Do nothing of the sort, mother.
The idea!

THE MOTHER. Please allow me, Clara. Have you
any pennies?

THE DAUGHTER. No. I've nothing smaller than sixpence.

THE FLOWER GIRL [*hopefully*] *I* can give you change
for a tanner, kind lady.

THE MOTHER [*to Clara*] Give it to me. [*Clara parts
reluctantly*]. Now [*to the girl*] This is for your flowers.

THE FLOWER GIRL. Thank you kindly, lady.

THE DAUGHTER. Make her give you the change. These things are only a penny a bunch.

THE MOTHER. Do hold your tongue, Clara. [*To the girl*]. You can keep the change.

THE FLOWER GIRL. Oh, thank you, lady.

THE MOTHER. Now tell me how you know that young gentleman's name.

THE FLOWER GIRL. I didnt.

THE MOTHER. I heard you call him by it. Dont try to deceive me.

THE FLOWER GIRL [*protesting*] Whos trying to deceive you? I called him Freddy or Charlie same as you might yourself if you was talking to a stranger and wished to be pleasant. [*She sits down beside her basket*].

THE DAUGHTER. Sixpence thrown away! Really, mamma, you might have spared Freddy that. [*She retreats in disgust behind the pillar*].

An elderly gentleman of the amiable military type rushes into shelter, and closes a dripping umbrella. He is in the same plight as Freddy, very wet about the ankles. He is in evening dress, with a light overcoat. He takes the place left vacant by the daughter's retirement.

THE GENTLEMAN. Phew!

THE MOTHER [*to the gentleman*] Oh, sir, is there any sign of its stopping?

THE GENTLEMAN. I'm afraid not. It started worse than ever about two minutes ago. [*He goes to the plinth beside the flower girl; puts up his foot on it; and stoops to turn down his trouser ends*].

THE MOTHER. Oh, dear! [*She retires sadly and joins her daughter*].

THE FLOWER GIRL [*taking advantage of the military gentleman's proximity to establish friendly relations with him*]. If it's worse it's a sign it's nearly over. So cheer up, Captain; and buy a flower off a poor girl.

THE GENTLEMAN. I'm sorry, I havnt any change.

THE FLOWER GIRL. I can give you change, Captain.

THE GENTLEMEN. For a sovereign? Ive nothing less.

THE FLOWER GIRL. Garn! Oh do buy a flower off me, Captain. I can change half-a-crown. Take this for tuppence.

THE GENTLEMAN. Now dont be troublesome: theres a good girl. [*Trying his pockets*] I really havnt any change—Stop: heres three hapence, if thats any use to you [*he retreats to the other pillar*].

THE FLOWER GIRL [*disappointed, but thinking three halfpence better than nothing*] Thank you, sir.

THE BYSTANDER [*to the girl*] You be careful: give him a flower for it. Theres a bloke here behind taking down every blessed word youre saying. [*All turn to the man who is taking notes*].

THE FLOWER GIRL [*springing up terrified*] I aint done nothing wrong by speaking to the gentleman. Ive a right to sell flowers if I keep off the kerb. [*Hysterically*] I'm a respectable girl: so help me, I never spoke to him except to ask him to buy a flower off me. [*General hubbub, mostly sympathetic to the flower girl, but deprecating her excessive sensibility. Cries of* Dont start hollerin. Whos hurting you? Nobody's going to touch you. Whats the good of fussing? Steady on. Easy, easy, *etc., come from the elderly staid spectators, who pat her comfortingly. Less patient ones bid her shut her head, or ask her roughly what is wrong with her. A remoter group, not knowing what the matter is, crowd in and increase the noise with question and answer:* Whats the row? What she do? Where is he? A tec taking her down. What! him? Yes: him over there: Took money off the gentleman, *etc. The flower girl, dis-*

traught and mobbed, breaks through them to the gentle-man, crying wildly] Oh, sir, dont let him charge me. You dunno what it means to me. Theyll take away my character and drive me on the streets for speaking to gentlemen. They—

THE NOTE TAKER [*coming forward on her right, the rest crowding after him*] There, there, there, there! whos hurting you, you silly girl? What do you take me for?

THE BYSTANDER. It's all right: hes a gentleman: look at his boots. [*Explaining to the note taker*] She thought you was a copper's nark, sir.

THE NOTE TAKER [*with quick interest*] Whats a copper's nark?

THE BYSTANDER [*inapt at definition*] It's a—well, it's a copper's nark, as you might say. What else would you call it? A sort of informer.

THE FLOWER GIRL [*still hysterical*] I take my Bible oath I never said a word—

THE NOTE TAKER [*overbearing but good-humored*] Oh, shut up, shut up. Do I look like a policeman?

THE FLOWER GIRL [*far from reassured*] Then what did you take down my words for? How do I know whether you took me down right? You just shew me what youve wrote about me. [*The note taker opens his book and holds it steadily under her nose, though the pressure of the mob trying to read it over his shoulders would upset a weaker man*]. Whats that? That aint proper writing. I cant read that.

THE NOTE TAKER. I can. [*Reads, reproducing her pronunciation exactly*] "Cheer ap, Keptin; n' baw ya flahr orf a pore gel."

THE FLOWER GIRL [*much distressed*] It's because I called him Captain. I meant no harm. [*To the gentle-man*] Oh, sir, dont let him lay a charge agen me for a word like that. You—

THE GENTLEMAN. Charge! I make no charge. [*To

the note taker] Really, sir, if you are a detective, you need not begin protecting me against molestation by young women until I ask you. Anybody could see that the girl meant no harm.

THE BYSTANDERS GENERALLY [*demonstrating against police espionage*] Course they could. What business is it of yours? You mind your own affairs. He wants promotion, he does. Taking down people's words! Girl never said a word to him. What harm if she did? Nice thing a girl cant shelter from the rain without being insulted, etc., etc., etc. [*She is conducted by the more smypathetic demonstrators back to her plinth, where she resumes her seat and struggles with her emotion.*

THE BYSTANDER. He aint a tec. Hes a blooming busybody: thats what he is. I tell you, look at his boots.

THE NOTE TAKER [*turning on him genially*] And how are all your people down at Selsey?

THE BYSTANDER [*suspiciously*] Who told you my people come from Selsey?

THE NOTE TAKER. Never you mind. They did. [*To the girl*] How do you come to be up so far east? You were born in Lisson Grove.

THE FLOWER GIRL [*appalled*] Oh, what harm is there in my leaving Lisson Grove? It wasnt fit for a pig to live in; and I had to pay four-and-six a week. [*In tears*] Oh, boo—hoo—oo—

THE NOTE TAKER. Live where you like; but stop that noise.

THE GENTLEMAN [*to the girl*] Come, come! he cant touch you: you have a right to live where you please.

A SARCASTIC BYSTANDER [*thrusting himself between the note taker and the gentleman*] Park Lane, for instance. Id like to go into the Housing Question with you, I would.

THE FLOWER GIRL [*subsiding into a brooding melan-*

*choly over her basket, and talking very low-spiritedly
to herself*] I'm a good girl, I am.

THE SARCASTIC BYSTANDER [*not attending to her*]
Do you know where *I* come from?

THE NOTE TAKER [*promptly*] Hoxton.

*Titterings. Popular interest in the note taker's per-
formance increases.*

THE SARCASTIC ONE [*amazed*] Well, who said I didnt?
Bly me! You know everything, you do.

THE FLOWER GIRL [*still nursing her sense of injury*]
Aint no call to meddle with me, he aint.

THE BYSTANDER [*to her*] Of course he aint. Dont
you stand it from him. [*To the note taker*] See here:
what call have you to know about people what never
offered to meddle with you? Wheres your warrant?

SEVERAL BYSTANDERS [*encouraged by this seeming
point of law*] Yes: wheres your warrant?

THE FLOWER GIRL. Let him say what he likes. I
dont want to have no truck with him.

THE BYSTANDER. You take us for dirt under your
feet, dont you? Catch you taking liberties with a gentleman!

THE SARCASTIC BYSTANDER. Yes: tell h i m where
he come from if you want to go fortune-telling.

THE NOTE TAKER. Cheltenham, Harrow, Cambridge,
and India.

THE GENTLEMAN. Quite right. [*Great laughter.
Reaction in the note taker's favor. Exclamations of* He
knows all about it. Told him proper. Hear him tell the
toff where he come from? *etc.*]. May I ask, sir, do you
do this for your living at a music hall?

THE NOTE TAKER. Ive thought of that. Perhaps I
shall some day.

*The rain has stopped; and the persons on the outside
of the crowd begin to drop off.*

THE FLOWER GIRL [*resenting the reaction*] Hes no gentleman, he aint, to interfere with a poor girl.

THE DAUGHTER [*out of patience, pushing her way rudely to the front and displacing the gentleman, who politely retires to the other side of the pillar*] What on earth is Freddy doing? I shall get pneumonia if I stay in this draught any longer.

THE NOTE TAKER [*to himself, hastily making a note of her pronunciation of "monia"*] Earlscourt.

THE DAUGHTER [*violently*] Will you please keep your impertinent remarks to yourself?

THE NOTE TAKER. Did I say that out loud? I didnt mean to. I beg your pardon. Your mother's Epsom, unmistakeably.

THE MOTHER [*advancing between her daughter and the note taker*] How very curious! I was brought up in Largelady Park, near Epsom.

THE NOTE TAKER [*uproariously amused*] Ha! ha! What a devil of a name! Excuse me. [*To the daughter*] You want a cab, do you?

THE DAUGHTER. Dont dare speak to me.

THE MOTHER. Oh, please, please Clara. [*Her daughter repudiates her with an angry shrug and retires haughtily.*] We should be so grateful to you, sir, if you found us a cab. [*The note taker produces a whistle*]. Oh, thank you. [*She joins her daughter*].

The note taker blows a piercing blast.

THE SARCASTIC BYSTANDER. There! I knowed he was a plain-clothes copper.

THE BYSTANDER. That aint a police whistle: thats a sporting whistle.

THE FLOWER GIRL [*still preoccupied with her wounded feelings*] Hes no right to take away my character. My character is the same to me as any lady's.

THE NOTE TAKER. I dont know whether youve noticed it; but the rain stopped about two minutes ago.

THE BYSTANDER. So it has. Why didnt you say so before? and us losing our time listening to your silliness. [*He walks off towards the Strand*].

THE SARCASTIC BYSTANDER. I can tell where you come from. You come from Anwell. Go back there.

THE NOTE TAKER [*helpfully*] *H*anwell.

THE SARCASTIC BYSTANDER [*affecting great distinction of speech*] Thenk you, teacher. Haw haw! So long [*he touches his hat with mock respect and strolls off*].

THE FLOWER GIRL. Frightening people like that! How would he like it himself.

THE MOTHER. It's quite fine now, Clara. We can walk to a motor bus. Come. [*She gathers her skirts above her ankles and hurries off towards the Strand*].

THE DAUGHTER. But the cab—[*her mother is out of hearing*]. Oh, how tiresome! [*She follows angrily*].

All the rest have gone except the note taker, the gentleman, and the flower girl, who sits arranging her basket, and still pitying herself in murmurs.

THE FLOWER GIRL. Poor girl! Hard enough for her to live without being worrited and chivied.

THE GENTLEMAN [*returning to his former place on the note taker's left*] How do you do it, if I may ask?

THE NOTE TAKER. Simply phonetics. The science of speech. Thats my profession: also my hobby. Happy is the man who can make a living by his hobby! You can spot an Irishman or a Yorkshireman by his brogue. *I* can place any man within six miles. I can place him within two miles in London. Sometimes within two streets.

THE FLOWER GIRL. Ought to be ashamed of himself, unmanly coward!

THE GENTLEMAN. But is there a living in that?

THE NOTE TAKER. Oh yes. Quite a fat one. This is an age of upstarts. Men begin in Kentish Town with £80 a year, and end in Park Lane with a hundred thou-

sand. They want to drop Kentish Town; but they give
themselves away every time they open their mouths.
Now I can teach them—

THE FLOWER GIRL. Let him mind his own business
and leave a poor girl—

THE NOTE TAKER [*explosively*] Woman: cease this
detestable boohooing instantly; or else seek the shelter
of some other place of worship.

THE FLOWER GIRL [*with feeble defiance*] Ive a right
to be here if I like, same as you.

THE NOTE TAKER. A woman who utters such de-
pressing and disgusting sounds has no right to be anywhere—no right to live. Remember that you are a human being with a soul and the divine gift of articulate
speech: that your native language is the language of
Shakespear and Milton and The Bible; and dont sit
there crooning like a bilious pigeon.

THE FLOWER GIRL [*quite overwhelmed, and looking up
at him in mingled wonder and deprecation without daring
to raise her head*] Ah-ah-ah-ow-ow-ow-oo!

THE NOTE TAKER [*whipping out his book*] Heavens!
what a sound! [*He writes; then holds out the book and
reads, reproducing her vowels exactly*] Ah-ah-ah-ow-
ow-ow-oo!

THE FLOWER GIRL [*tickled by the performance, and
laughing in spite of herself*] Garn!

THE NOTE TAKER. You see this creature with her
kerbstone English: the English that will keep her in
the gutter to the end of her days. Well, sir, in three
months I could pass that girl off as a duchess at an ambassador's garden party. I could even get her a place
as lady's maid or shop assistant, which requires better
English. Thats the sort of thing I do for commercial
millionaires. And on the profits of it I do genuine scientific work in phonetics, and a little as a poet on Miltonic lines.

THE GENTLEMAN.   I am myself a student of Indian dialects; and—

THE NOTE TAKER [*eagerly*] Are you?   Do you know Colonel Pickering, the author of Spoken Sanscrit?

THE GENTLEMAN.   I am Colonel Pickering.   Who are you?

THE NOTE TAKER.   Henry Higgins, author of Higgins's Universal Alphabet.

PICKERING [*with enthusiasm*] I came from India to meet you.

HIGGINS.   I was going to India to meet you.

PICKERING.   Where do you live?

HIGGINS.   27A Wimpole Street.   Come and see me to-morrow.

PICKERING.   I'm at the Carlton.   Come with me now and lets have a jaw over some supper.

HIGGINS.   Right you are.

THE FLOWER GIRL [*to Pickering, as he passes her*] Buy a flower, kind gentleman.   I'm short for my lodging.

PICKERING.   I really havnt any change.   I'm sorry [*he goes away*].

HIGGINS [*shocked at girl's mendacity*] Liar.   You said you could change half-a-crown.

THE FLOWER GIRL [*rising in desperation*] You ought to be stuffed with nails, you ought.   [*Flinging the basket at his feet*] Take the whole blooming basket for sixpence.

The church clock strikes the second quarter.

HIGGINS [*hearing in it the voice of God, rebuking him for his Pharisaic want of charity to the poor girl*] A reminder.   [*He raises his hat solemnly; then throws a handful of money into the basket and follows Pickering*].

THE FLOWER GIRL [*picking up a half-crown*] Ah-ow-ooh!   [*Picking up a couple of florins*] Aaah-ow-ooh!   [*Picking up several coins*] Aaaaaah-ow-ooh!   [*Picking up a half-sovereign*] Aaaaaaaaaaaah-ow ooh!!!

FREDDY [*springing out of a taxicab*] Got one at last.

Hallo! [*To the girl*] Where are the two ladies that were here?

THE FLOWER GIRL. They walked to the bus when the rain stopped.

FREDDY. And left me with a cab on my hands. Damnation!

THE FLOWER GIRL [*with grandeur*] Never you mind, young man. I'm going home in a taxi. [*She sails off to the cab. The driver puts his hand behind him and holds the door firmly shut against her. Quite understanding his mistrust, she shews him her handful of money.* Eightpence aint no object to me, Charlie. [*He grins and opens the door*]. Angel Court, Drury Lane, round the corner of Micklejohn's oil shop. Lets see how fast you can make her hop it. [*She gets in and pulls the door to with a slam as the taxicab starts*].

FREDDY. Well, I'm dashed!

ACT II

Next day at 11 a.m. Higgins's laboratory in Wimpole Street. It is a room on the first floor, looking on the street, and was meant for the drawing-room. The double doors are in the middle of the back wall; and persons entering find in the corner to their right two tall file cabinets at right angles to one another against the walls. In this corner stands a flat writing-table, on which are a phonograph, a laryngoscope, a row of tiny organ pipes with a bellows, a set of lamp chimneys for singing flames with burners attached to a gas plug in the wall by an indiarubber tube, several tuning-forks of different sizes, a life-size image of half a human head, showing in section the vocal organs, and a box containing a supply of wax cylinders for the phonograph.

Further down the room, on the same side, is a fireplace, with a comfortable leather-covered easy-chair at the side of the hearth nearest the door, and a coal-scuttle. There is a clock on the mantelpiece. Between the fireplace and the phonograph table is a stand for newspapers.

On the other side of the central door, to the left of the visitor, is a cabinet of shallow drawers. On it is a telephone and the telephone directory. The corner beyond, and most of the side wall, is occupied by a grand piano, with the keyboard at the end furthest from the door, and a bench for the player extending the full length of the keyboard. On the piano is a dessert dish heaped with fruit and sweets, mostly chocolates.

The middle of the room is clear. Besides the easy-chair, the piano bench, and two chairs at the phonograph

127

table, there is one stray chair. It stands near the fireplace. On the walls, engravings; mostly Piranesis and mezzotint portraits. No paintings.

Pickering is seated at the table, putting down some cards and a tuning-fork which he has been using. Higgins is standing up near him, closing two or three file drawers which are hanging out. He appears in the morning light as a robust, vital, appetizing sort of man of forty or thereabouts, dressed in a professional-looking black frock-coat with a white linen collar and black silk tie. He is of the energetic, scientific type, heartily, even violently interested in everything that can be studied as a scientific subject, and careless about himself and other people, including their feelings. He is, in fact, but for his years and size, rather like a very impetuous baby "taking notice" eagerly and loudly, and requiring almost as much watching to keep him out of unintended mischief. His manner varies from genial bullying when he is in a good humor to stormy petulance when anything goes wrong; but he is so entirely frank and void of malice that he remains likeable even in his least reasonable moments.

HIGGINS [*as he shuts the last drawer*] Well, I think thats the whole show.

PICKERING. It's really amazing. I havnt taken half of it in, you know.

HIGGINS. Would you like to go over any of it again?

PICKERING [*rising and coming to the fireplace, where he plants himself with his back to the fire*] No, thank you; not now. I'm quite done up for this morning.

HIGGINS [*following him, and standing beside him on his left*] Tired of listening to sounds?

PICKERING. Yes. It's a fearful strain. I rather fancied myself because I can pronounce twenty-four distinct vowel sounds; but your hundred and thirty beat me. I cant hear a bit of difference between most of them.

HIGGINS [*chuckling, and going over to the piano to eat sweets*] Oh, that comes with practice. You hear no difference at first; but you keep on listening, and presently you find theyre all as different as A from B. [*Mrs. Pearce looks in: she is Higgins's housekeeper*] Whats the matter?

MRS. PEARCE [*hesitating, evidently perplexed*] A young woman wants to see you, sir.

HIGGINS. A young woman! What does she want?

MRS. PEARCE. Well, sir, she says youll be glad to see her when you know what shes come about. Shes quite a common girl, sir. Very common indeed. I should have sent her away, only I thought perhaps you wanted her to talk into your machines. I hope Ive not done wrong; but really you see such queer people sometimes—youll excuse me, I'm sure, sir—

HIGGINS. Oh, thats all right, Mrs. Pearce. Has she an interesting accent?

MRS. PEARCE. Oh, something dreadful, sir, really. I dont know how you can take an interest in it.

HIGGINS [*to Pickering*] Lets have her up. Shew her up, Mrs. Pearce [*he rushes across to his working table and picks out a cylinder to use on the phonograph*].

MRS. PEARCE [*only half resigned to it*] Very well, sir. It's for you to say. [*She goes downstairs*].

HIGGINS. This is rather a bit of luck. I'll shew you how I make records. We'll set her talking; and I'll take it down first in Bell's visible Speech; then in broad Romic; and then we'll get her on the phonograph so that you can turn her on as often as you like with the written transcript before you.

MRS. PEARCE [*returning*] This is the young woman, sir.

The flower girl enters in state. She has a hat with three ostrich feathers, orange, sky-blue, and red. She

17

has a nearly clean apron, and the shoddy coat has been tidied a little. The pathos of this deplorable figure, with its innocent vanity and consequential air, touches Pickering, who has already straightened himself in the presence of Mrs. Pearce. But as to Higgins, the only distinction he makes between men and women is that when he is neither bullying nor exclaiming to the heavens against some featherweight cross, he coaxes women as a child coaxes its nurse when it wants to get anything out of her.

HIGGINS [*brusquely, recognizing her with unconcealed disappointment, and at once, babylike, making an intolerable grievance of it*] Why, this is the girl I jotted down last night. Shes no use: Ive got all the records I want of the Lisson Grove lingo; and I'm not going to waste another cylinder on it. [*To the girl*] Be off with you: I dont want you.

THE FLOWER GIRL. Dont you be so saucy. You aint heard what I come for yet. [*To Mrs. Pearce, who is waiting at the door for further instruction*] Did you tell him I come in a taxi?

MRS. PEARCE. Nonsense, girl! what do you think a gentleman like Mr. Higgins cares what you came in?

THE FLOWER GIRL. Oh, we are proud! He aint above giving lessons, not him: I heard him say so. Well, I aint come here to ask for any compliment; and if my money's not good enough I can go elsewhere.

HIGGINS. Good enough for what?

THE FLOWER GIRL. Good enough for ye-oo. Now you know, dont you? I'm come to have lessons, I am. And to pay for em too: make no mistake.

HIGGINS [*stupent*] Well ! ! ! [*Recovering his breath with a gasp*] What do you expect me to say to you?

THE FLOWER GIRL. Well, if you was a gentleman, you might ask me to sit down, I think. Dont I tell you I'm bringing you business?

Higgins. Pickering: shall we ask this baggage to sit down or shall we throw her out of the window?

The Flower Girl. [*running away in terror to the piano, where she turns at bay*] Ah-ah-ah-ow-ow-ow-oo! [*Wounded and whimpering*] I wont be called a baggage when Ive offered to pay like any lady.

Motionless, the two men stare at her from the other side of the room, amazed.

Pickering [*gently*] What is it you want, my girl?

The Flower Girl. I want to be a lady in a flower shop stead of selling at the corner of Tottenham Court Road. But they wont take me unless I can talk more genteel. He said he could teach me. Well, here I am ready to pay him—not asking any favor—and he treats me as if I was dirt.

Mrs. Pearce. How can you be such a foolish ignorant girl as to think you could afford to pay Mr. Higgins?

The Flower Girl. Why shouldnt I? I know what lessons cost as well as you do; and I'm ready to pay.

Higgins. How much?

The Flower Girl [*coming back to him, triumphant*] Now youre talking! I thought youd come off it when you saw a chance of getting back a bit of what you chucked at me last night. [*Confidentially*] Youd had a drop in, hadnt you?

Higgins [*peremptorily*] Sit down.

The Flower Girl. Oh, if youre going to make a compliment of it —

Higgins [*thundering at her*] Sit down.

Mrs. Pearce [*severely*] Sit down, girl. Do as youre told. [*She places the stray chair near the hearthrug between Higgins and Pickering, and stands behind it waiting for the girl to sit down*].

The Flower Girl. Ah-ah-ah-ow-ow-oo! [*She stands, half rebellious, half bewildered*].

Pickering [*very courteous*] Wont you sit down?

LIZA [*coyly*] Dont mind if I do.   [*She sits down. Pickering returns to the hearthrug*].

HIGGINS. Whats your name?

THE FLOWER GIRL. Liza Doolittle.

HIGGINS [*declaiming gravely*]

> Eliza, Elizabeth, Betsy and Bess,
> They went to the woods to get a birds nes':

PICKERING. They found a nest with four eggs in it:

HIGGINS.   They took one apiece, and left three in it.

They laugh heartily at their own wit.

LIZA. Oh, dont be silly.

MRS. PEARCE. You mustnt speak to the gentleman like that.

LIZA. Well, why wont he speak sensible to me?

HIGGINS. Come back to business. How much do you propose to pay me for the lessons?

LIZA. Oh, I know whats right. A lady friend of mine gets French lessons for eighteenpence an hour from a real French gentleman. Well, you wouldnt have the face to ask me the same for teaching me my own language as you would for French; so I wont give more than a shilling. Take it or leave it.

HIGGINS [*walking up and down the room, rattling his keys and his cash in his pockets*] You know, Pickering, if you consider a shilling, not as a simple shilling, but as a percentage of this girl's income, it works out as fully equivalent to sixty or seventy guineas from a millionaire.

PICKERING. How so?

HIGGINS. Figure it out. A millionaire has about £150 a day. She earns about half-a-crown.

LIZA [*haughtily*] Who told you I only—

HIGGINS [*continuing*] She offers me two-fifths of her day's income for a lesson. Two-fifths of a millionaire's income for a day would be somewhere about £60. It's handsome. By George, it's enormous! it's the biggest offer I ever had.

◁ LIZA [*rising, terrified*] Sixty pounds! What are you talking about? I never offered you sixty pounds. Where would I get—

HIGGINS. Hold your tongue.

◁ LIZA [*weeping*] But I aint got sixty pounds. Oh—

MRS. PEARCE. Dont cry, you silly girl. Sit down. Nobody is going to touch your money.

HIGGINS. Somebody is going to touch you, with a broomstick, if you dont stop snivelling. Sit down.

LIZA [*obeying slowly*] Ah-ah-ah-ow-oo-o! One would think you was my father.

HIGGINS. If I decide to teach you, I'll be worse than two fathers to you. Here [*he offers her his silk handkerchief*]!

LIZA. Whats this for?

HIGGINS. To wipe your eyes. To wipe any part of your face that feels moist. Remember: thats your handkerchief; and thats your sleeve. Dont mistake the one for the other if you wish to become a lady in a shop.

Liza, utterly bewildered, stares helplessly at him.

MRS. PEARCE. It's no use talking to her like that, Mr. Higgins: she doesnt understand you. Besides, youre quite wrong: she doesnt do it that way at all [*she takes the handkerchief*].

LIZA [*snatching it*] Here! You give me that handkerchief. He give it to me, not to you.

PICKERING [*laughing*] He did. I think it must be regarded as her property, Mrs. Pearce.

MRS. PEARCE [*resigning herself*] Serve you right, Mr. Higgins.

PICKERING. Higgins: I'm interested. What about the ambassador's garden party? I'll say youre the greatest teacher alive if you make that good. I'll bet you all the expenses of the experiment you cant do it. And I'll pay for the lessons.

LIZA. Oh, you are real good. Thank you, Captain.

HIGGINS [*tempted, looking at her*] It's almost irresistible. Shes so deliciously low—so horribly dirty—

LIZA [*protesting extremely*] Ah-ah-ah-ah-ow-ow-oo-oo!!! I aint dirty: I washed my face and hands afore I come, I did.

PICKERING. Youre certainly not going to turn her head with flattery, Higgins.

MRS. PEARCE [*uneasy*] Oh, dont say that, sir: theres more ways than one of turning a girl's head; and nobody can do it better than Mr. Higgins, though he may not always mean it. I do hope, sir, you wont encourage him to do anything foolish.

HIGGINS [*becoming excited as the idea grows on him*] What is life but a series of inspired follies? The difficulty is to find them to do. Never lose a chance: it doesnt come every day. I shall make a duchess of this draggle-tailed guttersnipe.

LIZA [*strongly deprecating this view of her*] Ah-ah-ah-ow-ow-oo!

HIGGINS [*carried away*] Yes: in six months—in three if she has a good ear and a quick tongue—I'll take her anywhere and pass her off as anything. We'll start today: now! this moment! Take her away and clean her, Mrs. Pearce. Monkey Brand, if it wont come off any other way. Is there a good fire in the kitchen?

MRS. PEARCE [*protesting*]. Yes; but—

HIGGINS [*storming on*] Take all her clothes off and burn them. Ring up Whiteley or somebody for new ones. Wrap her up in brown paper til they come.

LIZA. Youre no gentleman, youre not, to talk of such things. I'm a good girl, I am; and I know what the like of you are, I do.

HIGGINS. We want none of your Lisson Grove prudery here, young woman. Youve got to learn to behave like a duchess. Take her away, Mrs. Pearce. If she gives you any trouble wallop her.

LIZA [*springing up and running between Pickering and Mrs. Pearce for protection*] No! I'll call the police, I will.

MRS. PEARCE. But Ive no place to put her.

HIGGINS. Put her in the dustbin.

LIZA. Ah-ah-ah-ow-ow-oo!

PICKERING. Oh come, Higgins! be reasonable.

MRS. PEARCE [*resolutely*] You must be reasonable, Mr. Higgins: really you must. You cant walk over everybody like this.

Higgins, thus scolded, subsides. The hurricane is succeeded by a zephyr of amiable surprise.

HIGGINS [*with professional exquisiteness of modulation*] I walk over everybody! My dear Mrs. Pearce, my dear Pickering, I never had the slightest intention of walking over anyone. All I propose is that we should be kind to this poor girl. We must help her to prepare and fit herself for her new station in life. If I did not express myself clearly it was because I did not wish to hurt her delicacy, or yours.

Liza, reassured, steals back to her chair.

MRS. PEARCE [*to Pickering*] Well, did you ever hear anything like that, sir?

PICKERING [*laughing heartily*] Never, Mrs. Pearce: never.

HIGGINS [*patiently*] Whats the matter?

MRS. PEARCE. Well, the matter is, sir, that you cant take a girl up like that as if you were picking up a pebble on the beach.

HIGGINS. Why not?

MRS. PEARCE. Why not! But you dont know anything about her. What about her parents? She may be married.

LIZA. Garn!

HIGGINS. There! As the girl very properly says, Garn! Married indeed! Dont you know that a woman of that class looks a worn out drudge of fifty a year after shes married.

LIZA. Whood marry me?

HIGGINS [*suddenly resorting to the most thrillingly beautiful low tones in his best elocutionary style*] By George, Eliza, the streets will be strewn with the bodies of men shooting themselves for your sake before Ive done with you.

MRS. PEARCE. Nonsense, sir. You mustnt talk like that to her.

LIZA [*rising and squaring herself determinedly*] I'm going away. He's off his chump, he is. I dont want no balmies teaching me.

HIGGINS [*wounded in his tenderest point by her insensibility to his elocution*] Oh, indeed! I'm mad, am I? Very well, Mrs. Pearce: you neednt order the new clothes for her. Throw her out.

LIZA [*whimpering*] Nah-ow. You got no right to touch me.

MRS. PEARCE. You see now what comes of being saucy. [*Indicating the door*] This way, please.

LIZA [*almost in tears*] I didnt want no clothes. I wouldnt have taken them [*she throws away the handkerchief*]. I can buy my own clothes.

HIGGINS [*deftly retrieving the handkerchief and intercepting her on her reluctant way to the door*] Youre an ungrateful wicked girl. This is my return for offering to take you out of the gutter and dress you beautifully and make a lady of you.

MRS. PEARCE. Stop, Mr. Higgins. I wont allow it. It's you that are wicked. Go home to your parents, girl; and tell them to take better care of you.

LIZA. I aint got no parents. They told me I was big enough to earn my own living and turned me out.

MRS. PEARCE. Wheres your mother?

LIZA. I aint got no mother. Her that turned me out

was my sixth stepmother. But I done without them. And I'm a good girl, I am.

HIGGINS. Very well, then, what on earth is all this fuss about? The girl doesnt belong to anybody—is no use to anybody but me. [*He goes to Mrs. Pearce and begins coaxing*]. You can adopt her, Mrs. Pearce: I'm sure a daughter would be a great amusement to you. Now dont make any more fuss. Take her downstairs; and—

MRS. PEARCE. But whats to become of her? Is she to be paid anything? Do be sensible, sir.

HIGGINS. Oh, pay her whatever is necessary: put it down in the housekeeping book. [*Impatiently*] What on earth will she want with money? She'll have her food and her clothes. She'll only drink if you give her money.

LIZA [*turning on him*] Oh you are a brute. It's a lie: nobody ever saw the sign of liquor on me. [*She goes back to her chair and plants herself there defiantly*].

PICKERING [*in good-humored remonstrance*] Does it occur to you, Higgins, that the girl has some feelings?

HIGGINS [*looking critically at her*] Oh no, I dont think so. Not any feelings that we need bother about. [*Cheerily*] Have you, Eliza?

LIZA. I got my feelings same as anyone else.

HIGGINS [*to Pickering, reflectively*] You see the difficulty?

PICKERING. Eh? What difficulty?

HIGGINS. To get her to talk grammar. The mere pronunciation is easy enough.

LIZA. I dont want to talk grammar. I want to talk like a lady.

MRS. PEARCE. Will you please keep to the point, Mr. Higgins. I want to know on what terms the girl is to be here. Is she to have any wages? And what is to become of her when youve finished your teaching? You must look ahead a little.

HIGGINS [*impatiently*] Whats to become of her if I leave her in the gutter? Tell me that, Mrs. Pearce.

MRS. PEARCE. Thats her own business, not yours, Mr. Higgins.

HIGGINS. Well, when Ive done with her, we can throw her back into the gutter; and then it will be her own business again; so thats all right.

LIZA. Oh, youve no feeling heart in you: you dont care for nothing but yourself [*she rises and takes the floor resolutely*]. Here! Ive had enough of this. I'm going [*making for the door*]. You ought to be ashamed of yourself, you ought.

HIGGINS [*snatching a chocolate cream from the piano, his eyes suddenly beginning to twinkle with mischief*] Have some chocolates, Eliza.

LIZA [*halting, tempted*] How do I know what might be in them? Ive heard of girls being drugged by the like of you.

Higgins whips out his penknife; cuts a chocolate in two; puts one half into his mouth and bolts it; and offers her the other half.

HIGGINS. Pledge of good faith, Eliza. I eat one half: you eat the other. [*Liza opens her mouth to retort: he pops the half chocolate into it*]. You shall have boxes of them, barrels of them, every day. You shall live on them. Eh?

LIZA [*who has disposed of the chocolate after being nearly choked by it*] I wouldnt have ate it, only I'm too ladylike to take it out of my mouth.

HIGGINS. Listen, Eliza. I think you said you came in a taxi.

LIZA. Well, what if I did? Ive as good a right to take a taxi as anyone else.

HIGGINS. You have, Eliza; and in future you shall have as many taxis as you want. You shall go up and down and round the town in a taxi every day. Think of that, Eliza.

MRS. PEARCE. Mr. Higgins: youre tempting the girl. It's not right. She should think of the future.

HIGGINS. At her age! Nonsense! Time enough to think of the future when you havnt any future to think of. No, Eliza: do as this lady does: think of other people's futures; but never think of your own. Think of chocolates, and taxis, and gold, and diamonds.

LIZA. No: I dont want no gold and no diamonds. I'm a good girl, I am. [*She sits down again, with an attempt at dignity*].

HIGGINS. You shall remain so, Eliza, under the care of Mrs. Pearce. And you shall marry an officer in the Guards, with a beautiful moustache: the son of a marquis, who will disinherit him for marrying you, but will relent when he sees your beauty and goodness—

PICKERING. Excuse me, Higgins; but I really must interfere. Mrs. Pearce is quite right. If this girl is to put herself in your hands for six months for an experiment in teaching, she must understand thoroughly what shes doing.

HIGGINS. How can she? Shes incapable of understanding anything. Besides, do any of us understand what we are doing? If we did, would we ever do it?

PICKERING. Very clever, Higgins; but not sound sense. [*To Eliza*] Miss Doolittle—

LIZA [*overwhelmed*] Ah-ah-ow-oo!

HIGGINS. There! Thats all you get out of Eliza. Ah-ah-ow-oo! No use explaining. As a military man you ought to know that. Give her her orders: thats what she wants. Eliza: you are to live here for the next six months, learning how to speak beautifully, like a lady in a florist's shop. If youre good and do whatever youre told, you shall sleep in a proper bedroom, and have lots to eat, and money to buy chocolates and take rides in taxis. If youre naughty and idle you will sleep in the back kitchen among the black beetles, and be walloped by Mrs. Pearce with a broomstick. At the end of six months you shall go to Buckingham Palace in a carriage, beautifully dressed. If the King finds out youre not a lady, you will be taken by the police to the Tower of London, where your head will be cut off as a warning to other presumptuous flower girls. If you are not found out, you shall have a present of seven-and-sixpence to start life with as a lady in a shop. If you refuse this offer you will be a most ungrateful and wicked girl; and the angels will weep for you. [*To Pickering*] Now are you satisfied, Pickering? [*To Mrs. Pearce*] Can I put it more plainly and fairly, Mrs. Pearce?

MRS. PEARCE [*patiently*] I think youd better let me speak to the girl properly in private. I dont know that I can take charge of her or consent to the arrangement at all. Of course I know you dont mean her any harm; but when you get what you call interested in people's accents, you never think or care what may happen to them or you. Come with me, Eliza.

HIGGINS. Thats all right. Thank you, Mrs. Pearce. Bundle her off to the bath-room.

LIZA [*rising reluctantly and suspiciously*] Youre a great bully, you are. I wont stay here if I dont like. I wont let nobody wallop me. I never asked to go to Bucknam Palace, I didnt. I was never in trouble with the police, not me. I'm a good girl—

MRS. PEARCE. Dont answer back, girl. You dont understand the gentleman. Come with me. [*She leads the way to the door, and holds it open for Eliza*].

LIZA [*as she goes out*] Well, what I say is right. I wont go near the king, not if I'm going to have my head cut off. If I'd known what I was letting myself in for, I wouldnt have come here. I always been a good girl; and I never offered to say a word to him; and I dont owe him nothing; and I dont care; and I wont be put upon; and I have my feelings the same as anyone else—

Mrs. Pearce shuts the door; and Eliza's plaints are no longer audible. Pickering comes from the hearth to the chair and sits astride it with his arms on the back.

PICKERING. Excuse the straight question, Higgins. Are you a man of good character where women are concerned?

HIGGINS [*moodily*] Have you ever met a man of good character where women are concerned?

PICKERING. Yes: very frequently.

HIGGINS [*dogmatically, lifting himself on his hands to the level of the piano, and sitting on it with a bounce*] Well, I havnt. I find that the moment I let a woman make friends with me, she becomes jealous, exacting, suspicious, and a damned nuisance. I find that the moment I let myself make friends with a woman, I become selfish and tyrannical. Women upset everything. When you let them into your life, you find that the woman is driving at one thing and youre driving at another.

PICKERING. At what, for example?

HIGGINS [*coming off the piano restlessly*] Oh, Lord knows! I suppose the woman wants to live her own life; and the man wants to live his; and each tries to drag the other on to the wrong track. One wants to go north and the other south; and the result is that both have to go east, though they both hate the east wind. [*He sits down on the bench at the keyboard*]. So here I am, a confirmed old bachelor, and likely to remain so.

PICKERING [*rising and standing over him gravely*] Come, Higgins! You know what I mean. If I'm to be in this business I shall feel responsible for that girl. I hope it's understood that no advantage is to be taken of her position.

HIGGINS. What! That thing! Sacred, I assure you. [*Rising to explain*] You see, she'll be a pupil; and teaching would be impossible unless pupils were sacred. Ive taught scores of American millionairesses how to speak English: the best looking women in the world. I'm seasoned. They might as well be blocks of wood. *I* might as well be a block of wood. It's—

Mrs. Pearce opens the door. She has Eliza's hat in her hand. Pickering retires to the easy-chair at the hearth and sits down.

HIGGINS [*eagerly*] Well, Mrs. Pearce: is it all right?

MRS. PEARCE [*at the door*] I just wish to trouble you with a word, if I may, Mr. Higgins.

HIGGINS. Yes, certainly. Come in. [*She comes forward*]. Dont burn that, Mrs. Pearce. I'll keep it as a curiosity. [*He takes the hat*].

MRS. PEARCE. Handle it carefully, sir, please. I had to promise her not to burn it; but I had better put it in the oven for a while.

HIGGINS [*putting it down hastily on the piano*] Oh! thank you. Well, what have you to say to me?

PICKERING. Am I in the way?

MRS. PEARCE. Not at all, sir. Mr. Higgins: will you please be very particular what you say before the girl?

HIGGINS [*sternly*] Of course. I'm always particular about what I say. Why do you say this to me?

MRS. PEARCE [*unmoved*] No, sir: youre not at all particular when youve mislaid anything or when you get a little impatient. Now it doesnt matter before me: I'm used to it. But you really must not swear before the girl.

HIGGINS [*indignantly*] *I* swear! [*Most emphatically*] I never swear. I detest the habit. What the devil do you mean?

MRS. PEARCE [*stolidly*] Thats what I mean, sir. You swear a great deal too much. I dont mind your damning and blasting, and what the devil and where the devil and who the devil—

Higgins. Mrs. Pearce: this language from your lips! Really!

Mrs. Pearce [*not to be put off*]—but there is a certain word I must ask you not to use. The girl has just used it herself because the bath was too hot. It begins with the same letter as bath. She knows no better: she learnt it at her mother's knee. But she must not hear it from your lips.

Higgins [*loftily*] I cannot charge myself with having ever uttered it, Mrs. Pearce. [*She looks at him steadfastly. He adds, hiding an uneasy conscience with a judicial air*] Except perhaps in a moment of extreme and justifiable excitement.

Mrs. Pearce. Only this morning, sir, you applied it to your boots, to the butter, and to the brown bread.

Higgins. Oh, that! Mere alliteration, Mrs. Pearce, natural to a poet.

Mrs. Pearce. Well, sir, whatever you choose to call it, I beg you not to let the girl hear you repeat it.

Higgins. Oh, very well, very well. Is that all?

Mrs. Pearce. No, sir. We shall have to be very particular with this girl as to personal cleanliness.

Higgins. Certainly. Quite right. Most important.

Mrs. Pearce. I mean not to be slovenly about her dress or untidy in leaving things about.

Higgins [*going to her solemnly*] Just so. I intended to call your attention to that [*He passes on to Pickering, who is enjoying the conversation immensely*]. It is these little things that matter, Pickering. Take care of the pence and the pounds will take care of themselves is as true of personal habits as of money. [*He comes to anchor on the hearthrug, with the air of a man in an unassailable position*].

Mrs. Pearce. Yes, sir. Then might I ask you not to come down to breakfast in your dressing-gown, or at any rate not to use it as a napkin to the extent you do, sir. And if you would be so good as not to eat everything off the same plate, and to remember not to put the porridge saucepan out of your hand on the clean tablecloth, it would be a better example to the girl. You know you nearly choked yourself with a fishbone in the jam only last week.

HIGGINS [*routed from the hearthrug and drifting back to the piano*] I may do these things sometimes in absence of mind; but surely I dont do them habitually. [*Angrily*] By the way: my dressing-gown smells most damnably of benzine.

MRS. PEARCE. No doubt it does, Mr. Higgins. But if you will wipe your fingers—

HIGGINS [*yelling*] Oh very well, very well: I'll wipe them in my hair in future.

MRS. PEARCE. I hope youre not offended, Mr. Higgins.

HIGGINS [*shocked at finding himself thought capable of an unamiable sentiment*] Not at all, not at all. Youre quite right, Mrs. Pearce: I shall be particularly careful before the girl. Is that all?

MRS. PEARCE. No, sir. Might she use some of those Japanese dresses you brought from abroad? I really cant put her back into her old things.

HIGGINS. Certainly. Anything you like. Is that all?

MRS. PEARCE. Thank you, sir. Thats all. [*She goes out*].

HIGGINS. You know, Pickering, that woman has the most extraordinary ideas about me. Here I am, a shy, diffident sort of man. Ive never been able to feel really grown-up and tremendous, like other chaps. And yet shes firmly persuaded that I'm an arbitrary overbearing bossing kind of person. I cant account for it.

Mrs. Pearce returns.

MRS. PEARCE. If you please, sir, the trouble's beginning already. Theres a dustman downstairs, Alfred

Doolittle, wants to see you.   He says you have his daughter here.

PICKERING [*rising*] Phew! I say! [*He retreats to the hearthrug*].

HIGGINS [*promptly*] Send the blackguard up.

MRS. PEARCE. Oh, very well, sir. [*She goes out*].

PICKERING. He may not be a blackguard, Higgins.

HIGGINS. Nonsense.   Of course hes a blackguard.

PICKERING. Whether he is or not, I'm afraid we shall have some trouble with him.

HIGGINS [*confidently*] Oh no: I think not.   If theres any trouble he shall have it with me, not I with him.   And we are sure to get something interesting out of him.

PICKERING. About the girl?

HIGGINS. No.   I mean his dialect.

PICKERING. Oh!

MRS. PEARCE [*at the door*] Doolittle, sir. [*She admits Doolittle and retires*].

Alfred Doolittle is an elderly but vigorous dustman, clad in the costume of his profession, including a hat with a back brim covering his neck and shoulders. He has well marked and rather interesting features, and seems equally free from fear and conscience. He has a remarkably expressive voice, the result of a habit of giving vent to his feelings without reserve. His present pose is that of wounded honor and stern resolution.

DOOLITTLE [*at the door, uncertain which of the two gentlemen is his man*] Professor Higgins?

HIGGINS. Here.   Good morning.   Sit down.

DOOLITTLE. Morning, Governor. [*He sits down magisterially*] I come about a very serious matter, Governor.

HIGGINS [*to Pickering*] Brought up in Hounslow. Mother Welsh, I should think.   [*Doolittle opens his mouth, amazed.   Higgins continues*] What do you want, Doolittle?

18

DOOLITTLE [*menacingly*] I want my daughter: thats what I want. See?

HIGGINS. Of course you do. Youre her father, arnt you? You dont suppose anyone else wants her, do you? I'm glad to see you have some spark of family feeling left. Shes upstairs. Take her away at once.

DOOLITTLE [*rising, fearfully taken aback*] What!

HIGGINS. Take her away. Do you suppose I'm going to keep your daughter for you?

DOOLITTLE [*remonstrating*] Now, now, look here, Governor. Is this reasonable? Is it fairity to take advantage of a man like this? The girl belongs to me. You got her. Where do I come in? [*He sits down again*].

HIGGINS. Your daughter had the audacity to come to my house and ask me to teach her how to speak properly so that she could get a place in a flower-shop. This gentleman and my housekeeper have been here all the time. [*Bullying him*] How dare you come here and attempt to blackmail me? You sent her here on purpose.

DOOLITTLE [*protesting*] No, Governor.

HIGGINS. You must have. How else could you possibly know that she is here?

DOOLITTLE. Dont take a man up like that, Governor.

HIGGINS. The police shall take you up. This is a plant—a plot to extort money by threats. I shall telephone for the police [*he goes resolutely to the telephone and opens the directory*].

DOOLITTLE. Have I asked you for a brass farthing? I leave it to the gentleman here: have I said a word about money?

HIGGINS [*throwing the book aside and marching down on Doolittle with a poser*] What else did you come for?

DOOLITTLE [*sweetly*] Well, what would a man come for? Be human, Governor.

HIGGINS [*disarmed*] Alfred: did you put her up to it?

DOOLITTLE. So help me, Governor, I never did. I

take my Bible oath I aint seen the girl these two months past.

HIGGINS. Then how did you know she was here?

DOOLITTLE [*"most musical, most melancholy"*] I'll tell you, Governor, if youll only let me get a word in. I'm willing to tell you. I'm wanting to tell you. I'm waiting to tell you.

HIGGINS. Pickering: this chap has a certain natural gift of rhetoric. Observe the rhythm of his native wood-notes wild. "I'm willing to tell you: I'm wanting to tell you: I'm waiting to tell you." Sentimental rhetoric! thats the Welsh strain in him. It also accounts for his mendacity and dishonesty.

PICKERING. Oh, p l e a s e, Higgins: I'm west country myself. [*To Doolittle*] How did you know the girl was here if you didnt send her?

DOOLITTLE. It was like this, Governor. The girl took a boy in the taxi to give him a jaunt. Son of her landlady, he is. He hung about on the chance of her giving him another ride home. Well, she sent him back for her luggage when she heard you was willing for her to stop here. I met the boy at the corner of Long Acre and Endell Street.

HIGGINS. Public house. Yes?

DOOLITTLE. The poor man's club, Governor: why shouldnt I?

PICKERING. Do let him tell his story, Higgins.

DOOLITTLE. He told me what was up. And I ask you, what was my feelings and my duty as a father? I says to the boy, "You bring me the luggage," I says—

PICKERING. Why didnt you go for it yourself?

DOOLITTLE. Landlady wouldnt have trusted me with it, Governor. Shes that kind of woman: you know. I had to give the boy a penny afore he trusted me with it, the little swine. I brought it to her just to oblige you like, and make myself agreeable. Thats all.

HIGGINS. How much luggage?

DOOLITTLE. Musical instrument, Governor. A few pictures, a trifle of jewelry, and a bird-cage. She said she didnt want no clothes. What was I to think from that, Governor? I ask you as a parent what was I to think?

HIGGINS. So you came to rescue her from worse than death, eh?

DOOLITTLE [*appreciatively: relieved at being so well understood*] Just so, Governor. Thats right.

PICKERING. But why did you bring her luggage if you intended to take her away?

DOOLITTLE. Have I said a word about taking her away? Have I now?

HIGGINS [*determinedly*] Youre going to take her away, double quick. [*He crosses to the hearth and rings the bell*].

DOOLITTLE [*rising*] No, Governor. Dont say that. I'm not the man to stand in my girl's light. Heres a career opening for her, as you might say; and—

Mrs. Pearce opens the door and awaits orders.

HIGGINS. Mrs. Pearce: this is Eliza's father. He has come to take her away. Give her to him. [*He goes back to the piano, with an air of washing his hands of the whole affair*].

DOOLITTLE. No. This is a misunderstanding. Listen here—

MRS. PEARCE. He cant take her away, Mr. Higgins: how can he? You told me to burn her clothes.

DOOLITTLE. Thats right. I cant carry the girl through the streets like a blooming monkey, can I? I put it to you.

HIGGINS. You have put it to me that you want your daughter. Take your daughter. If she has no clothes go out and buy her some.

DOOLITTLE [*desperate*] Wheres the clothes she come in? Did I burn them or did your missus here?

MRS. PEARCE. I am the housekeeper, if you please. I have sent for some clothes for your girl. When they come you can take her away. You can wait in the kitchen. This way, please.

Doolittle, much troubled, accompanies her to the door; then hesitates; finally turns confidentially to Higgins.

DOOLITTLE. Listen here, Governor. You and me is men of the world, aint we?

HIGGINS. Oh! Men of the world, are we? Youd better go, Mrs. Pearce.

MRS. PEARCE. I think so, indeed, sir. [*She goes, with dignity*].

PICKERING. The floor is yours, Mr. Doolittle.

DOOLITTLE [*to Pickering*] I thank you, Governor. [*To Higgins, who takes refuge on the piano bench, a little overwhelmed by the proximity of his visitor; for Doolittle has a professional flavor of dust about him*]. Well, the truth is, Ive taken a sort of fancy to you, Governor; and if you want the girl, I'm not so set on having her back home again but what I might be open to an arrangement. Regarded in the light of a young woman, shes a fine handsome girl. As a daughter shes not worth her keep; and so I tell you straight. All I ask is my rights as a father; and youre the last man alive to expect me to let her go for nothing; for I can see youre one of the straight sort, Governor. Well, whats a five pound note to you? And whats Eliza to me? [*He returns to his chair and sits down judicially*].

PICKERING. I think you ought to know, Doolittle, that Mr. Higgins's intentions are entirely honorable.

DOOLITTLE. Course they are, Governor. If I thought they wasnt, Id ask fifty.

HIGGINS [*revolted*] Do you mean to say, you callous rascal, that you would sell your daughter for £50?

DOOLITTLE. Not in a general way I wouldnt; but to

oblige a gentleman like you I'd do do a good deal, I do assure you.

PICKERING. Have you no morals, man?

DOOLITTLE [*unabashed*] Cant afford them, Governor. Neither could you if you was as poor as me. Not that I mean any harm, you know. But if Liza is going to have a bit out of this, why not me too?

HIGGINS [*troubled*] I dont know what to do, Pickering. There can be no question that as a matter of morals it's a positive crime to give this chap a farthing. And yet I feel a sort of rough justice in his claim.

DOOLITTLE. Thats it, Governor. Thats all I say. A father's heart, as it were.

PICKERING. Well, I know the feeling; but really it seems hardly right—

DOOLITTLE. Dont say that, Governor. Dont look at it that way. What am I, Governors both? I ask you, what am I? I'm one of the undeserving poor: thats what I am. Think of what that means to a man. It means that hes up agen middle class morality all the time. If theres anything going, and I put in for a bit of it, it's always the same story: "Youre undeserving; so you cant have it." But my needs is as great as the most deserving widow's that ever got money out of six different charities in one week for the death of the same husband. I dont need less than a deserving man: I need more. I dont eat less hearty than him; and I drink a lot more. I want a bit of amusement, cause I'm a thinking man. I want cheerfulness and a song and a band when I feel low. Well, they charge me just the same for everything as they charge the deserving. What is middle class morality? Just an excuse for never giving me anything. Therefore, I ask you, as two gentlemen, not to play that game on me. I'm playing straight with you. I aint pretending to be deserving. I'm undeserving; and I mean to go on being undeserving. I like it; and thats the truth. Will you take advantage of a man's nature to do him out of the price of his own daughter what hes brought up and fed and clothed by the sweat of his brow until shes growed big enough to be interesting to you two gentlemen? Is five pounds unreasonable? I put it to you; and I leave it to you.

HIGGINS [*rising, and going over to Pickering*] Pickering: if we were to take this man in hand for three months, he could choose between a seat in the Cabinet and a popular pulpit in Wales.

PICKERING. What do you say to that, Doolittle?

DOOLITTLE. Not me, Governor, thank you kindly. Ive heard all the preachers and all the prime ministers—for I'm a thinking man and game for politics or religion or social reform same as all the other amusements—and I tell you it's a dog's life anyway you look at it. Undeserving poverty is my line. Taking one station in society with another, it's—it's—well, it's the only one that has any ginger in it, to my taste.

HIGGINS. I suppose we must give him a fiver.

PICKERING. He'll make a bad use of it, I'm afraid.

DOOLITTLE. Not me, Governor, so help me I wont. Dont you be afraid that I'll save it and spare it and live idle on it. There wont be a penny of it left by Monday: I'll have to go to work same as if I'd never had it. It wont pauperize me, you bet. Just one good spree for myself and the missus, giving pleasure to ourselves and employment to others, and satisfaction to you to think it's not been throwed away. You couldnt spend it better.

HIGGINS [*taking out his pocket book and coming between Doolittle and the piano*] This is irresistible. Lets give him ten. [*He offers two notes to the dustman*].

DOOLITTLE. No, Governor. She wouldnt have the heart to spend ten; and perhaps I shouldnt neither. Ten pounds is a lot of money: it makes a man feel prudent like; and then goodbye to happiness. You give me what

I ask you, Governor: not a penny more, and not a penny less.

PICKERING. Why dont you marry that missus of yours? I rather draw the line at encouraging that sort of immorality.

DOOLITTLE. Tell her so, Governor: tell her so. *I'm* willing. It's me that suffers by it. Ive no hold on her. I got to be agreeable to her. I got to give her presents. I got to buy her clothes something sinful. I'm a slave to that woman, Governor, just because I'm not her lawful husband. And she knows it too. Catch her marrying me! Take my advice, Governor: marry Eliza while shes young and dont know no better. If you dont youll be sorry for it after. If you do, she'll be sorry for it after; but better you than her, because youre a man, and shes only a woman and dont know how to be happy anyhow.

HIGGINS. Pickering: if we listen to this man another minute, we shall have no convictions left. [*To Doolittle*] Five pounds I think you said.

DOOLITTLE. Thank you kindly, Governor.

HIGGINS. Youre sure you wont take ten?

DOOLITTLE. Not now. Another time, Governor.

HIGGINS [*handing him a five-pound note*] Here you are.

DOOLITTLE. Thank you, Governor. Good morning. [*He hurries to the door, anxious to get away with his booty. When he opens it he is confronted with a dainty and exquisitely clean young Japanese lady in a simple blue cotton kimono printed cunningly with small white jasmine blossoms. Mrs. Pearce is with her. He gets out of her way deferentially and apologizes*]. Beg pardon, miss.

THE JAPANESE LADY. Garn! Dont you know your own daughter?

DOOLITTLE	*exclaiming*	Bly me! it's Eliza!
HIGGINS	*simul-*	Whats that! This!
PICKERING	*taneously*	By Jove!

LIZA. Dont I look silly?

HIGGINS. Silly?

MRS. PEARCE [*at the door*] Now, Mr. Higgins, please dont say anything to make the girl conceited about herself.

HIGGINS [*conscientiously*] Oh! Quite right, Mrs. Pearce. [*To Eliza*] Yes: damned silly.

MRS. PEARCE. Please, sir.

HIGGINS [*correcting himself*] I mean extremely silly.

LIZA. I should look all right with my hat on. [*She takes up her hat; puts it on; and walks across the room to the fireplace with a fashionable air*].

HIGGINS. A new fashion, by George! And it ought to look horrible!

DOOLITTLE [*with fatherly pride*] Well, I never thought she'd clean up as good looking as that, Governor. Shes a credit to me, aint she?

LIZA. I tell you, it's easy to clean up here. Hot and cold water on tap, just as much as you like, there is. Woolly towels, there is; and a towel horse so hot, it burns your fingers. Soft brushes to scrub yourself, and a wooden bowl of soap smelling like primroses. Now I know why ladies is so clean. Washing's a treat for them. Wish they saw what it is for the like of me!

HIGGINS. I'm glad the bath-room met with your approval.

LIZA. It didnt: not all of it, and I dont care who hears me say it. Mrs. Pearce knows.

HIGGINS. What was wrong, Mrs. Pearce?

MRS. PEARCE [*blandly*] Oh, nothing, sir. It doesnt matter.

LIZA. I had a good mind to break it. I didnt know which way to look. But I hung a towel over it, I did.

HIGGINS. Over what?

MRS. PEARCE. Over the looking-glass, sir.

HIGGINS. Doolittle: you have brought your daughter up too strictly.

DOOLITTLE. Me! I never brought her up at all, except to give her a lick of a strap now and again. Dont put it on me, Governor. She aint accustomed to it, you see: thats all. But she'll soon pick up your free-and-easy ways.

LIZA. I'm a good girl, I am; and I wont pick up no free and easy ways.

HIGGINS. Eliza: if you say again that youre a good girl, your father shall take you home.

LIZA. Not him. You dont know my father. All he come here for was to touch you for some money to get drunk on.

DOOLITTLE. Well, what else would I want money for? To put into the plate in church, I suppose. [*She puts out her tongue at him. He is so incensed by this that Pickering presently finds it necessary to step between them*]. Dont you give me none of your lip; and dont let me hear you giving this gentleman any of it neither, or youll hear from me about it. See?

HIGGINS. Have you any further advice to give her before you go, Doolittle? Your blessing, for instance.

DOOLITTLE. No, Governor: I aint such a mug as to put up my children to all I know myself. Hard enough to hold them in without that. If you want Eliza's mind improved, Governor, you do it yourself with a strap. So long, gentlemen. [*He turns to go*].

HIGGINS [*impressively*] Stop. Youll come regularly to see your daughter. It's your duty, you know. My brother is a clergyman; and he could help you in your talks with her.

DOOLITTLE [*evasively*] Certainly. I'll come, Governor. Not just this week, because I have a job at a distance. But later on you may depend on me. Afternoon, gentlemen. Afternoon, maam. [*He takes off his hat to*

Mrs. Pearce, who disdains the salutation and goes out. He winks at Higgins, thinking him probably a fellow-sufferer from Mrs. Pearce's difficult disposition, and follows her].

LIZA. Dont you believe the old liar. He'd as soon you set a bull-dog on him as a clergyman. You wont see him again in a hurry.

HIGGINS. I dont want to, Eliza. Do you?

LIZA. Not me. I dont want never to see him again, I dont. Hes a disgrace to me, he is, collecting dust, instead of working at his trade.

PICKERING. What is his trade, Eliza?

LIZA. Talking money out of other people's pockets into his own. His proper trade's a navvy; and he works at it sometimes too—for exercise—and earns good money at it. Aint you going to call me Miss Doolittle any more?

PICKERING. I beg your pardon, Miss Doolittle. It was a slip of the tongue.

LIZA. Oh, I dont mind; only it sounded so genteel. I should just like to take a taxi to the corner of Tottenham Court Road and get out there and tell it to wait for me, just to put the girls in their place a bit. I wouldnt speak to them, you know.

PICKERING. Better wait til we get you something really fashionable.

HIGGINS. Besides, you shouldnt cut your old friends now that you have risen in the world. Thats what we call snobbery.

LIZA. You dont call the like of them my friends now, I should hope. Theyve took it out of me often enough with their ridicule when they had the chance; and now I mean to get a bit of my own back. But if I'm to have fashionable clothes, I'll wait. I should like to have some. Mrs. Pearce says youre going to give me some to wear in bed at night different to what I wear in the day-time; but it do seem a waste of money when you could get something to shew. Besides, I never could fancy changing into cold things on a winter night.

MRS. PEARCE [*coming back*] Now, Eliza. The new things have come for you to try on.

LIZA. Ah-ow-oo-ooh! [*She rushes out*].

MRS. PEARCE [*following her*] Oh, dont rush about like that, girl [*She shuts the door behind her*].

HIGGINS. Pickering: we have taken on a stiff job.

PICKERING [*with conviction*] Higgins: we have.

ACT III

It is Mrs. Higgins's at-home day. Nobody has yet arrived. Her drawing-room, in a flat on Chelsea embankment, has three windows looking on the river; and the ceiling is not so lofty as it would be in an older house of the same pretension. The windows are open, giving access to a balcony with flowers in pots. If you stand with your face to the windows, you have the fireplace on your left and the door in the right-hand wall close to the corner nearest the windows.

Mrs. Higgins was brought up on Morris and Burne Jones; and her room, which is very unlike her son's room in Wimpole Street, is not crowded with furniture and little tables and nicknacks. In the middle of the room there is a big ottoman; and this, with the carpet, the Morris wall-papers, and the Morris chintz window curtains and brocade covers of the ottoman and its cushions, supply all the ornament, and are much too handsome to be hidden by odds and ends of useless things. A few good oil-paintings from the exhibitions in the Grosvenor Gallery thirty years ago (the Burne Jones, not the Whistler side of them) are on the walls. The only landscape is a Cecil Lawson on the scale of a Rubens. There is a portrait of Mrs. Higgins as she was when she defied fashion in her youth in one of the beautiful Rossettian costumes which, when caricatured by people who did not understand, led to the absurdities of popular estheticism in the eighteen-seventies.

In the corner diagonally opposite the door Mrs. Higgins, now over sixty and long past taking the trouble to

157

*dress out of the fashion, sits writing at an elegantly
simple writing-table with a bell button within reach of
her hand. There is a Chippendale chair further back in
the room between her and the window nearest her side.
At the other side of the room, further forward, is an
Elizabethan chair roughly carved in the taste of Inigo
Jones. On the same side a piano in a decorated case. The
corner between the fireplace and the window is occupied
by a divan cushioned in Morris chintz.*

It is between four and five in the afternoon.

*The door is opened violently; and Higgins enters with
his hat on.*

MRS. HIGGINS [*dismayed*] Henry [*scolding him*]!
What are you doing here to-day? It is my at-home day:
you promised not to come. [*As he bends to kiss her, she
takes his hat off, and presents it to him*].

HIGGINS. Oh bother! [*He throws the hat down on the
table*].

MRS. HIGGINS. Go home at once.

HIGGINS [*kissing her*] I know, mother. I came on purpose.

MRS. HIGGINS. But you mustnt. I'm serious, Henry.
You offend all my friends: they stop coming whenever
they meet you.

HIGGINS. Nonsense! I know I have no small talk; but
people dont mind. [*He sits on the settee*].

MRS. HIGGINS. Oh! dont they? Small talk indeed!
What about your large talk? Really, dear, you mustnt
stay.

HIGGINS. I must. Ive a job for you. A phonetic job.

MRS. HIGGINS. No use, dear. I'm sorry; but I cant
get round your vowels; and though I like to get pretty
postcards in your patent shorthand, I always have to read
the copies in ordinary writing you so thoughtfully send
me.

HIGGINS. Well, this isnt a phonetic job.

MRS. HIGGINS. You said it was.

HIGGINS. Not your part of it. Ive picked up a girl.

MRS. HIGGINS. Does that mean that some girl has picked you up?

HIGGINS. Not at all. I dont mean a love affair.

MRS. HIGGINS. What a pity!

HIGGINS. Why?

MRS. HIGGINS. Well, you never fall in love with anyone under forty-five. When will you discover that there are some rather nice-looking young women about?

HIGGINS. Oh, I cant be bothered with young women. My idea of a loveable woman is something as like you as possible. I shall never get into the way of seriously liking young women: some habits lie too deep to be changed. [*Rising abruptly and walking about, jingling his money and his keys in his trouser pockets*] Besides, theyre all idiots.

MRS. HIGGINS. Do you know what you would do if you really loved me, Henry?

HIGGINS. Oh bother! What? Marry, I suppose?

MRS. HIGGINS. No. Stop fidgeting and take your hands out of your pockets. [*With a gesture of despair, he obeys and sits down again*]. Thats a good boy. Now tell me about the girl.

HIGGINS. Shes coming to see you.

MRS. HIGGINS. I dont remember asking her.

HIGGINS. You didnt. *I* asked her. If youd known her you wouldnt have asked her.

MRS. HIGGINS. Indeed! Why?

HIGGINS. Well, it's like this. Shes a common flower girl. I picked her off the kerbstone.

MRS. HIGGINS. And invited her to my at-home!

HIGGINS [*rising and coming to her to coax her*] Oh, thatll be all right. Ive taught her to speak properly; and she has strict orders as to her behavior. Shes to keep to two subjects: the weather and everybody's health—

Fine day and How do you do, you know—and not to let herself go on things in general. That will be safe.

Mrs. Higgins. Safe! To talk about our health! about our insides! perhaps about our outsides! How could you be so silly, Henry?

Higgins [*impatiently*] Well, she must talk about something. [*He controls himself and sits down again*]. Oh, she'll be all right: dont you fuss. Pickering is in it with me. Ive a sort of bet on that I'll pass her off as a duchess in six months. I started on her some months ago; and shes getting on like a house on fire. I shall win my bet. She has a quick ear; and shes been easier to teach than my middle-class pupils because shes had to learn a complete new language. She talks English almost as you talk French.

Mrs. Higgins. Thats satisfactory, at all events.

Higgins. Well, it is and it isnt.

Mrs. Higgins. What does that mean?

Higgins. You see, Ive got her pronunciation all right; but you have to consider not only how a girl pronounces, but what she pronounces; and thats where—

They are interrupted by the parlor-maid, announcing guests.

The Parlor-Maid. Mrs. and Miss Eynsford Hill. [*She withdraws*].

Higgins. Oh Lord! [*He rises; snatches his hat from the table; and makes for the door; but before he reaches it his mother introduces him*].

Mrs. and Miss Eynsford Hill are the mother and daughter who sheltered from the rain in Covent Garden. The mother is well bred, quiet, and has the habitual anxiety of straitened means. The daughter has acquired a gay air of being very much at home in society: the bravado of genteel poverty.

Mrs. Eynsford Hill [*to Mrs. Higgins*] How do you do? [*They shake hands*].

Miss Eynsford Hill. How d'you do? [*She shakes*].

Mrs. Higgins [*introducing*] My son Henry.

Mrs. Eynsford Hill. Your celebrated son! I have so longed to meet you, Professor Higgins.

Higgins [*glumly, making no movement in her direction*] Delighted. [*He backs against the piano and bows brusquely*].

Miss Eynsford Hill [*going to him with confident familiarity*] How do you do?

Higgins [*staring at her*] Ive seen you before somewhere. I havnt the ghost of a notion where; but Ive heard your voice. [*Drearily*] It doesnt matter. Youd better sit down.

Mrs. Higgins. I'm sorry to say that my celebrated son has no manners. You mustnt mind him.

Miss Eynsford Hill [*gaily*] I dont. [*She sits in the Elizabethan chair*].

Miss Eynsford Hill [*a little bewildered*] Not at all. [*She sits on the ottoman between her daughter and Mrs. Higgins, who has turned her chair away from the writing-table*].

Higgins. Oh, have I been rude? I didnt mean to be.

He goes to the central window, through which, with his back to the company, he contemplates the river and the flowers in Battersea Park on the opposite bank as if they were a frozen desert.

The parlor-maid returns, ushering in Pickering.

The Parlor-Maid. Colonel Pickering [*She withdraws*].

Pickering. How do you do, Mrs. Higgins?

Mrs. Higgins. So glad youve come. Do you know Mrs. Eynsford Hill—Miss Eynsford Hill? [*Exchange of bows. The Colonel brings the Chippendale chair a little forward between Mrs. Hill and Mrs. Higgins, and sits down*].

19

PICKERING. Has Henry told you what weve come for?

HIGGINS [*over his shoulder*] We were interrupted: damn it!

MRS. HIGGINS. Oh Henry, Henry, really!

MRS. EYNSFORD HILL [*half rising*] Are we in the way?

MRS. HIGGINS [*rising and making her sit down again*] No, no. You couldnt have come more fortunately: we want you to meet a friend of ours.

HIGGINS [*turning hopefully*] Yes, by George! We want two or three people. Youll do as well as anybody else.

The parlor-maid returns, ushering Freddy.

THE PARLOR-MAID. Mr. Eynsford Hill.

HIGGINS [*almost audibly, past endurance*] God of Heaven! another of them.

FREDDY [*shaking hands with Mrs. Higgins*] Ahdedo?

MRS. HIGGINS. Very good of you to come. [*Introducing*] Colonel Pickering.

FREDDY [*bowing*] Ahdedo?

MRS. HIGGINS. I dont think you know my son, Professor Higgins.

FREDDY [*going to Higgins*] Ahdedo?

HIGGINS [*looking at him much as if he were a pick-pocket*] I'll take my oath Ive met you before somewhere. Where was it?

FREDDY. I dont think so.

HIGGINS [*resignedly*] It dont matter, anyhow. Sit down.

He shakes Freddy's hand, and almost slings him on the ottoman with his face to the windows; then comes round to the other side of it.

HIGGINS. Well, here we are, anyhow! [*He sits down on the ottoman next Mrs. Eynsford Hill, on her left*]. And now, what the devil are we going to talk about until Eliza comes?

Mrs. Higgins. Henry: you are the life and soul of the Royal Society's soirées; but really youre rather trying on more commonplace occasions.

Higgins. Am I? Very sorry. [*Beaming suddenly*] I suppose I am, you know. [*Uproariously*] Ha, ha!

Miss Eynsford Hill [*who considers Higgins quite eligible matrimonially*] I sympathize. *I* havnt any small talk. If people would only be frank and say what they really think!

Higgins [*relapsing into gloom*] Lord forbid!

Mrs. Eynsford Hill [*taking up her daughter's cue*] But why?

Higgins. What they think they ought to think is bad enough, Lord knows; but what they really think would break up the whole show. Do you suppose it would be really agreeable if I were to come out now with what *I* really think?

Miss Eynsford Hill [*gaily*] Is it so very cynical?

Higgins. Cynical! Who the dickens said it was cynical? I mean it wouldnt be decent.

Mrs. Eynsford Hill [*seriously*] Oh! I'm sure you dont mean that, Mr. Higgins.

Higgins. You see, we're all savages, more or less. We're supposed to be civilized and cultured—to know all about poetry and philosophy and art and science, and so on; but how many of us know even the meanings of these names? [*To Miss Hill*] What do you know of poetry? [*To Mrs. Hill*] What do you know of science? [*Indicating Freddy*] What does he know of art or science or anything else? What the devil do you imagine I know of philosophy?

Mrs. Higgins [*warningly*] Or of manners, Henry?

The Parlor-Maid [*opening the door*] Miss Doolittle. [*She withdraws*].

Higgins [*rising hastily and running to Mrs. Higgins*] Here she is, mother. [*He stands on tiptoe and makes signs over his mother's head to Eliza to indicate to her which lady is her hostess*].

Eliza, who is exquisitely dressed, produces an impression of such remarkable distinction and beauty as she enters that they all rise, quite fluttered. Guided by Higgins's signals, she comes to Mrs. Higgins with studied grace.

Liza [*speaking with pedantic correctness of pronunciation and great beauty of tone*] How do you do, Mrs. Higgins? [*She gasps slightly in making sure of the H in Higgins, but is quite successful*]. Mr. Higgins told me I might come.

Mrs. Higgins [*cordially*] Quite right: I'm very glad indeed to see you.

Pickering. How do you do, Miss Doolittle?

Liza [*shaking hands with him*] Colonel Pickering, is it not?

Mrs. Eynsford Hill. I feel sure we have met before, Miss Doolittle. I remember your eyes.

Liza. How do you do? [*She sits down on the ottoman gracefully in the place just left vacant by Higgins*].

Mrs. Eynsford Hill [*introducing*] My daughter Clara.

Liza. How do you do?

Clara [*impulsively*] How do you do? [*She sits down on the ottoman beside Eliza, devouring her with her eyes*].

Freddy [*coming to their side of the ottoman*] Ive certainly had the pleasure.

Mrs. Eynsford Hill [*introducing*] My son Freddy.

Liza. How do you do?

Freddy bows and sits down in the Elizabethan chair, infatuated.

Higgins [*suddenly*] By George, yes: it all comes back to me! [*They stare at him*]. Covent Garden! [*Lamentably*] What a damned thing!

MRS. HIGGINS. Henry, please! [*He is about to sit on the edge of the table*]. Dont sit on my writing-table: youll break it.

HIGGINS [*sulkily*] Sorry.

He goes to the divan, stumbling into the fender and over the fire-irons on his way; extricating himself with muttered imprecations; and finishing his disastrous journey by throwing himself so impatiently on the divan that he almost breaks it. Mrs. Higgins looks at him, but controls herself and says nothing.

A long and painful pause ensues.

MRS. HIGGINS [*at last, conversationally*] Will it rain, do you think?

LIZA. The shallow depression in the west of these islands is likely to move slowly in an easterly direction. There are no indications of any great change in the barometrical situation.

FREDDY. Ha! ha! how awfully funny!

LIZA. What is wrong with that, young man? I bet I got it right.

FREDDY. Killing!

MRS. EYNSFORD HILL. I'm sure I hope it wont turn cold. Theres so much influenza about. It runs right through our whole family regularly every spring.

LIZA [*darkly*] My aunt died of influenza: so they said.

MRS. EYNSFORD HILL [*clicks her tongue sympathetically*]!!!

LIZA [*in the same tragic tone*] But it's my belief they done the old woman in.

MRS. HIGGINS [*puzzled*] Done her in?

LIZA. Y-e-e-e-es, Lord love you! Why should she die of influenza? She come through diphtheria right enough the year before. I saw her with my own eyes. Fairly blue with it, she was. They all thought she was dead; but my father he kept ladling gin down her throat til she came to so sudden that she bit the bowl off the spoon.

Mrs. Eynsford Hill [*startled*] Dear me!

Liza [*piling up the indictment*] What call would a woman with that strength in her have to die of influenza? What become of her new straw hat that should have come to me? Somebody pinched it; and what I say is, them as pinched it done her in.

Mrs. Eynsford Hill. What does doing her in mean?

Higgins [*hastily*] Oh, thats the new small talk. To do a person in means to kill them.

Mrs. Eynsford Hill [*to Eliza, horrified*] You surely dont believe that your aunt was killed?

Liza. ~~Do I not~~! Them she lived with would have killed her for a hat-pin, let alone a hat.

Mrs. Eynsford Hill. But it cant have been right for your father to pour spirits down her throat like that. It might have killed her.

Liza. Not her. Gin was mother's milk to her. Besides, he'd poured so much down his own throat that he knew the good of it.

Mrs. Eynsford Hill. Do you mean that he drank?

Liza. Drank! My word! Something chronic.

Mrs. Eynsford Hill. How dreadful for you!

Liza. Not a bit. It never did him no harm what I could see. But then he did not keep it up regular. [*Cheerfully*] On the burst, as you might say, from time to time. And always more agreeable when he had a drop in. When he was out of work, my mother used to give him fourpence and tell him to go out and not come back until he'd drunk himself cheerful and loving-like. Theres lots of women has to make their husbands drunk to make them fit to live with. [*Now quite at her ease*] You see, it's like this. If a man has a bit of a conscience, it always takes him when he's sober; and then it makes him low-spirited. A drop of booze just takes that off and makes him happy. [*To Freddy, who is in convul-*

sions of suppressed laughter] Here! what are you sniggering at?

FREDDY. The new small talk. You do it so awfully well.

LIZA. If I was doing it proper, what was you laughing at? [*To Higgins*] Have I said anything I oughtnt?

MRS. HIGGINS [*interposing*] Not at all, Miss Doolittle.

LIZA. Well, thats a mercy, anyhow. [*Expansively*] What I always say is—

HIGGINS [*rising and looking at his watch*] Ahem!

LIZA [*looking round at him; taking the hint; and rising*] Well: I must go. [*They all rise. Freddy goes to the door*]. So pleased to have met you. Good-bye. [*She shakes hands with Mrs. Higgins*].

MRS. HIGGINS. Good-bye.

LIZA. Good-bye, Colonel Pickering.

PICKERING. Good-bye, Miss Doolittle. [*They shake hands*].

LIZA [*nodding to the others*] Good-bye, all.

FREDDY [*opening the door for her*] Are you walking across the Park, Miss Doolittle? If so—

LIZA. Walk! Not bloody likely. [*Sensation*]. I am going in a taxi. [*She goes out*].

Pickering gasps and sits down. Freddy goes out on the balcony to catch another glimpse of Eliza.

MRS. EYNSFORD HILL [*suffering from shock*] Well, I really cant get used to the new ways.

CLARA [*throwing herself discontentedly into the Elizabethan chair*]. Oh, it's all right, mamma, quite right. People will think we never go anywhere or see anybody if you are so old-fashioned.

MRS. EYNSFORD HILL. I daresay I am very old-fashioned; but I do hope you wont begin using that expression, Clara. I have got accustomed to hear you talking about men as rotters, and calling everything filthy and beastly; though I do think it horrible and unladylike. But this last is really too much. Dont you think so, Colonel Pickering?

PICKERING. Dont ask me. Ive been away in India for several years; and manners have changed so much that I sometimes dont know whether I'm at a respectable dinner-table or in a ship's forecastle.

CLARA. It's all a matter of habit. Theres no right or wrong in it. Nobody means anything by it. And it's so quaint, and gives such a smart emphasis to things that are not in themselves very witty. I find the new small talk delightful and quite innocent.

MRS. EYNSFORD HILL [*rising*] Well, after that, I think it's time for us to go.

Pickering and Higgins rise.

CLARA [*rising*] Oh yes: we have three at-homes to go to still. Good-bye, Mrs. Higgins. Good-bye, Colonel Pickering. Good-bye, Professor Higgins.

HIGGINS [*coming grimly at her from the divan, and accompanying her to the door*] Good-bye. Be sure you try on that small talk at the three at-homes. Dont be nervous about it. Pitch it in strong.

CLARA [*all smiles*] I will. Good-bye. Such nonsense, all this early Victorian prudery!

HIGGINS [*tempting her*] Such damned nonsense!

CLARA. Such bloody nonsense!

MRS. EYNSFORD HILL [*convulsively*] Clara!

CLARA. Ha! ha! [*She goes out radiant, conscious of being thoroughly up to date, and is heard descending the stairs in a stream of silvery laughter*].

FREDDY [*to the heavens at large*] Well, I ask you— [*He gives it up, and comes to Mrs. Higgins*]. Good-bye.

MRS. HIGGINS [*shaking hands*] Good-bye. Would you like to meet Miss Doolittle again?

FREDDY [*eagerly*] Yes, I should, most awfully.

MRS. HIGGINS. Well, you know my days.

FREDDY. Yes. Thanks awfully. Good-bye. [*He goes out*].

MRS. EYNSFORD HILL. Good-bye, Mr. Higgins.

HIGGINS. Good-bye. Good-bye.

MRS. EYNSFORD HILL [*to Pickering*] It's no use. I shall never be able to bring myself to use that word.

PICKERING. Dont. It's not compulsory, you know. Youll get on quite well without it.

MRS. EYNSFORD HILL. Only, Clara is so down on me if I am not positively reeking with the latest slang. Good-bye.

PICKERING. Good-bye [*They shake hands*].

MRS. EYNSFORD HILL [*to Mrs. Higgins*] You mustnt mind Clara. [*Pickering, catching from her lowered tone that this is not meant for him to hear, discreetly joins Higgins at the window*]. We're so poor! and she gets so few parties, poor child! She doesnt quite know. [*Mrs. Higgins, seeing that her eyes are moist, takes her hand sympathetically and goes with her to the door*]. But the boy is nice. Dont you think so?

MRS. HIGGINS. Oh, quite nice. I shall always be delighted to see him.

MRS. EYNSFORD HILL. Thank you, dear. Good-bye. [*She goes out*].

HIGGINS [*eagerly*] Well? Is Eliza presentable [*he swoops on his mother and drags her to the ottoman, where she sits down in Eliza's place with her son on her left*]?

Pickering returns to his chair on her right.

MRS. HIGGINS. You silly boy, of course shes not presentable. Shes a triumph of your art and of her dressmaker's; but if you suppose for a moment that she doesnt give herself away in every sentence she utters, you must be perfectly cracked about her.

PICKERING. But dont you think something might be

done? I mean something to eliminate the sanguinary element from her conversation.

MRS. HIGGINS. Not as long as she is in Henry's hands.

HIGGINS [*aggrieved*] Do you mean that my language is improper?

MRS. HIGGINS. No, dearest: it would be quite proper —say on a canal barge; but it would not be proper for her at a garden party.

HIGGINS [*deeply injured*] Well I must say—

PICKERING [*interrupting him*] Come, Higgins: you must learn to know yourself. I havnt heard such language as yours since we used to review the volunteers in Hyde Park twenty years ago.

HIGGINS [*sulkily*] Oh, well, if you say so, I suppose I dont always talk like a bishop.

MRS. HIGGINS [*quieting Henry with a touch*] Colonel Pickering: will you tell me what is the exact state of things in Wimpole Street?

PICKERING [*cheerfully: as if this completely changed the subject*] Well, I have come to live there with Henry. We work together at my Indian Dialects; and we think it more convenient—

MRS. HIGGINS. Quite so. I know all about that: it's an excellent arrangement. But where does this girl live?

HIGGINS. With us, of course. Where would she live?

MRS. HIGGINS. But on what terms? Is she a servant? If not, what is she?

PICKERING [*slowly*] I think I know what you mean, Mrs. Higgins.

HIGGINS. Well, dash me if *I* do! Ive had to work at the girl every day for months to get her to her present pitch. Besides, shes useful. She knows where my things are, and remembers my appointments and so forth.

MRS. HIGGINS. How does your housekeeper get on with her?

HIGGINS. Mrs. Pearce? Oh, shes jolly glad to get so

much taken off her hands; for before Eliza came, she used to have to find things and remind me of my appointments. But shes got some silly bee in her bonnet about Eliza. She keeps saying "You dont think, sir": doesnt she, Pick?

PICKERING. Yes: thats the formula. "You dont think, sir." Thats the end of every conversation about Eliza.

HIGGINS. As if I ever stop thinking about the girl and her confounded vowels and consonants. I'm worn out, thinking about her, and watching her lips and her teeth and her tongue, not to mention her soul, which is the quaintest of the lot.

MRS. HIGGINS. You certainly are a pretty pair of babies, playing with your live doll.

HIGGINS. Playing! The hardest job I ever tackled: make no mistake about that, mother. But you have no idea how frightfully interesting it is to take a human being and change her into a quite different human being by creating a new speech for her. It's filling up the deepest gulf that separates class from class and soul from soul.

PICKERING [drawing his chair closer to Mrs. Higgins and bending over to her eagerly] Yes: it's enormously interesting. I assure you, Mrs. Higgins, we take Eliza very seriously. Every week—every day almost—there is some new change. [Closer again] We keep records of every stage—dozens of gramophone disks and photographs—

HIGGINS [assailing her at the other ear] Yes, by George: it's the most absorbing experiment I ever tackled. She regularly fills our lives up; doesnt she, Pick?

PICKERING. We're always talking Eliza.

HIGGINS. Teaching Eliza.

PICKERING. Dressing Eliza.

MRS. HIGGINS. What!

HIGGINS. Inventing new Elizas.

HIGGINS.		You know, she has the most extraordinary quickness of ear:
[*speaking together*]		
PICKERING.		I assure you, my dear Mrs. Higgins, that girl
HIGGINS.		just like a parrot. Ive tried her with every
PICKERING.		is a genius. She can play the piano quite beautifully.
HIGGINS.		possible sort of sound that a human being can make—
PICKERING.		We have taken her to classical concerts and to music
HIGGINS.		Continental dialects, African dialects, Hottentot
PICKERING.		halls; and it's all the same to her: she plays everything
HIGGINS.		clicks, things it took me years to get hold of; and
PICKERING.		she hears right off when she comes home, whether it's
HIGGINS.		she picks them up like a shot, right away, as if she had
PICKERING.		Beethoven and Brahms or Lehar and Lionel Monckton;
HIGGINS.		been at it all her life.
PICKERING.		though six months ago, she'd never as much as touched a piano—

MRS. HIGGINS [*putting her fingers in her ears, as they are by this time shouting one another down with an intolerable noise*] Sh-sh-sh—sh! [*They stop*].

PICKERING. I beg your pardon. [*He draws his chair back apologetically*].

HIGGINS. Sorry. When Pickering starts shouting nobody can get a word in edgeways.

MRS. HIGGINS. Be quiet, Henry. Colonel Pickering: dont you realize that when Eliza walked into Wimpole Street, something walked in with her?

PICKERING. Her father did. But Henry soon got rid of him.

MRS. HIGGINS. It would have been more to the point if her mother had. But as her mother didnt something else did.

PICKERING. But what?

MRS. HIGGINS [*unconsciously dating herself by the word*] A problem.

PICKERING. Oh, I see. The problem of how to pass her off as a lady.

HIGGINS. I'll solve that problem. Ive half solved it already.

MRS. HIGGINS. No, you two infinitely stupid male creatures: the problem of what is to be done with her afterwards.

HIGGINS. I dont see anything in that. She can go her own way, with all the advantages I have given her.

MRS. HIGGINS. The advantages of that poor woman who was here just now! The manners and habits that disqualify a fine lady from earning her own living without giving her a fine lady's income! Is that what you mean?

PICKERING [*indulgently, being rather bored*] Oh, that will be all right, Mrs. Higgins. [*He rises to go*].

HIGGINS [*rising also*] We'll find her some light employment.

PICKERING. Shes happy enough. Dont you worry about her. Good-bye. [*He shakes hands as if he were consoling a frightened child, and makes for the door*].

HIGGINS. Anyhow, theres no good bothering now. The things done. Good-bye, mother. [*He kisses her, and follows Pickering*].

PICKERING [*turning for a final consolation*] There are plenty of openings. We'll do whats right. Good-bye.

HIGGINS [*to Pickering as they go out together*] Let's take her to the Shakespear exhibition at Earls Court.

PICKERING. Yes: lets. Her remarks will be delicious.

HIGGINS. She'll mimic all the people for us when we get home.

PICKERING. Ripping. [*Both are heard laughing as they go downstairs*].

MRS. HIGGINS [*rises with an impatient bounce, and returns to her work at the writing-table. She sweeps a litter of disarranged papers out of her way; snatches a sheet of paper from her stationery case; and tries resolutely to write. At the third line she gives it up; flings down her pen; grips the table angrily and exclaims*] Oh, men! men!! men!!!

ACT IV

The Wimpole Street laboratory. Midnight. Nobody in the room. The clock on the mantelpiece strikes twelve. The fire is not alight: it is a summer night.

Presently Higgins and Pickering are heard on the stairs.

HIGGINS [*calling down to Pickering*] I say, Pick: lock up, will you. I shant be going out again.

PICKERING. Right. Can Mrs. Pearce go to bed? We dont want anything more, do we?

HIGGINS. Lord, no!

Eliza opens the door and is seen on the lighted landing in opera cloak, brilliant evening dress, and diamonds, with fan, flowers, and all accessories. She comes to the hearth, and switches on the electric lights there. She is tired: her pallor contrasts strongly with her dark eyes and hair; and her expression is almost tragic. She takes off her cloak; puts her fan and flowers on the piano; and sits down on the bench, brooding and silent. Higgins, in evening dress, with overcoat and hat, comes in, carrying a smoking jacket which he has picked up downstairs. He takes off the hat and overcoat; throws them carelessly on the newspaper stand; disposes of his coat in the same way; puts on the smoking jacket; and throws himself wearily into the easy-chair at the hearth. Pickering, similarly attired, comes in. He also takes off his hat and overcoat, and is about to throw them on Higgins's when he hesitates.

PICKERING. I say: Mrs. Pearce will row if we leave these things lying about in the drawing-room.

175

HIGGINS. Oh, chuck them over the bannisters into the hall. She'll find them there in the morning and put them away all right. She'll think we were drunk.

PICKERING. We are, slightly. Are there any letters?

HIGGINS. I didnt look. [*Pickering takes the overcoats and hats and goes down stairs. Higgins begins half singing half yawning an air from La Fanciulla del Golden West. Suddenly he stops and exclaims*] I wonder where the devil my slippers are!

Eliza looks at him darkly; then rises suddenly and leaves the room.

Higgins yawns again, and resumes his song.

Pickering returns, with the contents of the letter-box in his hand.

PICKERING. Only circulars, and this coroneted billet-doux for you. [*He throws the circulars into the fender, and posts himself on the hearthrug, with his back to the grate*].

HIGGINS [*glancing at the billet-doux*] Money-lender. [*He throws the letter after the circulars*].

Eliza returns with a pair of large down-at-heel slippers. She places them on the carpet before Higgins, and sits as before without a word.

HIGGINS [*yawning again*] Oh Lord! What an evening! What a crew! What a silly tomfoollery! [*He raises his shoe to unlace it, and catches sight of the slippers. He stops unlacing and looks at them as if they had appeared there of their own accord*]. Oh! theyre there, are they?

PICKERING [*stretching himself*] Well, I feel a bit tired. It's been a long day. The garden party, a dinner party, and the opera! Rather too much of a good thing. But youve won your bet, Higgins. Eliza did the trick, and something to spare, eh?

HIGGINS [*fervently*] Thank God it's over!

Eliza flinches violently; but they take no notice of her; and she recovers herself and sits stonily as before.

PICKERING. Were you nervous at the garden party? *I* was. Eliza didnt seem a bit nervous.

HIGGINS. Oh, she wasnt nervous. I knew she'd be all right. No: it's the strain of putting the job through all these months that has told on me. It was interesting enough at first, while we were at the phonetics; but after that I got deadly sick of it. If I hadnt backed myself to do it I should have chucked the whole thing up two months ago. It was a silly notion: the whole thing has been a bore.

PICKERING. Oh come! the garden party was frightfully exciting. My heart began beating like anything.

HIGGINS. Yes, for the first three minutes. But when I saw we were going to win hands down, I felt like a bear in a cage, hanging about doing nothing. The dinner was worse: sitting gorging there for over an hour, with nobody but a damned fool of a fashionable woman to talk to! I tell you, Pickering, never again for me. No more artificial duchesses. The whole thing has been simple purgatory.

PICKERING. Youve never been broken in properly to the social routine. [*Strolling over to the piano*] I rather enjoy dipping into it occasionally myself: it makes me feel young again. Anyhow, it was a great success: an immense success. I was quite frightened once or twice because Eliza was doing it so well. You see, lots of the real people cant do it at all: theyre such fools that they think style comes by nature to people in their position; and so they never learn. Theres always something professional about doing a thing superlatively well.

HIGGINS. Yes: thats what drives me mad: the silly people dont know their own silly business. [*Rising*] However, it's over and done with; and now I can go to bed at last without dreading tomorrow.

20

Eliza's beauty becomes murderous.

PICKERING. I think I shall turn in too. Still, it's been a great occasion: a triumph for you. Good-night. [*He goes*].

HIGGINS [*following him*] Good-night. [*Over his shoulder, at the door*] Put out the lights, Eliza; and tell Mrs. Pearce not to make coffee for me in the morning: I'll take tea. [*He goes out*].

Eliza tries to control herself and feel indifferent as she rises and walks across to the hearth to switch off the lights. By the time she gets there she is on the point of screaming. She sits down in Higgins's chair and holds on hard to the arms. Finally she gives way and flings herself furiously on the floor raging.

HIGGINS [*in despairing wrath outside*] What the devil have I done with my slippers? [*He appears at the door*].

LIZA [*snatching up the slippers, and hurling them at him one after the other with all her force*] There are your slippers. And there. Take your slippers; and may you never have a day's luck with them!

HIGGINS [*astounded*] What on earth—! [*He comes to her*]. Whats the matter? Get up. [*He pulls her up*]. Anything wrong?

LIZA [*breathless*] Nothing wrong—with y o u. Ive won your bet for you, havnt I? Thats enough for you. *I* dont matter, I suppose.

HIGGINS. Y o u won my bet! You! Presumptuous insect! *I* won it. What did you throw those slippers at me for?

LIZA. Because I wanted to smash your face. I'd like to kill you, you selfish brute. Why didnt you leave me where you picked me out of—in the gutter? You thank God it's all over, and that now you can throw me back again there, do you? [*She crisps her fingers frantically*].

HIGGINS [*looking at her in cool wonder*] The creature i s nervous, after all.

LIZA [*gives a suffocated scream of fury, and instinctively darts her nails at his face*]!!

HIGGINS [*catching her wrists*] Ah! would you? Claws in, you cat. How dare you shew your temper to me? Sit down and be quiet. [*He throws her roughly into the easy-chair*].

LIZA [*crushed by superior strength and weight*] Whats to become of me? Whats to become of me?

HIGGINS. How the devil do I know whats to become of you? What does it matter what becomes of you?

LIZA. You dont care. I know you dont care. You wouldnt care if I was dead. I'm nothing to you—not so much as them slippers.

HIGGINS [*thundering*] Those slippers.

LIZA [*with bitter submission*] Those slippers. I didnt think it made any difference now.

A pause. Eliza hopeless and crushed. Higgins a little uneasy.

HIGGINS [*in his loftiest manner*] Why have you begun going on like this? May I ask whether you complain of your treatment here?

LIZA. No.

HIGGINS. Has anybody behaved badly to you? Colonel Pickering? Mrs. Pearce? Any of the servants?

LIZA. No.

HIGGINS. I presume you dont pretend that *I* have treated you badly.

LIZA. No.

HIGGINS. I am glad to hear it. [*He moderates his tone*]. Perhaps youre tired after the strain of the day. Will you have a glass of champagne? [*He moves towards the door*].

LIZA. No. [*Recollecting her manners*] Thank you.

HIGGINS [*good-humored again*] This has been coming on you for some days. I suppose it was natural for you to be anxious about the garden party. But thats all over

now. [*He pats her kindly on the shoulder.   She writhes*].
Theres nothing more to worry about.

LIZA. No. Nothing more for y o u to worry about. [*She suddenly rises and gets away from him by going to the piano bench, where she sits and hides her face*]. Oh God! I wish I was dead.

HIGGINS [*staring after her in sincere surprise*] Why? in heaven's name, why? [*Reasonably, going to her*] Listen to me, Eliza. All this irritation is purely subjective.

LIZA. I dont understand. I'm too ignorant.

HIGGINS. It's only imagination. Low spirits and nothing else. Nobody's hurting you. Nothing's wrong. You go to bed like a good girl and sleep it off. Have a little cry and say your prayers: that will make you comfortable.

LIZA. I heard y o u r prayers. "Thank God it's all over!"

HIGGINS [*impatiently*] Well, dont you thank God it's all over? Now you are free and can do what you like.

LIZA [*pulling herself together in desperation*] What am I fit for? What have you left me fit for? Where am I to go? What am I to do? Whats to become of me?

HIGGINS [*enlightened, but not at all impressed*] Oh, thats whats worrying you, is it? [*He thrusts his hands into his pockets, and walks about in his usual manner, rattling the contents of his pockets, as if condescending to a trivial subject out of pure kindness*]. I shouldnt bother about it if I were you. I should imagine you wont have much difficulty in settling yourself somewhere or other, though I hadnt quite realized that you were going away. [*She looks quickly at him: he does not look at her, but examines the dessert stand on the piano and decides that he will eat an apple*].   You might marry, you know. [*He bites a large piece out of the apple, and munches it noisily*].   You see, Eliza, all men are not confirmed old bachelors like me and the Colonel. Most men are the marrying sort (poor devils!); and youre not bad-looking; it's quite a pleasure to look at you sometimes—not now, of course, because youre crying and looking as ugly as the very devil; but when youre all right and quite your-self, youre what I should call attractive. That is, to the people in the marrying line, you understand. You go to bed and have a good nice rest; and then get up and look at yourself in the glass; and you wont feel so cheap.

Eliza again looks at him, speechless, and does not stir.

The look is quite lost on him: he eats his apple with a dreamy expression of happiness, as it is quite a good one.

HIGGINS [*a genial afterthought occurring to him*] I daresay my mother could find some chap or other who would do very well.

LIZA. We were above that at the corner of Tottenham Court Road.

HIGGINS [*waking up*] What do you mean?

LIZA. I sold flowers. I didnt sell myself. Now youve made a lady of me I'm not fit to sell anything else. I wish youd left me where you found me.

HIGGINS [*slinging the core of the apple decisively into the grate*] Tosh, Eliza. Dont you insult human relations by dragging all this cant about buying and selling into it. You neednt marry the fellow if you dont like him.

LIZA. What else am I to do?

HIGGINS. Oh, lots of things. What about your old idea of a florist's shop? Pickering could set you up in one: hes lots of money. [*Chuckling*] He'll have to pay for all those togs you have been wearing today; and that, with the hire of the jewellery, will make a big hole in two hundred pounds. Why, six months ago you would have thought it the millennium to have a flower shop of your own. Come! youll be all right. I must clear off to bed: I'm devilish sleepy. By the way, I came down for something: I forget what it was.

LIZA. Your slippers.

HIGGINS. Oh yes, of course. You shied them at me. [*He picks them up, and is going out when she rises and speaks to him*].

LIZA. Before you go, sir—

HIGGINS [*dropping the slippers in his surprise at her calling him Sir*] Eh?

LIZA. Do my clothes belong to me or to Colonel Pickering?

HIGGINS [*coming back into the room as if her question were the very climax of unreason*] What the devil use would they be to Pickering?

LIZA. He might want them for the next girl you pick up to experiment on.

HIGGINS [*shocked and hurt*] Is t h a t the way you feel towards us?

LIZA. I dont want to hear anything more about that. All I want to know is whether anything belongs to me. My own clothes were burnt.

HIGGINS. But what does it matter? Why need you start bothering about that in the middle of the night?

LIZA. I want to know what I may take away with me. I dont want to be accused of stealing.

HIGGINS [*now deeply wounded*] Stealing! You shouldnt have said that, Eliza. That shews a want of feeling.

LIZA. I'm sorry. I'm only a common ignorant girl; and in my station I have to be careful. There cant be any feelings between the like of you and the like of me. Please will you tell me what belongs to me and what doesn't?

HIGGINS [*very sulky*] You may take the whole damned

houseful if you like. Except the jewels. Theyre hired. Will that satisfy you? [*He turns on his heel and is about to go in extreme dudgeon*].

LIZA [*drinking in his emotion like nectar, and nagging him to provoke a further supply*] Stop, please. [*She takes off her jewels*]. Will you take these to your room and keep them safe? I dont want to run the risk of their being missing.

HIGGINS [*furious*] Hand them over. [*She puts them into his hands*]. If these belonged to me instead of to the jeweler, I'd ram them down your ungrateful throat. [*He perfunctorily thrusts them into his pockets, unconsciously decorating himself with the protruding ends of the chains*].

LIZA [*taking a ring off*] This ring isnt the jeweler's: it's the one you bought me in Brighton. I dont want it now. [*Higgins dashes the ring violently into the fireplace, and turns on her so threateningly that she crouches over the piano with her hands over her face, and exclaims*] Dont you hit me.

HIGGINS. Hit you! You infamous creature, how dare you accuse me of such a thing? It is you who have hit me. You have wounded me to the heart.

LIZA [*thrilling with hidden joy*] I'm glad. Ive got a little of my own back, anyhow.

HIGGINS [*with dignity, in his finest professional style*] You have caused me to lose my temper: a thing that has hardly ever happend to me before. I prefer to say nothing more tonight. I am going to bed.

LIZA [*pertly*] Youd better leave a note for Mrs. Pearce about the coffee; for she wont be told by me.

HIGGINS [*formally*] Damn Mrs. Pearce; and damn the coffee; and damn you; and damn my own folly in having lavished hard-earned knowledge and the treasure of my regard and intimacy on a heartless guttersnipe. [*He goes out with impressive decorum, and spoils it by slamming the door savagely*].

Eliza smiles for the first time; expresses her feelings by a wild pantomime in which an imitation of Higgins's exit is confused with her own triumph; and finally goes down on her knees on the hearthrug to look for the ring.

ACT V

Mrs. Higgins's drawing-room. She is at her writing-table as before. The parlor-maid comes in.

THE PARLOR-MAID [*at the door*] Mr. Henry, mam, is downstairs with Colonel Pickering.

MRS. HIGGINS. Well, shew them up.

THE PARLOR-MAID. Theyre using the telephone, mam. Telephoning to the police, I think.

MRS. HIGGINS. What!

THE PARLOR-MAID [*coming further in and lowering her voice*] Mr. Henry's in a state, mam. I thought I'd better tell you.

MRS. HIGGINS. If you had told me that Mr. Henry was not in a state it would have been more surprising. Tell them to come up when theyve finished with the police. I suppose hes lost something.

THE PARLOR-MAID. Yes, mam [*going*].

MRS. HIGGINS. Go upstairs and tell Miss Doolittle that Mr. Henry and the Colonel are here. Ask her not to come down till I send for her.

THE PARLOR-MAID. Yes, mam.

Higgins bursts in. He is, as the parlor-maid has said, in a state.

HIGGINS. Look here, mother: heres a confounded thing!

MRS. HIGGINS. Yes, dear. Good-morning. [*He checks his impatience and kisses her, whilst the parlor-maid goes out*]. What is it?

HIGGINS. Eliza's bolted.

MRS. HIGGINS [*calmly continuing her writing*] You must have frightened her.

HIGGINS. Frightened her! nonsense! She was left last night, as usual, to turn out the lights and all that; and instead of going to bed she changed her clothes and went right off: her bed wasnt slept in. She came in a cab for her things before seven this morning; and that fool Mrs. Pearce let her have them without telling me a word about it. What am I to do?

MRS. HIGGINS. Do without, I'm afraid, Henry. The girl has a perfect right to leave if she chooses.

HIGGINS [*wandering distractedly across the room*] But I cant find anything. I dont know what appointments Ive got. I'm— [*Pickering comes in. Mrs. Higgins puts down her pen and turns away from the writing-table*].

PICKERING [*shaking hands*] Good-morning, Mrs. Higgins. Has Henry told you? [*He sits down on the ottoman*].

HIGGINS. What does that ass of an inspector say? Have you offered a reward?

MRS. HIGGINS [*rising in indignant amazement*] You dont mean to say you have set the police after Eliza?

HIGGINS. Of course. What are the police for? What else could we do? [*He sits in the Elizabethan chair*].

PICKERING. The inspector made a lot of difficulties. I really think he suspected us of some improper purpose.

MRS. HIGGINS. Well, of course he did. What right have you to go to the police and give the girl's name as if she were a thief, or a lost umbrella, or something? Really! [*She sits down again, deeply vexed*].

HIGGINS. But we want to find her.

PICKERING. We cant let her go like this, you know, Mrs. Higgins. What were we to do?

MRS. HIGGINS. You have no more sense, either of you, than two children. Why—

The parlor-maid comes in and breaks off the conversation.

THE PARLOR-MAID. Mr. Henry: a gentleman wants to see you very particular. Hes been sent on from Wimpole Street.

HIGGINS. Oh, bother! I cant see anyone now. Who is it?

THE PARLOR-MAID. A Mr. Doolittle, sir.

PICKERING. Doolittle! Do you mean the dustman?

THE PARLOR-MAID. Dustman! Oh no, sir: a gentleman.

HIGGINS [*springing up excitedly*] By George, Pick, it's some relative of hers that shes gone to. Somebody we know nothing about. [*To the parlor-maid*] Send him up, quick.

THE PARLOR-MAID. Yes, sir. [*She goes*].

HIGGINS [*eagerly, going to his mother*] Genteel relatives! now we shall hear something. [*He sits down in the Chippendale chair*].

MRS. HIGGINS. Do you know any of her people?

PICKERING. Only her father: the fellow we told you about.

THE PARLOR-MAID [*announcing*] Mr. Doolittle. [*She withdraws*].

Doolittle enters. He is brilliantly dressed in a new fashionable frock-coat, with white waistcoat and grey trousers. A flower in his buttonhole, a dazzling silk hat, and patent leather shoes complete the effect. He is too concerned with the business he has come on to notice Mrs. Higgins. He walks straight to Higgins, and accosts him with vehement reproach.

DOOLITTLE [*indicating his own person*] See here! Do you see this? You done this.

HIGGINS. Done what, man?

DOOLITTLE. This, I tell you. Look at it. Look at this hat. Look at this coat.

PICKERING. Has Eliza been buying you clothes?

DOOLITTLE. Eliza! not she. Not half. Why would she buy me clothes?

MRS. HIGGINS. Good-morning, Mr. Doolittle. Wont you sit down?

DOOLITTLE [*taken aback as he becomes conscious that he has forgotten his hostess*] Asking your pardon, maam. [*He approaches her and shakes her proffered hand*]. Thank you. [*He sits down on the ottoman, on Pickering's right*]. I am that full of what has happened to me that I cant think of anything else.

HIGGINS. What the dickens has happened to you?

DOOLITTLE. I shouldnt mind if it had only happened to me: anything might happen to anybody and nobody to blame but Providence, as you might say. But this is something that you done to me: yes, you, Henry Higgins.

HIGGINS. Have you found Eliza? Thats the point.

DOOLITTLE. Have you lost her?

HIGGINS. Yes.

DOOLITTLE. You have all the luck, you have. I aint found her; but she'll find me quick enough now after what you done to me.

MRS. HIGGINS. But what has my son done to you, Mr. Doolittle?

DOOLITTLE. Done to me! Ruined me. Destroyed my happiness. Tied me up and delivered me into the hands of middle class morality.

HIGGINS [*rising intolerantly and standing over Doolittle*] Youre raving. Youre drunk. Youre mad. I gave you five pounds. After that I had two conversations with you, at half-a-crown an hour. Ive never seen you since.

DOOLITTLE. Oh! Drunk! am I? Mad! am I? Tell me this. Did you or did you not write a letter to an old blighter in America that was giving five millions to found

Moral Reform Societies all over the world, and that
wanted you to invent a universal language for him?

HIGGINS. What! Ezra D. Wannafeller! Hes dead.
[*He sits down again carelessly*].

DOOLITTLE. Yes: hes dead; and I'm done for. Now
did you or did you not write a letter to him to say that
the most original moralist at present in England, to
the best of your knowledge, was Alfred Doolittle, a
common dustman.

HIGGINS. Oh, after your last visit I remember making
some silly joke of the kind.

DOOLITTLE. Ah! you may well call it a silly joke. It
put the lid on me right enough. Just give him the chance
he wanted to shew that Americans is not like us: that
they recognize and respect merit in every class of life,
however humble. Them words is in his blooming will,
in which, Henry Higgins, thanks to your silly joking, he
leaves me a share in his Pre-digested Cheese Trust worth
three thousand a year on condition that I lecture for his
Wannafeller Moral Reform World League as often as
they ask me up to six times a year.

HIGGINS. The devil he does! Whew! [*Brightening
suddenly*] What a lark!

PICKERING. A safe thing for you, Doolittle. They
wont ask you twice.

DOOLITTLE. It aint the lecturing I mind. I'll lecture
them blue in the face, I will, and not turn a hair. It's
making a gentleman of me that I object to. Who asked
him to make a gentleman of me? I was happy. I was
free. I touched pretty nigh everybody for money when I
wanted it, same as I touched you, Henry Higgins. Now
I am worrited; tied neck and heels; and everybody
touches me for money. It's a fine thing for you, says my
solicitor. Is it? says I. You mean it's a good thing for you,
I says. When I was a poor man and had a solicitor
once when they found a pram in the dust cart, he got

me off, and got shut of me and got me shut of him as
quick as he could. Same with the doctors: used to shove
me out of the hospital before I could hardly stand on my
legs, and nothing to pay. Now they finds out that I'm
not a healthy man and cant live unless they looks after
me twice a day. In the house I'm not let do a hand's
turn for myself: somebody else must do it and touch me
for it. A year ago I hadnt a relative in the world except
two or three that wouldnt speak to me. Now Ive fifty,
and not a decent week's wages among the lot of them.
I have to live for others and not for myself: thats middle class morality. You talk of losing Eliza. Dont you be
anxious: I bet shes on my doorstep by this: she that could
support herself easy by selling flowers if I wasnt respectable.   And the next one to touch me will be you,
Henry Higgins. I'll have to learn to speak middle class
language from you, instead of speaking proper English.
Thats where youll come in; and I daresay thats what you
done it for.

Mrs. Higgins. But, my dear Mr. Doolittle, you need
not suffer all this if you are really in earnest. Nobody
can force you to accept this bequest. You can repudiate
it. Isnt that so, Colonel Pickering?

Pickering. I believe so.

Doolittle [*softening his manner in deference to her
sex*] Thats the tragedy of it, maam.   It's easy to say
chuck it; but I havent the nerve. Which of us has? We're
all intimidated.   Intimidated, maam: thats what we are.
What is there for me if I chuck it but the workhouse in
my old age? I have to dye my hair already to keep my
job as a dustman. If I was one of the deserving poor, and
had put by a bit, I could chuck it; but then why should
I, acause the deserving poor might as well be millionaires
for all the happiness they ever has.   They dont know
what happiness is. But I, as one of the undeserving poor,
have nothing between me and the pauper's uniform but

this here blasted three thousand a year that shoves me into the middle class. (Excuse the expression, maam: youd use it yourself if you had my provocation). Theyve got you every way you turn: it's a choice between the Skilly of the workhouse and the Char Bydis of the middle class; and I havnt the nerve for the workhouse.   Intimidated: thats what I am. Broke. Bought up. Happier men than me will call for my dust, and touch me for their tip; and I'll look on helpless, and envy them. And thats what your son has brought me to. [*He is overcome by emotion*].

MRS. HIGGINS. Well, I'm very glad youre not going to do anything foolish, Mr. Doolittle. For this solves the problem of Eliza's future. You can provide for her now.

DOOLITTLE [*with melancholy resignation*] Yes, maam: I'm expected to provide for everyone now, out of three thousand a year.

HIGGINS [*jumping up*] Nonsense! he cant provide for her. He shant provide for her. She doesnt belong to him. I paid him five pounds for her. Doolittle: either youre an honest man or a rogue.

DOOLITTLE [*tolerantly*] A little of both, Henry, like the rest of us: a little of both.

HIGGINS. Well, you took that money for the girl; and you have no right to take her as well.

MRS. HIGGINS. Henry: dont be absurd. If you really want to know where Eliza is, she is upstairs.

HIGGINS [*amazed*] Upstairs!!! Then I shall jolly soon fetch her downstairs. [*He makes resolutely for the door*].

MRS. HIGGINS [*rising and following him*] Be quiet, Henry. Sit down.

HIGGINS. I—

MRS. HIGGINS. Sit down, dear; and listen to me.

HIGGINS. Oh very well, very well, very well. [*He throws himself ungraciously on the ottoman, with his face towards the windows*]. But I think you might have told me this half an hour ago.

MRS. HIGGINS. Eliza came to me this morning. She passed the night partly walking about in a rage, partly trying to throw herself into the river and being afraid to, and partly in the Carlton Hotel. She told me of the brutal way you two treated her.

HIGGINS [*bounding up again*] What!

PICKERING [*rising also*] My dear Mrs. Higgins, shes been telling you stories. We didnt treat her brutally. We hardly said a word to her; and we parted on particularly good terms. [*Turning on Higgins*]. Higgins did you bully her after I went to bed?

HIGGINS. Just the other way about. She threw my slippers in my face. She behaved in the most outrageous way. I never gave her the slightest provocation. The slippers came bang into my face the moment I entered the room—before I had uttered a word. And used perfectly awful language.

PICKERING [*astonished*] But why? What did we do to her?

MRS. HIGGINS. I think I know pretty well what you did. The girl is naturally rather affectionate, I think. Isnt she, Mr. Doolittle?

DOOLITTLE. Very tender-hearted, maam. Takes after me.

MRS. HIGGINS. Just so. She had become attached to you both. She worked very hard for you, Henry! I dont think you quite realize what anything in the nature of brain work means to a girl like that. Well, it seems that when the great day of trial came, and she did this wonderful thing for you without making a single mistake, you two sat there and never said a word to her, but talked together of how glad you were that it was all over and how you had been bored with the whole thing. And then you were surprised because she threw your slippers at you! *I* should have thrown the fire-irons at you.

HIGGINS. We said nothing except that we were tired and wanted to go to bed. Did we, Pick?

PICKERING [*shrugging his shoulders*] That was all.

MRS. HIGGINS [*ironically*] Quite sure?

PICKERING. Absolutely. Really, that was all.

MRS. HIGGINS. You didn't thank her, or pet her, or admire her, or tell her how splendid she'd been.

HIGGINS [*impatiently*] But she knew all about that. We didnt make speeches to her, if thats what you mean.

PICKERING [*conscience stricken*] Perhaps we were a little inconsiderate. Is she very angry?

MRS. HIGGINS [*returning to her place at the writing-table*] Well, I'm afraid she wont go back to Wimpole Street, especially now that Mr. Doolittle is able to keep up the position you have thrust on her; but she says she is quite willing to meet you on friendly terms and to let bygones be bygones.

HIGGINS [*furious*] Is she, by George? Ho!

MRS. HIGGINS. If you promise to behave yourself, Henry, I'll ask her to come down. If not, go home; for you have taken up quite enough of my time.

HIGGINS. Oh, all right. Very well. Pick: you behave yourself. Let us put on our best Sunday manners for this creature that we picked out of the mud. [*He flings himself sulkily into the Elizabethan chair*].

DOOLITTLE [*remonstrating*] Now, now, Henry Higgins! have some consideration for my feelings as a middle class man.

MRS. HIGGINS. Remember your promise, Henry. [*She presses the bell-button on the writing-table*]. Mr. Doolittle: will you be so good as to step out on the balcony for a moment. I dont want Eliza to have the shock of your news until she has made it up with these two gentlemen. Would you mind?

21

DOOLITTLE. As you wish, lady. Anything to help Henry to keep her off my hands. [*He disappears through the window*].

The parlor-maid answers the bell. Pickering sits down in Doolittle's place.

MRS. HIGGINS. Ask Miss Doolittle to come down, please.

THE PARLOR-MAID. Yes, mam. [*She goes out*].

MRS. HIGGINS. Now, Henry: be good.

HIGGINS. I am behaving myself perfectly.

PICKERING. He is doing his best, Mrs. Higgins.

A pause. Higgins throws back his head; stretches out his legs; and begins to whistle.

MRS. HIGGINS. Henry, dearest, you dont look at all nice in that attitude.

HIGGINS [*pulling himself together*] I was not trying to look nice, mother.

MRS. HIGGINS. It doesnt matter, dear. I only wanted to make you speak.

HIGGINS. Why?

MRS. HIGGINS. Because you cant speak and whistle at the same time.

Higgins groans. Another very trying pause.

HIGGINS [*springing up, out of patience*] Where the devil is that girl? Are we to wait here all day?

Eliza enters, sunny, self-possessed, and giving a staggeringly convincing exhibition of ease of manner. She carries a little work-basket, and is very much at home. Pickering is too much taken aback to rise.

LIZA. How do you do, Professor Higgins? Are you quite well?

HIGGINS [*choking*] Am I— [*He can say no more*].

LIZA. But of course you are: you are never ill. So glad to see you again, Colonel Pickering. [*He rises hastily; and they shake hands*]. Quite chilly this morning, isnt it? [*She sits down on his left. He sits beside her*].

HIGGINS. Dont you dare try this game on me. I taught
it to you; and it doesnt take me in. Get up and come
home; and dont be a fool.

*Eliza takes a piece of needlework from her basket, and
begins to stitch at it, without taking the least notice of
this outburst.*

MRS. HIGGINS. Very nicely put, indeed, Henry. No
woman could resist such an invitation.

HIGGINS. You let her alone, mother. Let her speak for
herself. You will jolly soon see whether she has an idea
that I havnt put into her head or a word that I havnt
put into her mouth. I tell you I have created this thing
out of the squashed cabbage leaves of Covent Garden;
and now she pretends to play the fine lady with me.

MRS. HIGGINS [*placidly*] Yes, dear; but youll sit down,
wont you?

Higgins sits down again, savagely.

LIZA [*to Pickering, taking no apparent notice of Higgins, and working away deftly*] Will you drop me altogether now that the experiment is over, Colonel Pickering?

PICKERING. Oh dont. You mustnt think of it as an experiment. It shocks me, somehow.

LIZA. Oh, I'm only a squashed cabbage leaf—

PICKERING [*impulsively*] No.

LIZA [*continuing quietly*]—but I owe so much to you
that I should be very unhappy if you forgot me.

PICKERING. It's very kind of you to say so, Miss Doolittle.

LIZA. It's not because you paid for my dresses. I know
you are generous to everybody with money. But it was
from you that I learnt really nice manners; and that is
what makes one a lady, isnt it? You see it was so very
difficult for me with the example of Professor Higgins always before me. I was brought up to be just like him,
unable to control myself, and using bad language on the

slightest provocation. And I should never have known that ladies and gentlemen didnt behave like that if you hadnt been there.

HIGGINS. Well!!

PICKERING. Oh, thats only his way, you know. He doesnt mean it.

LIZA. Oh, *I* didnt mean it either, when I was a flower girl. It was only my way. But you see I did it; and thats what makes the difference after all.

PICKERING. No doubt. Still, he taught you to speak; and I couldnt have done that, you know.

LIZA [*trivially*] Of course: that is his profession.

HIGGINS. Damnation!

LIZA [*continuing*] It was just like learning to dance in the fashionable way: there was nothing more than that in it. But do you know what began my real education?

PICKERING. What?

LIZA [*stopping her work for a moment*] Your calling me Miss Doolittle that day when I first came to Wimpole Street. That was the beginning of self-respect for me. [*She resumes her stitching*]. And there were a hundred little things you never noticed, because they came naturally to you. Things about standing up and taking off your hat and opening door—

PICKERING. Oh, that was nothing.

LIZA. Yes: things that shewed you thought and felt about me as if I were something better than a scullery-maid; though of course I know you would have been just the same to a scullery-maid if she had been let in the drawing-room. You never took off your boots in the dining room when I was there.

PICKERING. You mustnt mind that. Higgins takes off his boots all over the place.

LIZA. I know. I am not blaming him. It is his way, isnt it? But it made such a difference to me that you didnt do it. You see, really and truly, apart from the things

anyone can pick up (the dressing and the proper way
of speaking, and so on), the difference between a lady
and a flower girl is not how she behaves, but how shes
treated. I shall always be a flower girl to Professor Higgins, because he always treats me as a flower girl, and
always will; but I know I can be a lady to you, because
you always treat me as a lady, and always will.

MRS. HIGGINS. Please dont grind your teeth, Henry.

PICKERING. Well, this is really very nice of you, Miss
Doolittle.

LIZA. I should like you to call me Eliza, now, if you
would.

PICKERING. Thank you. Eliza, of course.

LIZA. And I should like Professor Higgins to call me
Miss Doolittle.

HIGGINS.   I'll see you damned first.

MRS. HIGGINS. Henry! Henry!

PICKERING [*laughing*] Why dont you slang back at
him? Dont stand it. It would do him a lot of good.

LIZA. I cant. I could have done it once; but now I cant
go back to it. Last night, when I was wandering about, a
girl spoke to me; and I tried to get back into the old
way with her; but it was no use. You told me, you know,
that when a child is brought to a foreign country, it picks
up the language in a few weeks, and forgets its own.
Well, I am a child in your country.   I have forgotten
my own language, and can speak nothing but yours.
Thats the real break-off with the corner of Tottenham
Court Road.   Leaving Wimpole Street finishes it.

PICKERING [*much alarmed*] Oh! but youre coming
back to Wimpole Street, arnt you? Youll forgive Higgins?

HIGGINS [*rising*] Forgive! Will she, by George! Let
her go. Let her find out how she can get on without us.
She will relapse into the gutter in three weeks without
me at her elbow.

Doolittle appears at the centre window.   With a look of dignified reproach at Higgins, he comes slowly and silently to his daughter, who, with her back to the window, is unconscious of his approach.

PICKERING. Hes incorrigible, Eliza. You wont relapse, will you?

LIZA. No: Not now. Never again. I have learnt my lesson. I dont believe I could utter one of the old sounds if I tried. [*Doolittle touches her on her left shoulder. She drops her work, losing her self-possession utterly at the spectacle of her father's splendor*] A-a-a-a-a-ah-owooh!

HIGGINS [*with a crow of triumph*] Aha! Just so. A-a-a-a-ahowooh! A-a-a-a-ahowooh! A-a-a-a-ahowooh! Victory! Victory! [*He throws himself on the divan, folding his arms, and spraddling arrogantly*].

DOOLITTLE. Can you blame the girl? Dont look at me like that, Eliza. It aint my fault. Ive come into some money.

LIZA. You must have touched a millionaire this time, dad.

DOOLITTLE. I have. But I'm dressed something special today. I'm going to St. George's, Hanover Square. Your stepmother is going to marry me.

LIZA [*angrily*] Youre going to let yourself down to marry that low common woman!

PICKERING [*quietly*] He ought to, Eliza. [*To Doolittle*] Why has she changed her mind?

DOOLITTLE [*sadly*] Intimidated, Governor. Intimidated. Middle class morality claims its victim. Wont you put on your hat, Liza, and come and see me turned off?

LIZA. If the Colonel says I must, I—I'll [*almost sobbing*] I'll demean myself. And get insulted for my pains, like enough.

DOOLITTLE. Dont be afraid: she never comes to words

with anyone now, poor woman! respectability has broke
all the spirit out of her.

PICKERING [*squeezing Eliza's elbow gently*] Be kind
to them, Eliza. Make the best of it.

LIZA [*forcing a little smile for him through her vexa-
tion*] Oh well, just to shew theres no ill feeling.   I'll be
back in a moment. [*She goes out*].

DOOLITTLE [*sitting down beside Pickering*] I feel uncommon nervous about the ceremony, Colonel.   I wish
youd come and see me through it.

PICKERING. But youve been through it before, man.
You were married to Eliza's mother.

DOOLITTLE. Who told you that, Colonel?

PICKERING. Well, nobody told me. But I concluded—
naturally—

DOOLITTLE. No: that aint the natural way, Colonel:
it's only the middle class way. My way was always the
undeserving way. But dont say nothing to Eliza. She
dont know: I always had a delicacy about telling her.

PICKERING. Quite right. We'll leave it so, if you dont
mind.

DOOLITTLE. And youll come to the church, Colonel,
and put me through straight?

PICKERING. With pleasure. As far as a bachelor can.

MRS. HIGGINS. May I come, Mr. Doolittle? I should
be very sorry to miss your wedding.

DOOLITTLE.   I should indeed be honored by your condescension, maam; and my poor old woman would take it
as a tremenjous compliment. Shes been very low, thinking
of the happy days that are no more.

MRS. HIGGINS [*rising*] I'll order the carriage and get
ready. [*The men rise, except Higgins*]. I shant be more
than fifteen minutes. [*As she goes to the door Eliza comes
in, hatted and buttoning her gloves*]. I'm going to the
church to see your father married, Eliza. You had better

come in the brougham with me. Colonel Pickering can go on with the bridegroom.

Mrs. Higgins goes out. Eliza comes to the middle of the room between the centre window and the ottoman. Pickering joins her.

DOOLITTLE. Bridegroom! What a word! It makes a man realize his position, somehow. [*He takes up his hat and goes towards the door*].

PICKERING. Before I go, Eliza, do forgive him and come back to us.

LIZA. I dont think papa would allow me. Would you, dad?

DOOLITTLE [*sad but magnanimous*] They played you off very cunning, Eliza, them two sportsmen. If it had been only one of them, you could have nailed him. But you see, there was two; and one of them chaperoned the other, as you might say. [*To Pickering*] It was artful of you, Colonel; but I bear no malice: I should have done the same myself. I been the victim of one woman after another all my life; and I dont grudge you two getting the better of Eliza. I shant interfere. It's time for us to go, Colonel. So long, Henry. See you in St. George's, Eliza. [*He goes out*].

PICKERING [*coaxing*] Do stay with us, Eliza. [*He follows Doolittle*].

Eliza goes out on the balcony to avoid being alone with Higgins. He rises and joins her there. She immediately comes back into the room and makes for the door; but he goes along the balcony quickly and gets his back to the door before she reaches it.

HIGGINS. Well, Eliza, youve had a bit of your own back, as you call it. Have you had enough? and are you going to be reasonable? Or do you want any more?

LIZA. You want me back only to pick up your slippers and put up with your tempers and fetch and carry for you.

HIGGINS. I havnt said I wanted you back at all.

LIZA. Oh, indeed. Then what are we talking about?

HIGGINS. About you, not about me. If you come back I shall treat you just as I have always treated you. I cant change my nature; and I dont intend to change my manners. My manners are exactly the same as Colonel Pickering's.

LIZA. Thats not true. He treats a flower girl as if she was a duchess.

HIGGINS. And I treat a duchess as if she was a flower girl.

LIZA. I see. [*She turns away composedly, and sits on the ottoman, facing the window*]. The same to everybody.

HIGGINS. Just so.

LIZA. Like father.

HIGGINS [*grinning, a little taken down*] Without accepting the comparison at all points, Eliza, it's quite true that your father is not a snob, and that he will be quite at home in any station of life to which his eccentric destiny may call him. [*Seriously*] The great secret, Eliza, is not having bad manners or good manners or any other particular sort of manners, but having the same manner for all human souls: in short, behaving as if you were in Heaven, where there are no third-class carriages, and one soul is as good as another.

LIZA. Amen. You are a born preacher.

HIGGINS [*irritated*] The question is not whether I treat you rudely, but whether you ever heard me treat anyone else better.

LIZA [*with sudden sincerity*] I dont care how you treat me. I dont mind your swearing at me. I dont mind a black eye: Ive had one before this. But [*standing up and facing him*] I wont be passed over.

HIGGINS. Then get out of my way; for I wont stop for you. You talk about me as if I were a motor bus.

LIZA. So you are a motor bus: all bounce and go, and no consideration for anyone. But I can do without you: dont think I cant.

HIGGINS. I know you can. I told you you could.

LIZA [*wounded, getting away from him to the other side of the ottoman with her face to the hearth*] I know you did, you brute. You wanted to get rid of me.

HIGGINS. Liar.

LIZA. Thank you. [*She sits down with dignity*].

HIGGINS. You never asked yourself, I suppose, whether *I* could do without y o u.

LIZA [*earnestly*] Dont you try to get round me. Youll h a v e to do without me.

HIGGINS [*arrogant*] I can do without anybody. I have my own soul: my own spark of divine fire. But [*with sudden humility*] I shall miss you, Eliza. [*He sits down near her on the ottoman*]. I have learnt something from your idiotic notions: I confess that humbly and gratefully. And I have grown accustomed to your voice and appearance. I like them, rather.

LIZA. Well, you have both of them on your gramophone and in your book of photographs. When you feel lonely without me, you can turn the machine on. It's got no feelings to hurt.

HIGGINS. I cant turn your soul on. Leave me those feelings; and you can take away the voice and the face. They are not you.

LIZA. Oh, you a r e a devil. You can twist the heart in a girl as easy as some could twist her arms to hurt her. Mrs. Pearce warned me. Time and again she has wanted to leave you; and you always got round her at the last minute. And you dont care a bit for her. And you dont care a bit for me.

HIGGINS. I care for life, for humanity; and you are a part of it that has come my way and been built into my house. What more can you or anyone ask?

LIZA. I wont care for anybody that doesnt care for me.

HIGGINS. Commercial principles, Eliza. Like [*reproducing her Covent Garden pronunciation with professional exactness*] s'yollin voylets [selling violets], isnt it?

LIZA. Dont sneer at me. It's mean to sneer at me.

HIGGINS. I have never sneered in my life. Sneering doesnt become either the human face or the human soul. I am expressing my righteous contempt for Commercialism. I dont and wont trade in affection. You call me a brute because you couldnt buy a claim on me by fetching my slippers and finding my spectacles. You were a fool: I think a woman fetching a man's slippers is a disgusting sight: did I ever fetch y o u r slippers? I think a good deal more of you for throwing them in my face. No use slaving for me and then saying you want to be cared for: who cares for a slave? If you come back, come back for the sake of good fellowship; for youll get nothing else. Youve had a thousand times as much out of me as I have out of you; and if you dare to set up your little dog's tricks of fetching and carrying slippers against my creation of a Duchess Eliza, I'll slam the door in your silly face.

LIZA. What did you do it for if you didnt care for me?

HIGGINS [*heartily*] Why, because it was my job.

LIZA. You never thought of the trouble it would make for me.

HIGGINS. Would the world ever have been made if its maker had been afraid of making trouble? Making life means making trouble. Theres only one way of escaping trouble; and thats killing things. Cowards, you notice, are always shrieking to have troublesome people killed.

LIZA. I'm no preacher: I dont notice things like that. I notice that you dont notice me.

HIGGINS [*jumping up and walking about intolerantly*] Eliza: youre an idiot. I waste the treasures of my Miltonic mind by spreading them before you. Once for all, understand that I go my way and do my work without caring twopence what happens to either of us. I am not intimidated, like your father and your stepmother. So you can come back or go to the devil: which you please.

LIZA. What am I to come back for?

HIGGINS [*bouncing up on his knees on the ottoman and leaning over it to her*] For the fun of it. Thats why I took you on.

LIZA [*with averted face*] And you may throw me out tomorrow if I dont do everything you want me to?

HIGGINS. Yes; and you may walk out tomorrow if I dont do everything y o u want me to.

LIZA. And live with my stepmother?

HIGGINS. Yes, or sell flowers.

LIZA. Oh! if I only c o u l d go back to my flower basket! I should be independent of both you and father and all the world! Why did you take my independence from me? Why did I give it up? I'm a slave now, for all my fine clothes.

HIGGINS. Not a bit. I'll adopt you as my daughter and settle money on you if you like. Or would you rather marry Pickering?

LIZA [*looking fiercely round at him*] I wouldnt marry y o u if you asked me; and youre nearer my age than what he is.

HIGGINS [*gently*] Than he is: not "than what he is."

LIZA [*losing her temper and rising*] I'll talk as I like. Youre not my teacher now.

HIGGINS [*reflectively*] I dont suppose Pickering would, though. Hes as confirmed an old bachelor as I am.

LIZA. Thats not what I want; and dont you think it. Ive always had chaps enough wanting me that way. Freddy Hill writes to me twice and three times a day, sheets and sheets.

HIGGINS [*disagreeably surprised*] Damn his impudence! [*He recoils and finds himself sitting on his heels*].

LIZA.   He has a right to if he likes, poor lad. And he does love me.

HIGGINS [*getting off the ottoman*] You have no right to encourage him.

LIZA.   Every girl has a right to be loved.

HIGGINS.   What! By fools like that?

LIZA.   Freddy's not a fool. And if hes weak and poor and wants me, may be hed make me happier than my betters that bully me and dont want me.

HIGGINS.   Can he m a k e anything of you? Thats the point.

LIZA.   Perhaps I could make something of him. But I never thought of us making anything of one another; and you never think of anything else. I only want to be natural.

HIGGINS.   In short, you want me to be as infatuated about you as Freddy? Is that it?

LIZA.   No I dont. Thats not the sort of feeling I want from you. And dont you be too sure of yourself or of me. I could have been a bad girl if I'd liked. Ive seen more of some things than you, for all your learning. Girls like me can drag gentlemen down to make love to them easy enough. And they wish each other dead the next minute.

HIGGINS.   Of course they do. Then what in thunder are we quarrelling about?

LIZA [*much troubled*] I want a little kindness. I know I'm a common ignorant girl, and you a book-learned gentleman; but I'm not dirt under your feet. What I done [*correcting herself*] what I did was not for the dresses and the taxis: I did it because we were pleasant together and I come—came—to care for you; not to want you to make love to me, and not forgetting the difference between us, but more friendly like.

HIGGINS. Well, of course. Thats just how I feel. And how Pickering feels. Eliza: youre a fool.

LIZA. Thats not a proper answer to give me [*she sinks on the chair at the writing-table in tears*].

HIGGINS. It's all youll get until you stop being a common idiot. If youre going to be a lady, youll have to give up feeling neglected if the men you know dont spend half their time snivelling over you and the other half giving you black eyes. If you cant stand the coldness of my sort of life, and the strain of it, go back to the gutter. Work til you are more a brute than a human being; and then cuddle and squabble and drink til you fall asleep. Oh, it's a fine life, the life of the gutter. It's real: it's warm: it's violent: you can feel it through the thickest skin: you can taste it and smell it without any training or any work. Not like Science and Literature and Classical Music and Philosophy and Art. You find me cold, un-feeling, selfish, dont you? Very well: be off with you to the sort of people you like. Marry some sentimental hog or other with lots of money, and a thick pair of lips to kiss you with and a thick pair of boots to kick you with. If you cant appreciate what youve got, youd better get what you can appreciate.

LIZA [*desperate*] Oh, you are a cruel tyrant. I cant talk to you: you turn everything against me: I'm always in the wrong. But you know very well all the time that youre nothing but a bully. You know I cant go back to the gutter, as you call it, and that I have no real friends in the world but you and the Colonel. You know well I couldnt bear to live with a low common man after you two; and it's wicked and cruel of you to insult me by pre-tending I could. You think I must go back to Wimpole Street because I have nowhere else to go but father's. But dont you be too sure that you have me under your feet to be trampled on and talked down. I'll marry Freddy, I will, as soon as hes able to support me.

HIGGINS [*sitting down beside her*] Rubbish! you shall marry an ambassador. You shall marry the Governor-General of India or the Lord-Lieutenant of Ireland, or somebody who wants a deputy-queen. I'm not going to have my masterpiece thrown away on Freddy.

LIZA. You think I like you to say that. But I havnt forgot what you said a minute ago; and I wont be coaxed round as if I was a baby or a puppy. If I cant have kindness, I'll have independence.

HIGGINS.   Independence? Thats middle class blasphemy. We are all dependent on one another, every soul of us on earth.

LIZA [*rising determinedly*] I'll let you see whether I'm dependent on you. If you can preach, I can teach. I'll go and be a teacher.

HIGGINS. Whatll you teach, in heaven's name?

LIZA. What you taught me. I'll teach phonetics.

HIGGINS. Ha! Ha! Ha!

LIZA. I'll offer myself as an assistant to Professor Nepean.

HIGGINS [*rising in a fury*] What! That impostor! that humbug! that toadying ignoramus! Teach him my methods! my discoveries! You take one step in his direction and I'll wring your neck. [*He lays hands on her*]. Do you hear?

LIZA [*defiantly non-resistant*] Wring away. What do I care? I knew youd strike me some day. [*He lets her go, stamping with rage at having forgotten himself, and recoils so hastily that he stumbles back into his seat on the ottoman*]. Aha! Now I know how to deal with you. What a fool I was not to think of it before! You cant take away the knowledge you gave me. You said I had a finer ear than you. And I can be civil and kind to people, which is more than you can. Aha! Thats done you, Henry Higgins, it has. Now I dont care that [*snapping her fingers*] for your bullying and your big talk. I'll advertize it in the papers that your duchess is only a flower girl that you taught, and that she'll teach anybody to be a duchess just the same in six months for a thousand guineas. Oh, when I think of myself crawling under your feet and being trampled on and called names, when all the time I had only to lift up my finger to be as good as you, I could just kick myself.

HIGGINS [*wondering at her*] You damned impudent slut, you! But it's better than snivelling; better than fetching slippers and finding spectacles, isnt it? [*Rising*] By George, Eliza, I said I'd make a woman of you; and I have. I like you like this.

LIZA. Yes: you turn round and make up to me now that I'm not afraid of you, and can do without you.

HIGGINS. Of course I do, you little fool. Five minutes ago you were like a millstone round my neck. Now youre a tower of strength: a consort battleship. You and I and Pickering will be three old bachelors together instead of only two men and a silly girl.

Mrs. Higgins returns, dressed for the wedding. Eliza instantly becomes cool and elegant.

MRS. HIGGINS. The carriage is waiting, Eliza. Are you ready?

LIZA. Quite. Is the Professor coming?

MRS. HIGGINS. Certainly not. He cant behave himself in church. He makes remarks out loud all the time on the clergyman's pronunciation.

LIZA. Then I shall not see you again, Professor. Good bye. [*She goes to the door*].

MRS. HIGGINS [*coming to Higgins*] Good-bye, dear.

HIGGINS. Good-bye, mother. [*He is about to kiss her, when he recollects something*]. Oh, by the way, Eliza, order a ham and a Stilton cheese, will you? And buy me a pair of reindeer gloves, number eights, and a tie

to match that new suit of mine, at Eale & Binman's. You
can choose the color. [*His cheerful, careless, vigorous
voice shows that he is incorrigible*].

LIZA [*disdainfully*] Buy them yourself. [*She sweeps
out*].

MRS. HIGGINS. I'm afraid youve spoiled that girl, Henry. But never mind, dear: I'll buy you the tie and gloves.

HIGGINS [*sunnily*] Oh, dont bother. She'll buy em all
right enough. Good-bye.

*They kiss. Mrs. Higgins runs out. Higgins, left alone,
rattles his cash in his pocket; chuckles; and disports
himself in a highly self-satisfied manner.*

*　　*　　*　　*　　*　　*　　*

The rest of the story need not be shown in action, and
indeed, would hardly need telling if our imaginations
were not so enfeebled by their lazy dependence on the
ready-mades and reach-me-downs of the ragshop in which
Romance keeps its stock of "happy endings" to misfit
all stories. Now, the history of Eliza Doolittle, though
called a romance because of the transfiguration it records
seems exceedingly improbable, is common enough. Such
transfigurations have been achieved by hundreds of resolutely ambitions young women since Nell Gwynne set
them the example by playing queens and fascinating kings
in the theatre in which she began by selling oranges.
Nevertheless, people in all directions have assumed, for
no other reason than that she became the heroine of a
romance, that she must have married the hero of it. This
is unbearable, not only because her little drama, if acted
on such a thoughtless assumption, must be spoiled, but
because the true sequel is patent to anyone with a sense
of human nature in general, and of feminine instinct in
particular.

Eliza, in telling Higgins she would not marry him if
he asked her, was not coquetting: she was announcing a

22

well-considered decision. When a bachelor interests, and dominates, and teaches, and becomes important to a spinster, as Higgins with Eliza, she always, if she has character enough to be capable of it, considers very seriously indeed whether she will play for becoming that bachelor's wife, especially if he is so little interested in marriage that a determined and devoted woman might capture him if she set herself resolutely to do it. Her decision will depend a good deal on whether she is really free to choose; and that, again, will depend on her age and income. If she is at the end of her youth, and has no security for her livelihood, she will marry him because she must marry anybody who will provide for her. But at Eliza's age a good-looking girl does not feel that pressure: she feels free to pick and choose. She is therefore guided by her instinct in the matter. Eliza's instinct tells her not to marry Higgins. It does not tell her to give him up. It is not in the slightest doubt as to his remaining one of the strongest personal interests in her life. It would be very sorely strained if there was another woman likely to supplant her with him. But as she feels sure of him on that last point, she has no doubt at all as to her course, and would not have any, even if the difference of twenty years in age, which seems so great to youth, did not exist between them.

As our own instincts are not appealed to by her conclusion, let us see whether we cannot discover some reason in it. When Higgins excused his indifference to young women on the ground that they had an irresistible rival in his mother, he gave the clue to his inveterate old-bachelordom. The case is uncommon only to the extent that remarkable mothers are uncommon. If an imaginative boy has a sufficiently rich mother who has intelligence, personal grace, dignity of character without harshness, and a cultivated sense of the best art of her time to enable her to make her house beautiful, she sets a standard for him against which very few women can struggle, besides effecting for him a disengagement of his affections, his sense of beauty, and his idealism from his specifically sexual impulses. This makes him a standing puzzle to the huge number of uncultivated people who have been brought up in tasteless homes by commonplace or disagreeable parents, and to whom, consequently, literature, painting, sculpture, music, and affectionate personal relations come as modes of sex if they come at all. The word passion means nothing else to them; and that Higgins could have a passion for phonetics and idealize his mother instead of Eliza, would seem to them absurd and unnatural. Nevertheless, when we look round and see that hardly anyone is too ugly or disagreeable to find a wife or a husband if he or she wants one, whilst many old maids and bachelors are above the average in quality and culture, we cannot help suspecting that the disentanglement of sex from the associations with which it is so commonly confused, a disentanglement which persons of genius achieve by sheer intellectual analysis, is sometimes produced or aided by parental fascination.

Now, though Eliza was incapable of thus explaining to herself Higgins's formidable powers of resistance to the charm that prostrated Freddy at the first glance, she was instinctively aware that she could never obtain a complete grip of him, or come between him and his mother (the first necessity of the married woman). To put it shortly, she knew that for some mysterious reason he had not the makings of a married man in him, according to her conception of a husband as one to whom she would be his nearest and fondest and warmest interest. Even had there been no mother-rival, she would still have refused to accept an interest in herself that was secondary to philosophic interests. Had Mrs. Higgins died, there would still have been Milton and the Universal Alphabet. Landor's remark that to those who have the greatest power of loving, love is a secondary affair, would not have recommended Landor to Eliza. Put that along with her resentment of Higgins's domineering superiority, and her mistrust of his coaxing cleverness in getting round her and evading her wrath when he had gone too far with his impetuous bullying, and you will see that Eliza's instinct had good grounds for warning her not to marry her Pygmalion.

And now, whom did Eliza marry? For if Higgins was a predestinate old bachelor, she was most certainly not a predestinate old maid. Well, that can be told very shortly to those who have not guessed it from the indications she has herself given them.

Almost immediately after Eliza is stung into proclaiming her considered determination not to marry Higgins, she mentions the fact that young Mr. Frederick Eynsford Hill is pouring out his love for her daily through the post. Now Freddy is young, practically twenty years younger than Higgins: he is a gentleman (or, as Eliza would qualify him, a toff), and speaks like one; he is nicely dressed, is treated by the Colonel as an equal, loves her unaffectedly, and is not her master, nor ever likely to dominate her in spite of his advantage of social standing. Eliza has no use for the foolish romantic tradition that all women love to be mastered, if not actually bullied and beaten. "When you go to women," says Nietzsche, "take your whip with you." Sensible despots have never confined that precaution to women: they have taken their whips with them when they have dealt with men, and been slavishly idealized by the men over whom they have flourished the whip much more than by women. No doubt there are slavish women as well as slavish men; and women, like men, admire those that are stronger than themselves. But to admire a strong person and to live under that strong person's thumb are two different things. The weak may not be admired and hero-worshipped; but they are by no means disliked or shunned; and they never seem to have the least difficulty in marrying people who are too good for them. They may fail in emergencies; but life is not one long emergency: it is mostly a string of situations for which no exceptional strength is needed, and with which even rather weak people can cope if they have a stronger partner to help them out. Accordingly, it is a truth everywhere in evidence that strong people, masculine or feminine, not only do not marry stronger people, but do not shew any preference for them in selecting their friends. When a lion meets another with a louder roar "the first lion thinks the last a bore." The man or woman who feels strong enough for two, seeks for every other quality in a partner than strength.

The converse is also true. Weak people want to marry strong people who do not frighten them too much; and this often leads them to make the mistake we describe metaphorically as "biting off more than they can chew." They want too much for too little; and when the bargain is unreasonable beyond all bearing, the union becomes impossible: it ends in the weaker party being either discarded or borne as a cross, which is worse. People who are not only weak, but silly or obtuse as well, are often in these difficulties.

This being the state of human affairs, what is Eliza fairly sure to do when she is placed between Freddy and Higgins? Will she look forward to a lifetime of fetching Higgins's slippers or to a lifetime of Freddy fetching hers? There can be no doubt about the answer. Unless Freddy is biologically repulsive to her, and Higgins biologically attractive to a degree that overwhelms all her other instincts, she will, if she marries either of them, marry Freddy.

And that is just what Eliza did.

Complications ensued; but they were economic, not

romantic. Freddy had no money and no occupation. His mother's jointure, a last relic of the opulence of Largelady Park, had enabled her to struggle along in Earlscourt with an air of gentility, but not to procure any serious secondary education for her children, much less give the boy a profession. A clerkship at thirty shillings a week was beneath Freddy's dignity, and extremely distasteful to him besides. His prospects consisted of a hope that if he kept up appearances somebody would do something for him. The something appeared vaguely to his imagination as a private secretaryship or a sinecure of some sort. To his mother it perhaps appeared as a marriage to some lady of means who could not resist her boy's niceness. Fancy her feelings when he married a flower girl who had become déclassée under extraordinary circumstances which were now notorious!

It is true that Eliza's situation did not seem wholly ineligible. Her father, though formerly a dustman, and now fantastically disclassed, had become extremely popular in the smartest society by a social talent which triumphed over every prejudice and every disadvantage. Rejected by the middle class, which he loathed, he had shot up at once into the highest circles by his wit, his dustmanship (which he carried like a banner), and his Nietzschean transcendence of good and evil. At intimate ducal dinners he sat on the right hand of the Duchess; and in country houses he smoked in the pantry and was made much of by the butler when he was not feeding in the dining-room and being consulted by cabinet ministers. But he found it almost as hard to do all this on four thousand a year as Mrs. Eynsford Hill to live in Earlscourt on an income so pitiably smaller that I have not the heart to disclose its exact figure. He absolutely refused to add the last straw to his burden by contributing to Eliza's support.

Thus Freddy and Eliza, now Mr. and Mrs. Eynsford

Hill, would have spent a penniless honeymoon but for a wedding present of £500 from the Colonel to Eliza. It lasted a long time because Freddy did not know how to spend money, never having had any to spend, and Eliza, socially trained by a pair of old bachelors, wore her clothes as long as they held together and looked pretty, without the least regard to their being many months out of fashion. Still, £500 will not last two young people for ever; and they both knew, and Eliza felt as well, that they must shift for themselves in the end. She could quarter herself on Wimpole Street because it had come to be her home; but she was quite aware that she ought not to quarter Freddy there, and that it would not be good for his character if she did.

Not that the Wimpole Street bachelors objected. When she consulted them, Higgins declined to be bothered about her housing problem when that solution was so simple. Eliza's desire to have Freddy in the house with her seemed of no more importance than if she had wanted an extra piece of bedroom furniture. Pleas as to Freddy's character, and the moral obligation on him to earn his own living, were lost on Higgins. He denied that Freddy had any character, and declared that if he tried to do any useful work some competent person would have the trouble of undoing it: a procedure involving a net loss to the community, and great unhappiness to Freddy himself, who was obviously intended by Nature for such light work as amusing Eliza, which, Higgins declared, was a much more useful and honorable occupation than working in the city. When Eliza referred again to her project of teaching phonetics, Higgins abated not a jot of his violent opposition to it. He said she was not within ten years of being qualified to meddle with his pet subject; and as it was evident that the Colonel agreed with him, she felt she could not go against them in this grave matter, and that she had no right, without Higgins's consent, to exploit the knowledge he had given her; for his knowledge seemed to her as much his private property as his watch: Eliza was no communist. Besides, she was superstitiously devoted to them both, more entirely and frankly after her marriage than before it.

It was the Colonel who finally solved the problem, which had cost him much perplexed cogitation. He one day asked Eliza, rather shyly, whether she had quite given up her notion of keeping a flower shop. She replied that she had thought of it, but had put it out of her head, because the Colonel had said, that day at Mrs. Higgins's, that it would never do. The Colonel confessed that when he said that, he had not quite recovered from the dazzling impression of the day before. They broke the matter to Higgins that evening. The sole comment vouchsafed by him very nearly led to a serious quarrel with Eliza. It was to the effect that she would have in Freddy an ideal errand boy.

Freddy himself was next sounded on the subject. He said he had been thinking of a shop himself; though it had presented itself to his pennilessness as a small place in which Eliza should sell tobacco at one counter whilst he sold newspapers at the opposite one. But he agreed that it would be extraordinarily jolly to go early every morning with Eliza to Covent Garden and buy flowers on the scene of their first meeting: a sentiment which earned him many kisses from his wife. He added that he had always been afraid to propose anything of the sort, because Clara would make an awful row about a step that must damage her matrimonial chances, and his mother could not be expected to like it after clinging for so many years to that step of the social ladder on which retail trade is impossible.

This difficulty was removed by an event highly unexpected by Freddy's mother. Clara, in the course of her incursions into those artistic circles which were the highest within her reach, discovered that her conversational qualifications were expected to include a grounding in the novels of Mr. H. G. Wells. She borrowed them in various directions so energetically that she swallowed them all within two months. The result was a conversion of a kind quite common today. A modern Acts of the Apostles would fill fifty whole Bibles if anyone were capable of writing it.

Poor Clara, who appeared to Higgins and his mother as a disagreeable and ridiculous person, and to her own mother as in some inexplicable way a social failure, had never seen herself in either light; for, though to some extent ridiculed and mimicked in West Kensington like everybody else there, she was accepted as a rational and normal—or shall we say inevitable?—sort of human being. At worst they called her The Pusher; but to them no more than to herself had it ever occurred that she was pushing the air, and pushing it in a wrong direction. Still, she was not happy. She was growing desperate. Her one asset, the fact that her mother was what the Epsom greengrocer called a carriage lady had no exchange value, apparently. It had prevented her from getting educated, because the only education she could have afforded was education with the Earlscourt greengrocer's daughter. It had led her to seek the society of her mother's class; and that class simply would not have her, because she was much poorer than the greengrocer, and, far from being able to afford a maid, could not afford even a housemaid, and had to scrape along at home with an illiberally treated general servant. Under such circumstances nothing could give her an air of being a genuine product of Largelady Park. And yet its tradition made her regard a marriage with anyone within her reach as an unbearable humiliation. Commercial people and professional people in a small way were odious to her. She ran after painters and novelists; but she did not charm them; and her bold attempts to pick up and practise artistic and literary talk irritated them. She was, in short, an utter failure, an ignorant, incompetent, pretentious, unwelcome, penniless, useless little snob; and though she did not admit these disqualifications (for nobody ever faces unpleasant truths of this kind until the possibility of a way out dawns on them) she felt their effects too keenly to be satisfied with her position.

Clara had a startling eyeopener when, on being suddenly wakened to enthusiasm by a girl of her own age who dazzled her and produced in her a gushing desire to take her for a model, and gain her friendship, she discovered that this exquisite apparition had graduated from the gutter in a few months' time. It shook her so violently, that when Mr. H. G. Wells lifted her on the point of his puissant pen, and placed her at the angle of view from which the life she was leading and the society to which she clung appeared in its true relation to real human needs and worthy social structure, he effected a conversion and a conviction of sin comparable to the most sensational feats of General Booth or Gypsy Smith. Clara's snobbery went bang. Life suddenly began to move with her. Without knowing how or why, she began to make friends and enemies. Some of the acquaintances to whom she had been a tedious or indifferent or ridiculous affliction, dropped her: others became cordial. To her amazement she found that some "quite nice" people were saturated with Wells, and that this accessibility to ideas was the secret of their niceness. People she had thought deeply religious, and had tried to conciliate on that tack with disastrous results, suddenly took an interest in her, and revealed a hostility to conventional religion which she had never conceived possible except among the most desperate characters. They made her read Galsworthy; and Galsworthy ex-

posed the vanity of Largelady Park and finished her.
It exasperated her to think that the dungeon in which
she had languished for so many unhappy years had been
unlocked all the time, and that the impulses she had so
carefully struggled with and stifled for the sake of keeping well with society, were precisely those by which
alone she could have come into any sort of sincere human
contact. In the radiance of these discoveries, and the
tumult of their reaction, she made a fool of herself as
freely and conspicuously as when she so rashly adopted
Eliza's expletive in Mrs. Higgins's drawing-room; for
the new-born Wellsian had to find her bearings almost
as ridiculously as a baby; but nobody hates a baby for
its ineptitudes, or thinks the worse of it for trying to
eat the matches; and Clara lost no friends by her follies.
They laughed at her to her face this time; and she had
to defend herself and fight it out as best she could.

When Freddy paid a visit to Earlscourt (which he
never did when he could possibly help it) to make the
desolating announcement that he and his Eliza were
thinking of blackening the Largelady scutcheon by opening a shop, he found the little household already con-
vulsed by a prior announcement from Clara that she
also was going to work in an old furniture shop in Dover
Street, which had been started by a fellow Wellsian.
This appointment Clara owed, after all, to her old social
accomplishment of Push. She had made up her mind
that, cost what it might, she would see Mr. Wells in the
flesh; and she had achieved her end at a garden party.
She had better luck than so rash an enterprise deserved.
Mr. Wells came up to her expectations. Age had not
withered him, nor could custom stale his infinite variety
in half an hour. His pleasant neatness and compactness,
his small hands and feet, his teeming ready brain, his
unaffected accessibility, and a certain fine apprehensive-
ness which stamped him as susceptible from his topmost

hair to his tipmost toe, proved irresistible. Clara talked
of nothing else for weeks and weeks afterwards. And
as she happened to talk to the lady of the furniture shop,
and that lady also desired above all things to know Mr.
Wells and sell pretty things to him, she offered Clara a
job on the chance of achieving that end through her.

And so it came about that Eliza's luck held, and the
expected opposition to the flower shop melted away. The
shop is in the arcade of a railway station not very far
from the Victoria and Albert Museum; and if you live in
that neighborhood you may go there any day and buy
a buttonhole from Eliza.

Now here is a last opportunity for romance. Would
you not like to be assured that the shop was an immense
success, thanks to Eliza's charms and her early business
experience in Covent Garden? Alas! the truth is the
truth: the shop did not pay for a long time, simply because Eliza and her Freddy did not know how to keep it.
True, Eliza had not to begin at the very beginning: she
knew the names and prices of the cheaper flowers; and
her elation was unbounded when she found that Freddy,
like all youths educated at cheap, pretentious, and
thoroughly inefficient schools, knew a little Latin. It was
very little, but enough to make him appear to her a Por-
son or Bentley, and to put him at his ease with botanical
nomenclature. Unfortunately he knew nothing else; and
Eliza, though she could count money up to eighteen
shillings or so, and had acquired a certain familiarity
with the language of Milton from her struggles to
qualify herself for winning Higgins's bet, could not
write out a bill without utterly disgracing the establish-
ment. Freddy's power of stating in Latin that Balbus
built a wall and that Gaul was divided into three parts
did not carry with it the slightest knowledge of accounts
or business: Colonel Pickering had to explain to him
what a cheque book and a bank account meant. And the

pair were by no means easily teachable. Freddy backed up Eliza in her obstinate refusal to believe that they could save money by engaging a bookkeeper with some knowledge of the business. How, they argued, could you possibly save money by going to extra expense when you already could not make both ends meet? But the Colonel, after making the ends meet over and over again, at last gently insisted; and Eliza, humbled to the dust by having to beg from him so often, and stung by the uproarious derision of Higgins, to whom the notion of Freddy succeeding at anything was a joke that never palled, grasped the fact that business, like phonetics, has to be learned.

On the piteous spectacle of the pair spending their evenings in shorthand schools and polytechnic classes, learning bookkeeping and typewriting with incipient junior clerks, male and female, from the elementary schools, let me not dwell. There were even classes at the London School of Economics, and a humble personal appeal to the director of that institution to recommend a course bearing on the flower business. He, being a humorist, explained to them the method of the celebrated Dickensian essay on Chinese Metaphysics by the gentleman who read an article on China and an article on Metaphysics and combined the information. He suggested that they should combine the London School with Kew Gardens. Eliza, to whom the procedure of the Dickensian gentleman seemed perfectly correct (as in fact it was) and not in the least funny (which was only her ignorance) took his advice with entire gravity. But the effort that cost her the deepest humiliation was a request to Higgins, whose pet artistic fancy, next to Milton's verse, was caligraphy, and who himself wrote a most beautiful Italian hand, that he would teach her to write. He declared that she was congenitally incapable of forming a single letter worthy of the least of Milton's words; but she persisted; and again he suddenly threw himself into the task of teaching her with a combination of stormy intensity, concentrated patience, and occasional bursts of interesting disquisition on the beauty and nobility, the august mission and destiny, of human handwriting. Eliza ended by acquiring an extremely uncommercial script which was a positive extension of her personal beauty, and spending three times as much on stationery as anyone else because certain qualities and shapes of paper became indispensable to her. She could not even address an envelope in the usual way because it made the margins all wrong.

Their commercial school days were a period of disgrace and despair for the young couple. They seemed to be learning nothing about flower shops. At last they gave it up as hopeless, and shook the dust of the shorthand schools, and the polytechnics, and the London School of Economics from their feet for ever. Besides, the business was in some mysterious way beginning to take care of itself. They had somehow forgotten their objections to employing other people. They came to the conclusion that their own way was the best, and that they had really a remarkable talent for business. The Colonel, who had been compelled for some years to keep a sufficient sum on current account at his bankers to make up their deficits, found that the provision was unnecessary: the young people were prospering. It is true that there was not quite fair play between them and their competitors in trade. Their week-ends in the country cost them nothing, and saved them the price of their Sunday dinners; for the motor car was the Colonel's; and he and Higgins paid the hotel bills. Mr. F. Hill, florist and greengrocer (they soon discovered that there was money in asparagus; and asparagus led to other vegetables), had an air which stamped the business as classy; and in private life he was still Frederick Eynsford Hill, Esquire. Not that there was any swank about him: nobody but Eliza knew that he had been christened Frederick Challoner. Eliza herself swanked like anything.

That is all. That is how it has turned out. It is astonishing how much Eliza still manages to meddle in the housekeeping at Wimpole Street in spite of the shop and her own family. And it is notable that though she never nags her husband, and frankly loves the Colonel as if she were his favorite daughter, she has never got out of the habit of nagging Higgins that was established on the fatal night when she won his bet for him. She snaps his head off on the faintest provocation, or on none. He no longer dares to tease her by assuming an abysmal inferiority of Freddy's mind to his own. He storms and bullies and derides; but she stands up to him so ruthlessly that the Colonel has to ask her from time to time to be kinder to Higgins; and it is the only request of his that brings a mulish expression into her face. Nothing but some emergency or calamity great enough to break down all likes and dislikes, and throw them both back on their common humanity—and may they be spared any such trial!—will ever alter this. She knows that Higgins does not need her, just as her father did not need her. The very scrupulousness with which he told her that day that he had become used to having her there, and dependent on her for all sorts of little services, and that he should miss her if she went away (it would never have occurred to Freddy or the Colonel to say anything of the sort) deepens her inner certainty that she is "no more to him than them slippers", yet she has a sense, too, that his indifference is deeper than the infatuation of commoner souls. She is immensely interested in him. She has even secret mischievous moments in which she wishes she could get him alone, on a desert island, away from all ties and with nobody else in the world to consider, and just drag him off his pedestal and see him making love like any common man. We all have private imaginations of that sort. But when it comes to business, to the life that she really leads as distinguished from the life of dreams and fancies, she likes Freddy and she likes the Colonel; and she does not like Higgins and Mr. Doolittle. Galatea never does quite like Pygmalion: his relation to her is too godlike to be altogether agreeable.